Contents

Roadblocked

ROADBLOCKED

Joe Biden's Rocky Transition to the Presidency

Heath Brown

University Press of Kansas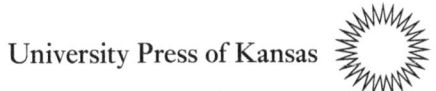

Published by the University Press of Kansas (Lawrence, Kansas 66045), which
was organized by the Kansas Board of Regents and is operated and funded by
Emporia State University, Fort Hays State University, Kansas State University,
Pittsburg State University, the University of Kansas, and Wichita State University

Library of Congress Cataloging-in-Publication Data

Names: Brown, Heath A., author.
Title: Roadblocked : Joe Biden's rocky transition to the presidency / Heath
  Brown.
Description: Lawrence: University Press of Kansas, 2024. | Includes
  bibliographical references and index.
Identifiers: LCCN 2023041534 (print) | LCCN 2023041535 (ebook)
  ISBN 9780700636570 (cloth)
  ISBN 9780700637072 (paperback)
  ISBN 9780700636587 (ebook)
Subjects: LCSH: United State—Politics and government—2021– |
  Presidents—United States—Transition periods. | Presidents—United
  States—History—21st century. | Biden, Joseph R., Jr. | BISAC:
  POLITICAL SCIENCE / American Government / Executive Branch |
  POLITICAL SCIENCE / American Government / National
Classification: LCC E916 .B76 2024 (print) | LCC E916 (ebook) | DDC
  973.934—dc23/eng/20231211
LC record available at https://lccn.loc.gov/2023041534.
LC ebook record available at https://lccn.loc.gov/2023041535.

British Library Cataloguing-in-Publication Data is available.

Acknowledgments

Roadblocked began at the same time the Biden-Harris transition started, but it faced none of the blocks in the road faced by the incoming administration in 2020. The book is the product of the exact opposite: a helpful editor and publisher, cooperative graduate students and generous colleagues, and a supportive and loving family. David Congdon at the University Press of Kansas and several anonymous reviewers believed in my vision for the book and are integral to its publication.

John Jay College of Criminal Justice master's students Denise Clarke, Tyler Brockington, and Fariza Majidova all gave extensive time to help collect data used in chapters 2 and 6. Kathleen Dunn Tenpas from the Brookings Institution shared data used in chapter 2. Colleagues, including Niambi Carter, Jonathan Keller, Alex Garlick, Brian Cook, Aaron Smith-Walter, John Torpey, Boris Heersink, Sam Workman, and Elizabeth Nisbet, provided important feedback on the manuscript at various points. I benefited from the chance to present a portion of the analysis from the book to the Human Rights Workshop at the CUNY Graduate Center. Though they will go unnamed, hundreds of people aided this project by sitting for interviews about their experiences during the 2020–2021 transition. Portions of chapters 3 and 5 were previously published with permission in the *Presidential Studies Quarterly* and the *Journal of Social Equity and Public Administration*.

Most importantly, my family inspired and motivated me to write this book. My son, Finn, regularly reminded me to think deeply about the future and preserving the world in which he and his friends will live. My wife, Kate Storey, guided me through writing this book by modeling rigorous research and sound writing. I wrote and rewrote each word in the book to make her proud.

Roadblocked

Introduction

At 3 p.m. everyone's calendar beeped.

Members of the transition team were scheduled to log on to a video call for a seven-minute workout. The music thumped: the Greatest Hits of the 1970s and '80s played from someone's cell phone.[1] First, jumping jacks, then push-ups, as the team—really a group of strangers—got sweaty together in their business clothes, building the camaraderie needed for this unthinkably difficult job.

Sonia Chessen—who'd spent nearly a decade at the Pew Charitable Trusts—led the workouts, but Cecilia Munoz was the one in charge, waving at the kids at play in the corner of home offices. "It makes a difference to understand ourselves as part of a team unified around advancing the boss' agenda and the country's agenda," Munoz surmised (Bravender 2021). Munoz was a pro and an insider, having served eight years in the Obama administration before taking on the role of director of domestic and economic policy on the Biden-Harris transition team months in advance of the November election. On loan from a think tank, New America, where she'd been a senior adviser since Donald Trump took over the White House, Munoz knew the monumental task ahead of them to prepare to govern during a pandemic.

Munoz was a logical, if not curious, choice. Few could compete with her experience, but many were aghast at her record. Nearly five thousand people signed a petition sponsored by the group Familia: Trans Queen Liberation Movement, to bar President Biden from appointing Munoz to his administration once the transition ended (Action Network 2020). To Familia, Munoz was one of the architects of a cruel policy of deportation during Obama's eight years in the presidency. Appointing Munoz to the transition team meant Joe Biden was lying during the campaign when he told Jorge Ramos (2020) on Univision that deporting three million people was "a big mistake." It meant Biden wasn't the progressive Democrat he claimed to be.[2]

But like so many thorny policy issues, immigration advocates were a disparate group. Five board members from UnidosUS (formerly the National Council of La Raza, where Munoz had worked earlier in her career) applauded the appointment, explaining in a public letter: "Latinos could not have a more qualified, authentic, and effective voice at the Biden transition table" (Bazan et al. 2020). Equating Munoz with those opposed to immigration and immigrants, like President Trump's chief immigration adviser, Stephen Miller, was ill-informed, outrageous, and textbook demagoguery, according to UnidosUS. Munoz was the right person for the job.

UnidosUS and Familia weren't the only groups vying for influence during the 2020–2021 transition. The National Sheriffs' Association also had been asked for its opinion. Sheriff Mark Dannels, who'd worked for four decades as a cop, now was one of the fourteen thousand members of the association and head of its Border Security committee.[3] He knew his way around this chaotic interregnum between presidents as well as the recent history of federal immigration policy. He also knew that Joe Biden pledged to halt construction of a wall along the US-Mexico border, a signature issue of the Trump presidency and his failed reelection campaign.

When Biden's transition team invited him to talk, Dannels told them about the successes his members had had over the past four years enforcing border security: things were working at the border. He left feeling optimistic that they'd heard what he had to say on behalf of the association (Porier 2021). "You hope that if you put in the time and effort, they're going to listen. I thought they were. Somewhere in there, politics started," Dannels later said to a reporter (Porier 2021).

As Dannels feared, within hours of being sworn in and as the official transition wrapped up, the first thing President Biden did was to pause all border wall construction (Biden 2021). He directed federal officials to evaluate the legality of the wall and to halt funding. Not a day into his administration, and the president had made good on a campaign pledge and satisfied at least some of his supporters, but not Dannels and the other members of his association.

Across dozens of issues, similar stories unfolded. Harried volunteers, most working safely at home, coordinated the transition of the forty-sixth president of the United States under the direction of Jeff Zients and Yohannes Abraham. As COVID-19 raged—1,007 Americans died on the date Biden was declared the winner of the election—over one thousand experts dissected how the new administration could be up-and-running in less than one hundred days. The governance challenge of the transition period had always been immense, but 2020 was especially challenging in a mind-boggling number of ways: from the array of pressing public health, economic, and foreign policy issues related to surviving the pandemic to the practical issue of coordinating schedules for volunteers spread across the country and maintaining cyber security (Kaufman 2021). This was why Biden had begun planning months earlier, secretly establishing the 501(c)(4) nonprofit named the PT Fund Inc. on May 1, 2020, to begin fundraising to support his distant transition plan (Goldmacher 2020).

Never, however, had the political challenge of the transition period been so dire. Despite Biden being declared winner several days after the election, sitting president Trump refused to concede the outcome, the first sitting president to do so. He insisted the election had been rigged and that the transition wouldn't start until fraud was uncovered and he was declared the winner.

Attention shifted to the General Services Administration (GSA), an integral but historically uncontroversial player in the transition. Starting after the party conventions, the GSA has the statutory responsibility to help prepare all eligible candidates to be ready to govern, should they win. GSA staff had been doing just this since the summer with representatives for both Biden and Trump. But when it came time for the process of *ascertainment*—when the GSA officially disburses federal funds to the apparent winner of the election—administrator Emily Murphy waited. Weeks passed, with the transition team's access to the government severely limited and public funds unavailable; celebrities Leonardo DiCaprio, Shonda Rhimes, and Scarlett Johansson chipped in to make up the gap (Levinthal and Bravender 2021). Whereas past transitions would have already commenced meetings with federal bureaucrats by this time, Biden's team had to hold back, leading the president-elect to say, "More people may die if we don't coordinate" (Levinthal and Bravender 2021; Chalfant 2020). Speculation soon mounted that Trump was behind Murphy's wavering, yet when she finally released the resources on November 23, Murphy explained she was just doing her job, no influence or favoritism at all (Murphy 2020).

Now flush with $7 million in federal funds, the Biden team could do away with its precautionary color-coded spreadsheets: red for officials in the government they couldn't talk to; yellow for think-tank experts and former federal officials they could (Bravender 2021). They now had the green light to rapidly move ahead with transition planning. Agency review teams conferred virtually with senior bureaucrats and outgoing Trump appointees. Cabinet nominations quickly came from the personnel team: Antony Blinken to run State, Alejandro Mayorkas at Homeland Security, Avril Haines to direct National Intelligence, and Linda Thomas-Greenfield as ambassador to the United Nations. As with previous transitions, these foreign policy posts were deemed the most important positions for maintaining peace and stability during the transition period. This initial batch of nominees also reflected the close attention the transition team paid to tracking personnel metrics such as the race, gender, and background of cabinet members as well as to the influence of powerful groups like WestExec Advisors, where several Biden appointees had recently been employed (Bender and Meyer 2020; Bravender 2021).

Yet the fear of foreign attack during the transfer of power, so long the worry of federal officials, subsided as the threat from domestic terror rose (Bohn 2003). Just twelve years earlier, while newly elected Barack Obama joined President George W. Bush for coffee in the White House, the incoming and outgoing national security teams huddled in the Situation Room over intelligence of a potential threat from the extremist group al-Shabaab (Kumar 2017). The threat never materialized, but the close coordination between the Bush and Obama teams remained a testament to how transitions had evolved over time, from loosely planned affairs among sometimes petty rivals to an institutionalized, well-funded, and cooperative endeavor to safely ease the country into a new administration.

Not in 2020.

As Washington, DC, celebrated the holidays, Trump refused to concede, orchestrating a multistate effort to challenge the election results. At the Pentagon, acting secretary of defense Chris Miller halted cooperation between his department and the Biden-Harris team, claiming a two-week break had been agreed upon, according to news reports (Allen and Swan 2022). At the end of one meeting to share intelligence on threats to the country, a Trump political appointee said to members of the transition team: "You guys are not legitimate, so I'm not sharing this information."[4] Biden, who didn't received his first intelligence briefing until November 30, weeks after it was expected, said there were roadblocks at the Office of Management and Budget as well (Whipple 2023).

And then, on January 6, 2021, as Congress met to certify the final election results and officially declare Joe Biden and Kamala Harris the winners, rioters attacked the Capitol. What was supposed to be a matter-of-fact vote in Congress became a crime scene as hundreds stormed into the Capitol Building, a coordinated domestic effort to head off the impending inauguration and transfer of power. The two-hundred-year history of peaceful, orderly presidential transitions was over.

The waning days of the Trump administration were filled with many firsts and never-befores. The presidential transition period, nearly always a humdrum affair dominated by meetings and memos, was just such a case. Political scientist Martha Kumar's book *Before the Oath* (2017) is a testament to this point: 2008–2009 was lauded for the cooperation between administrations that played out with a predictable, organized, and efficient transition, despite vocal disagreements between groups advising the new president. The year 2020 was different. How did the incoming Biden-Harris team manage to prepare for governance amid a global pandemic and unrealized coup d'etat? How did it reconcile the competing factions within the Democratic Party, each grappling with historic challenges of climate change, racial justice, and immigration? Why did progressive groups, like the Poor People's Movement, the Immigration Hub, and the Sunrise Movement, win on some parts of the agenda and lose badly on others?

In answering these questions, we learn about the tension between campaigning and governing; the interplay between parties, groups, and movements; and trade-offs between descriptive and substantive representation (Jones 1998). The transition period also presents a case to closely inspect influence, power, and secrecy, all central themes of the study of politics and government. This inspection reveals that many of the norms of democracy in the United States are fragile, much more prone to disruption than experts have portrayed in the past. If the transfer of power is a hallmark of democracy, and in 2020 that transfer was so uncertain, future transitions must be approached with much more trepidation. There may be a need for better regulations and rules on ascertainment by the GSA, on sharing information between the outgoing and incoming administration, and on who has a seat at the table with the transition team (Herz and Shaw 2021). Some of those changes were made by Congress in the final days of 2022.

Rule changes, though, may not be sufficient to withstand domestic terror threats that disregard the rule of law in favor of raw autocratic demonstrations of power and violence. Securing democracy during trying times may demand a better understanding of what is at stake during the transition of power: a revival of the spirit of cooperation of adversaries like George W. Bush and Barack Obama and adherence to democratic norms demonstrated in the past. This book enriches this understanding with a deep study of how a variety of actors descended on Washington during the weeks after the 2020 election, only some committed to peace. By spotlighting how think tanks like New America, civil rights groups like UnidosUS, and trade associations like the National Sheriffs' Association wrestled for control of the future of the country during this transition period, we can better understand how transitions work, fail, and reconcile conflict. And by placing this competition of ideas of hundreds of political groups into the context of past transitions and the contemporary interplay between polarized political parties, much is revealed about influence, power, and the institutions of democracy.

The story of the Biden-Harris transition plays out over the next six chapters and conclusion, each motivated by a question or questions. Chapter 1 centers on a historic question: how have the key features of presidential transitions changed over time? It maps the history and development of presidential transitions in the United States with particular attention to the period of 1960 to 1980, when many of the most important elements of the transition period became institutionalized and politicized. Chapter 2 focuses on two questions: Who served on the Biden-Harris team? And was this different from who had served during previous transitions? To answer these questions, I compare those in leadership positions on recent transition teams as well as the thousands of volunteers on agency review teams serving the four previous transitions (Clinton, Bush, Obama, and Trump). Chapter 3 looks closer at the parts of the Biden-Harris transition team focused on economic issues, referencing more than seventy-five original qualitative interviews and archival material. How did leaders of the transition team organize the 2020 Biden-Harris transition, and what did that organization do for the key priorities of the candidates? From this chapter, we can see the inner working of this organized, efficient, yet secretive transition.

Chapters 4 and 5 present two case studies that shift the focus from the inside to the outside of the transition. The first compares groups advocating within two stable policy domains: foreign policy and education. Did groups gain access and influence with the Biden-Harris team? The second chapter compares groups advocating for a policy domain in the spotlight in 2020: racial justice and equity. Based on extensive interviews, each case study chapter seeks an answer to the question, How does the access and influence of groups vary in these different policy domains? Chapter 6 examines groups more generally using a statistical analysis, rather than qualitative, to answer two questions: How did groups—associations, think tanks, and advocacy organizations—seek to influence the Biden-Harris transition team? Was this different from past transitions? To figure this out, I rely on original data gleaned from approximately five hundred letters submitted to the Obama, Trump, and Biden transition teams. The conclusion returns to the issue of immigration that started the book to understand what transpired before, during, and after the 2020 transition and look ahead to planning for a possible transition in 2024 and beyond.

CHAPTER 1

A Model of Access and Influence during Presidential Transitions

On Friday, January 13, 2017, in the Eisenhower Executive Office Building next to the White House, thirty members of the Trump transition team faced a pandemic: H9N2 was spreading through London, Jakarta, and Seoul and heading for the United States. It was a fictional public health emergency created by White House experts to prepare incoming Trump cabinet officials for an unlikely, but real, threat to the country. Suggestive of their attentiveness, Commerce Secretary-nominee Wilbur Ross seemed to be dozing through the exercise (Toosi, Lippman, and Diamond 2020).

Two months earlier, just days after the election, public health groups including the Infectious Diseases Society of America advised the Trump transition team of an identical concern, urging it to prioritize preparation and funding for the chance this might happen in the early days of the administration (Infectious Disease Society of America 2016). History suggests the advice was largely ignored, and Trump shelved the White House's National Security Council Directorate for Global Health Security and Biodefense the following year.

Four years later, Joe Biden and Kamala Harris faced a very real pandemic, but their transition team was initially blocked from consulting with federal officials at key agencies like the Office of Management and Budget and Department of Defense. Outside groups again offered advice, often filtered through the transition team's COVID-19 Advisory Board. One coalition of groups, the Consortium for Citizens with Disabilities, sent several letters to the team, including one with a list of eight recommendations on everything from required data collection to expanding access to personal protective equipment (PPE) and developing a new national strategy to address the harm the pandemic had on Black, Indigenous, and people of color (BIPOC) (Consortium for Citizens with Disabilities 2020). The seven-page letter came with examples of recent scientific studies, statistics, and twenty-three footnotes. The heads of fifteen groups co-signed the letter, offering in conclusion: "If you are taking meeting requests at this time, we would like to schedule a meeting to discuss the issues in this letter with you."

The pandemic wasn't the only issue for the incoming administration to fret over, nor were public health groups the only ones ready to share their views. Yet, when the Biden-Harris transition team, running short on time because of the obstruction from the White House, invited the Reverend William Barber to a meeting, they didn't expect his response: "No we can't meet like that" (Jenkins 2020).

Since 2018, Barber had not merely run an interest group but led a broad national movement of hundreds of anti-poverty groups: the new Poor People's Campaign. Months earlier, when then-candidate Joe Biden spoke at an event Barber had organized, the future president said: "I promised you that we'd not only talk about (poverty), but that we'd do something about it together" (Jenkins 2020).

"Who (do) you want to bring?" the transition team replied. Barber recalled the movement's original leader, Dr. Martin Luther King Jr.: "I remember what he said in the Poor People's Campaign: 'I'm taking poor people to the Capitol and we're going to stay there until the nation shifts'" (The Brian Lehrer Show 2021). Someone who attended the eventual meeting later said they thought some on the transition team were afraid to say "no" to Barber; that he'd expose them as breaking one of Biden's promises.[1] Barber needed thirty invites and, luckily for the transition team, the meeting would be held virtually, so a bigger conference room need not be booked.

On the December 17 video call were several key officials on the Biden-Harris team, reflecting the typical structure of a transition: day-to-day operations, White House planning, personnel, and policy review. Congressman Cedric Richmond, one of the five transition co-chairs, was there. From the fifteen-person transition advisory board, Ambassador Susan Rice was on the call, as was a close friend of President-elect Biden, Ambassador Mark Gitenstein, who'd once lobbied for the US Chamber of Commerce and AT&T. Yohannes Abraham, executive director of the team, dialed in, as did issue experts, like Cecilia Munoz, who was heading up domestic policy for the transition.

This was a high-profile set of officials, an accurate reflection of who typically represents the transition team at this type of meeting, a mix of party loyalists, policy experts, and former lobbyists. The representatives also showed Biden and Harris's commitment to diversity on the transition team, with as many women as men and many people of color. In 2020 this was not surprising from an incoming Democratic presidential administration: for four decades gender and racial parity had been a stated goal.

Joining Barber and his co-chair, the Reverend Dr. Liz Theoharis, was a much less conventional array of experts. The Poor People's Campaign had, in fact, partnered with some think-tank experts, like John Cavanaugh, the director of the Institute for Policy Studies, and Thea Lee, the president of the Economic Policy Institute, to write a fourteen-point policy plan pushing for poverty relief through a steep increase in the federal minimum wage, a single-payer universal health-care program, and student debt relief (Poor People's Campaign 2021). That officials from think tanks based in DC presented a detailed policy proposal was itself nothing new for the transition period. This was the right time to make big asks.

It was the backgrounds of the other attendees, and what they shared, at the ninety-minute meeting—twice the length the team originally allotted—that were so different. "What we do is we put people in the room, we believe in the agency of poor and low wealth people," said Barber. So, Zillah Wesley from Washington, DC talked about her challenges dealing with the Coronavirus while she managed other health problems. Kenia Alcocer, an organizer with Union de Vecinos from Los Angeles, explained her status as an undocumented mother of two and the importance of tenant rights. Sara Fearrington from North Carolina recounted periods of homelessness despite working since she was seven years old and her efforts as a union organizer to push for a $15 minimum wage. And Chris Olive, a veteran from Washington State, recounted his own substance abuse and experiences advocating for the one in sixteen residents of Aberdeen, WA, who were living without sufficient housing.

This was a break from the past, a change in the tone from a typical interaction with a transition team, so often focused on policy details, data, and facts. These personal accounts, rich in emotion, seemed to make a difference for at least one member of the transition team on the call. Reverend Theoharis later related: "(Cecilia Munoz) deeply appreciated that we pulled this meeting together, and said it's not often, in fact it's not happened in her life before, to have impacted folk talking about the stories that they come from and the solutions" (Poor People's Campaign 2020).

The 2020–2021 transition was then an unusual mixture of more of the same and something very different. This was alright for Reverend Barber, who had come to expect the unexpected: "We come out of a tradition where in 1964 Lyndon Baines Johnson who got elected was a segregationist, but the movement turned him into a civil rights President" (The Brian Lehrer Show 2021). Barber aimed to convince this new president with a resume no more radical than Johnson's when he came into office. "We have to push," Barber said, and to do so in a way that might seem shocking to a transition team steeped in convention and the status quo: "We have to put a face on poverty."

To understand Barber's unconventional approach, though, this anecdote must be placed into the longer history of past presidential transitions and evolving Democratic Party politics. How, for example, does the transition period fit into the larger democratic process of transferring executive power and authority? More specifically, why does the transition team even set up meetings with groups outside the campaign, like Barber's, since they are so short on time and federal law doesn't require them to? The short answer is that each transition, distinct in many ways from the last, demonstrates longer patterns of party politics in Washington and the changing influence of groups, ideology, and new policy ideas. The transition period was first institutionalized by Congress, then later politicized by groups allied with each party, leading to a process that favors insiders over outsiders, except in unusual circumstances.

Who's Got Time to Advise the New President?

Fall 2020 was unlike any autumn in recent US history. In the last month of the presidential campaign, there were 24,000 COVID-related deaths, and on Election Day, more than a thousand died.[2] Amid this raging pandemic, with many exhausted from a two-year campaign, even the most interested group had to figure out whether it had the time to lobby the newly elected president and vice president.

What seems to have helped *groups*—that is, formal organizations that represent a constituency interested in public policy including trade associations, labor unions, and member-based groups as well as non–constituency-based policy organizations like think tanks, research institutes, and legal research centers (Halpin, Fraussen, and Nownes 2018)—to answer this question in 2020, as it had in past transitions, was whether they'd be listened to. Nobody wants to waste their breath.

In 2016, Donald Trump's lawyer Michael Cohen "begged" him to read a report written by advisers to Mitt Romney about sound transition planning (Cohen 2020). Trump refused; after all, he'd called Romney a "fool" and a "stiff" in the past (Conway 2016). Sensing this, when Omarosa Manigault invited civil rights leaders to advise Trump during the same transition, they refused (Manigault 2019). To be fair, Trump didn't trust anyone: he fired the person he'd asked to prepare for the 2016 transition, New Jersey governor Chris Christie, days after he won the election. And, to be even fairer, perhaps anticipating he'd make over sixteen thousand misleading claims while in office, Trump gave scant reasons for anyone to trust him (Kessler, Rizzo, and Kelly 2021).

Research by political scientists backs up these anecdotes: policymakers, including presidents, aren't open to hearing from all groups but typically have close friends and trusted allies (Holyoke 2004; Miller 2022). Mutually beneficial relationships form between groups and policymakers that share interests as well as beliefs about policy and personnel (Furnas et al. 2022). For example, following eight years of limited access to the Nixon and Ford White Houses, political scientist Jack Walker (1991) showed that nearly half of citizen groups reported more cooperation with the White House after an ally, Democrat Jimmy Carter, was elected in 1976. In comparison, just a quarter of business groups believed the same. Four years later, the reverse happened. Business associations were ascendant as the fortunes of various groups shifted following Republican Ronald Reagan's election, according to political scientists Kay Schlozman and John Tierney (1986).

And this isn't just about money and the crude exchange of financial support for influence. Most groups, in fact, don't give campaign contributions; many don't even have the funds to hire a lobbyist, let alone the explicitly political mission to permit it (Baumgartner et al. 2009; Drutman 2015). Instead, information is the coin of the realm in Washington (Baumgartner and Jones 2015). When a policymaker finds a group that it can trust to supply information, a relationship is born, what political scientists Richard Hall and Alan Deardorff (2006) called "legislative subsidy" to refer to the costs groups incur on behalf of policymakers to collect, analyze, and share information (Hojnacki and Kimball 1998). It isn't that money doesn't matter, it's just that many groups don't have any to give, and when it comes to the transition period, the big-ticket items that mattered during the campaign, like paid political advertisements, national organizing, and various forms of digital media, are no longer needed compared to information.

An incoming president needs information to help with the thousands of decisions that they must make. One person involved in the 2020 transition said: "You more or less only have three months . . . to build a plane, fly a plane, land a plane . . . that plane, being the massive apparatus that is the federal government."[3] This is the essence of what makes presidential transitions different from transitions in control of Congress, and what makes presidential transitions increasingly important as the size of the executive branch and expectations about presidents as policymakers have grown (Neustadt 1960; Schlesinger 2004; Howell 2003; Rudalevige 2005). Though civil service rules mean the vast majority of federal employees keep their jobs after a transition, the Center for Presidential Transitions estimates up to four thousand positions may be filled by a new president: a little less than a third (30%) of those require Senate confirmation, with many others in the White House and across federal departments (Center for Presidential Transitions n.d.). This set of so-called *political appointees*, who oversee the execution of the president's agenda and ongoing work of federal agencies, turns over each time a new president is elected.

When it comes to that policy agenda, the transition formally begins after a campaign in which a typical candidate makes policy promise after policy promise. This is, of course, how they get elected. POLITIFACT tracked more than five hundred campaign promises Barack Obama made in 2008, many about policy change (POLITIFACT n.d.). Even if a presidential candidate didn't intend to follow through on each one—Obama fulfilled 47 percent over two terms, and Trump 23 percent in one term—this suggests a transition period dominated by figuring out which policies will top the agenda and where the president-elect can act unilaterally once in office (Shogan 2004; Howell 2003).

Yet, it's not just hot-button campaign issues that the new president must address. Hundreds of other issues—what some scholars call *non-salient issues*—must be addressed as well (Burstein 2006). Add to that preparing an initial budget proposal, reorganizing federal agencies and the White House, and addressing unexpected calamities like a flailing economy or a public health crisis, and the transition period is an overwhelming catalog of decisions, big and small.

These decision-making demands also explain why the transition period isn't focused on the type of persuasion that is so central to political scientist Richard Neustadt's (1960) seminal view of the president once in office. The president-elect's actions during the transition period come with fewer of the checks and balances imposed after the inauguration, so there's less pressure (and fewer incentives) to bargain with Congress, especially during an era of rising polarization and partisan gridlock on Capitol Hill. This is, in part, because during the transition the president-elect is just that—not yet president. So, while the decisions during the transition period are incredibly important, such as organizing the future White House, developing a policy agenda, and making thousands of appointments that don't require Senate confirmation, most aren't the types of decisions that fall within presidential authority under the Constitution. Even the preparation of the initial executive orders, a focus of much activity before the inauguration, requires almost no cooperation with Congress and others outside the transition team. Finally, while new rules have moved the transition closer to the official work of government, the transition team remains a private organization and the president-elect a private citizen. With less need to persuade Congress, more control over unilateral decisions (Christenson and Kriner 2020), and a press corps undergoing its own transition (Jones 1998), there are also fewer reasons to court the public with frequent press events or to "Go Public," in the words of political scientist Samuel Kernell (2007). To this point, during the pre-election transition period in 2020, the Biden-Harris transition team had a single person covering press issues, according to one high-ranking transition official.[4]

As a consequence of these peculiar features of the transition period, unlike after the president has been sworn into office and the full support of the vast federal bureaucracy is at their disposal, the president-elect has little time but considerable need for help prior to January 20 (Workman 2015; Resh 2014).

Much of that help comes from—is delegated to—members of the transition team, once a small team of close advisers, by the twenty-first century a small army of volunteers and short-term employees. Bill Clinton brought in a core team of forty-five overseen by Vernon Jordan and Warren Christopher as well as hundreds more volunteering to review what was happening at each federal agency. Donald Trump's team topped two hundred, and Joe Biden's was even bigger.

A large team of volunteers, however, won't have all the right information about every nook and cranny of the vast federal government. Groups do.

Take the example of the Clinton-Gore transition in 1992–1993. During a campaign speech to the US Conference of Mayors in June, Clinton promised a "bold plan" to stimulate the struggling economy, including $20 billion in new infrastructure spending for the next four years (*New York Times* 1992). After he was elected, though, it was unclear to the transition team whether the states could actually spend that much money in the coming year, risking the stimulus going to waste. To solve this problem, the transition team turned to the group that could figure this out quickly, the American Association of State Highway and Transportation Officials—commonly known in Washington as AASHTO—which surveyed its members in all fifty states and reported back to the transition team that states would in fact be able to spend the money (US Congress 1992).

Interest groups, trade associations, think tanks, labor unions, and civil society organizations of every shape and size, like AASHTO, possess this type of prized information, and if they don't have it, they can collect it quickly. This is why so many of their staff end up chosen as trusted volunteers on the transition team or called in to advise on key decisions.

But who to trust?

Broadly speaking, the first people you trust are the ones who helped you get the job, not those career bureaucrats with an expertise in policy and governance who remained neutral during the election and remain wary after it (Resh 2015; Heclo 1977). And, not your voters, who've been loyal, but lack expert policy knowledge. Instead, it is the groups that claim to represent them that can be trusted most. The UCLA School of Political Parties suggests that parties serve as broad umbrellas of what are called "intense policy-demanders" (Cohen et al. 2008, 30). That is, groups with particular demands or views on what goes on in Washington, everything from who is going to be the party's presidential candidate to what is the ideal budget of the Environmental Protection Agency to how to restructure the Department of Health and Human Services. Each party has an array of "intense-policy demanding" groups camped out under their umbrella that help them make these decisions, even if most of these groups are, officially speaking, nonpartisan.

We can think of these groups colloquially as *insiders*. They are insiders in the sense that they operate in close (or strong) connection to party leaders and in contrast with *outsiders*, which operate with fewer (or weaker) connections to party leaders. Insider groups are offered *access*, that most prized and scarce resource in Washington. Access to the important meetings. Access to the right people. Access to—in the words of Lin-Manuel Miranda's Aaron Burr—"the room where it happens."

Throughout the remainder of the book, access is *the* central concept.

Access is a quickly returned text message, an invitation to the right dinner, or a decision-maker's personal number saved in your phone. Access is scarce and therefore valuable. Access is the last seat at the conference room table. You know you have access if someone in power has shared big news with you just before it drops on social media for the world to read. Access is not easily defined, but for outsider groups that never have an email returned or never get an invite to that meeting, they know they have little of it.

Access doesn't equal influence, exactly.

To have influence, to have the power to change the mind of someone with authority, you must possess something of value to share. In exchange for access, and potential influence over party decisions, some groups help candidates win elections by contributing money, endorsing candidates, and rallying voters, and then later help those elected officials do their jobs once in office. Other groups have novel information needed by new presidents to make important decisions. In this way, access is not the same thing as influence, but it is related because access affords more chances to gain trust. The more often a group has the access to interact with the party, the more comfortable they become with each other, sealing a mutually beneficial and trusting relationship (Peterson 1992). This may be why, on the one hand, some evidence suggests congressional staffers are no more likely to grant a meeting to a lobbyist than a constituent (other evidence shows campaign donors may be given extra access), but at the same time Democratic staffers favor information provided by liberal think tanks and Republican staffers from conservative think tanks (Furnas et al. 2022; Kalla and Broockman 2016). Constituents may have access, but it's the party's insider groups that possess the information needed to influence decisions.

It may even be the case that if the relationship is extremely close, group access may appear to *decline* while influence *rises*. This is what political scientists Kyuwon Lee and Hye Young You (2023) found in research on lobbying of the US Trade Representative (USTR). Paradoxically, Lee and You showed when a company had a close associate working at the USTR, its lobbying spending went down, apparent evidence that their access might also be declining, yet its influence, in fact, was rising.

These patterns of trust and deep connections suggest why experienced groups have such an advantage over upstarts. Political scientist Matt Grossmann (2012) aptly described a system of *institutionalized pluralism* in which an interest group's longevity determines its resources and then its access and influence. Over time, groups become intertwined with parties, grow powerful, and the patterns of influence are rendered institutionalized, predictable, and stable. The famed "Revolving Door" of people in and out of government derives from this institutionalization, as groups stand to benefit from hiring those with prominent positions in the party and the real insider groups are the ones that have the money needed to pay them, too (LaPira and Thomas 2017). Thus, the basis of trust is often regular and repeated interactions, which show the policymaker that the group is on their side and should be given access to help over the long haul. These institutionalized patterns also reinforce the status-quo bias in federal public-policy making, as insiders typically work to protect their position to maintain policy rather than initiate disruptive policy change (Baumgartner and Jones 1993; Baumgartner et al. 2009).

Institutionalized Transition Pluralism

What has happened for transitions since the 1960s resembles Grossmann's more general depiction of policymaking. This is why in the past I've characterized the period as a form of *institutionalized transition pluralism* (Brown 2012). In this case, *institutionalization*, the second big concept of the book, followed from new policies on the transition process after Congress passed the Presidential Transition Act (PTA) of 1963.

Prior to this, transitions were largely informal—Woodrow Wilson took a month-long vacation in Bermuda following his election; Warren Harding cruised along the Florida coast in a houseboat after a trip to Panama to recuperate from his election ("Eleven Weeks between Presidents" 1960). The outgoing administration was required to abide by few rules, and the incoming even fewer, raising the chance that the transfer of power could go very badly, especially during the height of the Cold War.

The PTA took this ad hoc eleven-week stroll along the beach and turned it into an institution with the precision of a military tattoo, adhering to Douglass North's (2009) conception of an institution as a set of societal rules that provide stability and reduce uncertainty. Since then, additional policy changes to the PTA did just that, further reducing uncertainty by strengthening the rules of the transition period, including increasing federal funding for transition planning to candidates before the election as well as to the eventual winner before Inauguration Day (Jones 1998).

In the case of foreign affairs, incoming presidents had been in a particularly bad position prior to institutionalization of the transition period because the most pertinent information was classified, closely protected by national security officials, and thus largely unavailable to the transition team until after the inauguration. This "transition failure" contributed to "the Bay of Pigs Fiasco," one of the biggest missteps of the Kennedy presidency, according to political scientist Rebecca Friedman (2011). Today, federal law has institutionalized the sharing of classified information by expediting security clearances for foreign policy advisers of the major candidates. This assures, in normal circumstances, that classified briefings can commence immediately after the election.[5]

Subsequent policy changes further formalized the role of the General Services Administration (GSA) as the hub of transition planning, required the sitting president to establish interagency transition teams to coordinate a possible transition out of office months before the day of the election, and mandated federal support for secure communications and office space after the party conventions nominate a candidate (Herz and Shaw 2021). A leisurely vacation at the beach for the exhausted candidate is a thing of the past (Jones 1998).

Transition teams have responded accordingly, adopting similar structures, procedures, and timelines, often the result of federally mandated coordination between the outgoing and incoming White House. Whether it's a Republican or Democratic campaign, prior to the election—what's called the *pre-election transition period*—transition leaders quietly begin identifying potential appointees, mapping a plan for the White House, and figuring out how to translate campaign promises into federal policy (Kumar 2017). Small teams are established during this time, typically working separately from the campaign, but increasingly busy, better staffed, and integrated with the campaign as Election Day and the (*post-election*) transition period nears.

The institutionalization of the transition process has generally worked to the benefit of insider groups, those sufficiently well-resourced, experienced, and prepared to participate with the incoming administration. These groups know to be ready long before Election Day, stocked with policy reports and lists of names for key appointments, and available to meet with the transition team. Upstarts, sometimes caught up in the excitement of the campaign, often can't even figure out who's in charge of the transition until it's too late.

As a result of existing and trusting relationships, groups closely associated with each party get the prized seats at the transition table, pushing others to stand and wait, thereby winning the chance to influence the new administration, have a say in who is appointed, and gain control over the policy agenda. And research bears this out: during the 2008–2009 transition, groups aligned with the Democratic Party used significantly more transition tactics compared to groups that were not aligned, and, further, older organizations were significantly more likely to have someone appointed to the new Obama administration than newer organizations (Brown 2012). Institutionalization has advantaged party insiders, especially when they have an interest in maintaining the status quo.

An Opportunity for Outsiders

If this is how things usually work, we'd have little to explain why Reverend Barber's group lined up a meeting with the Biden-Harris transition team. It was just two years old at the time, hadn't given large campaign donations to the candidates, and had nobody placed on the inside circle of the Biden-Harris team. These types of factors have historically driven a wedge between presidents and social movement groups: indifference, suspicion, and ignorance on each side undermining close connections (Milkis and Tichenor 2019; Miroff 1981). What then explains why, despite the institutionalization of the transition period, new groups are ever given access and sometimes are even influential?

It could be that on the micro-level, groups like Reverend Barber's have just become savvier at overcoming institutional barriers to access during the transition, learning how to leverage the moral authority of a leader like Barber. On the macro-level, however, it may be that the Democratic Party isn't as powerful as it once was. Powerful, that is, in the sense of being able to use its institutions to patrol the edges of its umbrella, pushing out newcomers in favor of trusted friends and insiders. Lacking that power to keep order, parties—both Democratic and Republican—create unintended opportunities for new groups to insert themselves into party activities, especially during the transition period. This is consistent with the idea of "hollow parties" articulated by political scientists Daniel Schlozman and Sam Rosenfeld (2019). They focused on the polarized era in American politics starting in the 1970s when the distinctions between the two parties grew starker and the cost of campaigns skyrocketed. Polarization and the explosion of money in politics reshaped the parties, rendering them less responsible to the wishes of their voters and dismantling many of their historic functions. The parties of the past, along with their powerful party institutions, had been hollowed out.

Into the institutional hole, "para-party" groups on both the ideological left and right have arisen. On the political right, these groups, like the Koch brothers' Americans for Prosperity—well-resourced, but largely unaccountable—wield considerable influence through unrestricted campaign contributions, access to the media, and support for ideological think tanks. They've been integral to transitions, as well.

Take, as an example from the Republican Party, the case of the Heritage

Foundation, which broke through in 1980 from out of nowhere. It was a new-comer in so many ways, lacking the deep institutional ties of more established conservative groups, like the American Enterprise Institute (AEI) and the Hoover Institution, and possessing few of the financial resources of business associations to support the party's candidate. How exactly did Heritage do it?

Prior to 1980, ideology was kept far from the technical dimensions of the transition period, similar to how political scientists Stephen Skowronek, John Dearborn, and Desmond King (2022) characterized the "happy balance" found until the 1970s across other day-to-day functions of the federal government that depended on synthesizing complex information without interference from party or ideology.

Indicative of this nonpolitical environment, the Brookings Institution was the main think-tank shop in town, evenhandedly advising incoming presidential administrations for twenty years, both Democrats and Republicans (Brown 2012). During the 1960 campaign, Brookings convened representatives for each candidate—Brig. Gen. Robert E. Cushman Jr. for Nixon and Clark M. Clifford for Kennedy—to begin preparing for a transition after Eisenhower's two terms in the White House. Brookings president Robert Calkins explained that "it would be useful for an outside organization like Brookings to make an objective appraisal of certain administration and institutional problems involved in the transition," but he reassured everyone that "Brookings envisages its role as a modest one" (Brookings Institution 1960).

Brookings's outside, modest, and objective approach focused on the nuts and bolts of getting the president's administration up and working, explicitly leaving the politics aside (Jones 1998). This bipartisan imprimatur sealed the access needed to advise Kennedy after he won in 1960—Brookings's research associate Laurin Henry wrote to Clifford on November 11, "Congratulations on yesterday's announcement from Hyannisport [sic]!"—as well as Nixon eight years later. And in 1964 Congress even accepted Henry's advice for it to begin funding transition planning, demonstrating the think tank's integral role in institutionalizing this process (Brookings Institution 2008). Brookings had moved from outsider to insider, gaining access and influence in the process.

To be sure, one group's evenhanded advice is another group's self-interested opinion. By the 1970s conservatives had grown weary of the dominant role played by Brookings (Edwards 1997). Brookings's claim to ideological neutrality was greatly oversold, Heritage contended (Lamb 2005). Conservatives always lost out when the same group, committed to the same vision for public policy, got the inside track on advising everyone from Kennedy to Johnson to Nixon. Though he soon soured on the think tank, Nixon even appointed to his administration Henry Kissinger and Herbert Stein, who'd written essays for the 1968 Brookings transition report "Agenda for the Nation," the former chosen for National Security Affairs and the later for the Council of Economic Advisers (Troy 2017; Brookings Institution 2008).

With California governor Ronald Reagan in the race and a brand-new think tank just launched, things were going to change (Edwards 1997). How could Reagan trust Brookings to advise him on the transition when its advisers cared so little about the priorities of his conservative movement? Personnel *is* policy, everyone agreed at Heritage, and fidelity to the cause mattered most. If the conservative standard bearer, the American Enterprise Institute, was too slow to do it, with the deep pockets of Joseph Coors, Heritage would rebuild Washington on its own—and the transition was the place to start (Edwards 1997; Bjerre-Poulsen 1991).

To do so, Heritage organized a group of conservative scholars to draft a road map for the Reagan presidency to transform the federal government, should he win.[6] It eventually published a five-volume tome: three thousand pages of suggestions for the Reagan team, with essays on everything from defense spending to enterprise zones.

Heritage, though, wasn't simply focused on policy. James Hinish, author of the report's section on regulatory reform, wrote: "[Reagan's] most important weapon in the war against regulatory red-tape, paperwork and overkill is his appointment power" and that "the single most important qualification, however, must be that the appointee share the general philosophy and outlook of the President" (Heatherly 1981). Appointments made during the transition period were crucial to Heritage's vision for the future. This was because not only would those devoted political appointees share Reagan's vision for policy, they'd also share his disdain for government itself. He'd made this much clear at the end of his transition: "Government is the problem," he famously proclaimed during his inaugural address (Reagan 1981). Loyal personnel appointed during the transition wouldn't just oversee the federal government but also would check the impulses of government employees who were hostile to Reagan's agenda.

When Reagan won in November 1980, Heritage had the final copy, *Mandate for Leadership*, ready for the cabinet's first meeting. The book became a best-seller.

From that earliest point of the Reagan presidency, Heritage overturned precedent and the institutionalized practice of ideological neutrality on the part of think tanks during past transitions. It had the access to get fourteen of its staffers onto the Reagan transition team and, later, the influence associated with having three dozen Heritage-affiliated scholars appointed to the administration (Brown 2012).

Given Heritage's innovative transition strategy, it should come as no surprise that the Reagan presidency that unfolded over the next eight years has been lauded by scholars, including political scientist Charles O. Jones (1998), as transformational, and the start of a new era or regime, according to political scientist Stephen Skowronek (1997). The new governing philosophy of the Reagan era was the realization of the conservative movement's beliefs in individualism, preserving racial, gender, and religious hierarchies; deep distrust of government; and shrinking the social welfare state. It was a break from the Roosevelt era, a break from the institutionalized practice of non-politicized transitions, and it became the dominant presidential regime far into the twenty-first century (Jones 1998).

Across this Reagan era, then, two important things happened: first, the transition period grew even more *institutionalized*, with subsequent changes to the Presidential Transition Act to increase federal funding and promote greater planning; and, second, it became more *politicized* as who incoming administrations trusted to advise them was more strongly tied to ideology, deeply held convictions, and connections. Heritage's newcomer success in 1980 was the exception that proved the rule, as most transitions followed a pattern of institutionalized pluralism. Politicization helps explain why. Following Heritage's success in 1980, those helping with advice—those given access—were no longer just the disinterested research centers, like the Brookings Institution or even career bureaucrats with a wealth of information to share, but also so-called advocacy tanks tied to each party: Heritage for the Republicans and, for the Democratic Party, the left-of-center Democratic Leadership Conference (DLC) in 1992 and the Center for American Progress in 2008 (Resh 2015). Indicative of this, four decades on, it was Heritage again in 2016—not some new conservative upstart—that stocked the Trump transition team with sixteen volunteers and dozens of policy proposals (Mahler 2018; Milbank 2000).[7]

But the two national parties in the United States aren't mirror images of each other. Heritage's success owes much to the Republican Party's orientation to ideology as its center of gravity and pursuit of conservatism as its raison d'etre. Adapting the broad ideological aims of the conservative movement—maintaining racial, ethnic, and gender hierarchies, opposing the Soviet Union, and advancing American business—to a coherent policy agenda facilitated the emergence of a central group like Heritage.

Political scientists Matt Grossmann and David Hopkins (2016) assert that for the Democratic Party, it has long been about linking the interests of social groups, necessitating the coordination of various representative organizations with distinct policy agendas. Policy precedes ideology for Democrats. Although Democratic Party leaders sometimes allude to a common progressive ideal, since party realignment in the middle of the twentieth century they have been centrally concerned with representing the policy aims of women, African Americans, and labor, not a common ideology across groups (Schickler 2013; Grossmann and Dominguez 2009; Dark 2018). The party, then, has long been fixated on coalition, not ideological, management, limiting the chance for any single organization to dominate its agenda like Heritage has for Republicans (Troy 2017).

Take the case of the DLC and the Progressive Policy Institute, the twin organizations of New Democrats, founded in the mid-1980s to shift the Democratic Party's thinking away from New Deal progressivism and what the leaders called "liberal fundamentalism" in their 1989 call-to-action "The Politics of Evasion" (Galston and Kamarck 1989, 17). To the DLC, the Democratic Party was captured by "a coalition increasingly dominated by minority groups and white elites," with an outlook dominated by race, and a harmful orthodoxy on policies like abortion. Early DLC leaders William Galston and Elaine Kamarck (1989, 17) wrote that among Democratic voters there was "a profound division on the abortion question," but that it was "virtually unthinkable that a serious candidate for the Democratic presidential nomination would deviate far from the strict pro-choice position." They noted the same disconnects for affirmative action, crime, and poverty.

The DLC had a plan to do things differently, copying what Heritage had done in 1980 with *Mandate for Leadership*. Galston (2004) explained that *"Mandate for Change* (the title of the DLC transition report in 1992) . . . was imitation being the sincerest form of flattery." And just like how Heritage had its report ready in 1980: "[the DLC] would have something to put on the President-elect's desk the day after he was elected, and it would be a leaner, meaner version of what the Heritage Foundation had done for Reagan" (Galston 2004).

Bill Clinton had been a DLC fan since before he decided to run for the White House; he'd even agreed to serve as the organization's president. The DLC had Clinton's ear during the campaign and felt it had successfully moved the party's platform to the center, adding new policy alternatives to change welfare, education, and economic policy (Riley 2008). According to Michael Espy, a DLC-affiliated member of Congress and future secretary of agriculture: "[The Democratic Party] didn't see the DLC as a rival; they saw the DLC as an asset, because [the DLC] could do the think tank and the policy development and [the Democratic Party] would do the technical campaign mission. . . . It was very complementary" (Martin 2006).

Once Clinton won the election and the transition began, however, the DLC had access, yet its influence waned. Clinton named DLC founder Al From to run domestic policy planning for the transition team, but when Clinton arrived in Washington in December, he met with Marion Wright

Edelman of the Children's Defense Fund (CDF), first, not the DLC (Russell 2008). Looking back, Clinton's choice hardly seems like a death blow to an organization, but at the time it alarmed the DLC. The Children's Defense Fund had been a foil of the DLC, advancing policies that Kamarck called "old-fashioned, doomed-to-fail, bad-on-substance, bad politics" (Riley 2008). Clinton's decision to visit Wright Edelman's group first shocked the DLC and signaled the DLC wasn't Heritage.

For his part, Clinton couldn't have won without having a lot of friends. The declining influence also had to do with the DLC itself. Another early DLC leader, Al From, explained: "Unlike the Heritage Foundation when Reagan won, we didn't have this big cadre of intellectuals" (Riley 2007). The DLC got a few people in, most importantly Bruce Reed as the domestic policy director and several DLC-affiliated members of Congress into the cabinet, "But there weren't many of us. As the White House staff was put together, we had our recommendations but . . . there were not that many people with real New Democrat DNA in their blood" (Riley 2007).

And in hindsight it wasn't just that the DLC didn't have its people ready; the DLC didn't fully understand the party, even if they wanted to change it (Riley 2008). One of the recommendations from the DLC during the transition was to appoint loyalists to key positions, much as Heritage had advised twelve years earlier. When From met with Clinton during the first week of the transition, he advised the president-elect accordingly: "I think you ought to go with a test of loyalty to your programs and not worry about diversity" (Riley 2007). Nobody asked From for his feelings on appointments after that (Riley 2008).

Years later, in assessing whether the DLC succeeded in advising Clinton to make appointments based on fealty to the DLC policy agenda, Galston (2004) concluded: "Failure, failure on all fronts. The construction of the Cabinet was guided by other principles. The construction of the White House was guided by no principles at all."

Unlike Heritage's success at linking a new policy agenda to personnel, the DLC managed policy victories, some significant, but nothing larger. Importantly, on Clinton's signature first-term issue, his top priority, healthcare reform, the DLC hadn't taken a clear stand, and DLC leaders including From and Kamarck weren't chosen to lead on its design during the transition or within the White House.[8] The DLC could mimic Heritage's strategy, but it couldn't make the Democratic Party work like the Republican Party, especially on a "core" issue like health care that drew so many groups to the Clinton transition planning (LaPira, Thomas, and Baumgartner 2014).

By 1992–1993, according to Charles O. Jones (1998, 196), presidential transitions had been fully politicized; the historic distinction between campaigning and governing that Reagan had blurred, Clinton erased. This politicization meant more groups expected, and were given, access to the Clinton transition. Many of those groups, like the Children's Defense Fund, and others like the major labor unions, environmental groups, and medical associations, represented different constituencies with permanent positions in the party and had helped rally the voters Clinton needed to win. An upstart think tank short on resources, like the DLC, even with its intimate access to the new president, couldn't demand loyalty to a newly fashioned ideology for a party structured around something other than ideology.

A decade and a half later, another Democratic president was preparing for the White House. Barack Obama, who'd carefully navigated the politics of race during the campaign, found a winning policy agenda and a promise of hope and change. Again, just as in 1992, there was an upstart think tank allied with the candidate and ready to make that change happen. Unlike in 1992, the Center for American Progress (CAP) was well-staffed and well-resourced. With the ground set, Obama appeared on the cover of *Time* magazine and *The New Yorker* as the next FDR, the next transformational Democratic president.

Magazine covers, alas, aren't destiny, and several decisions shifted the path of the Obama administration from transformational to something else. For one, though the Obama campaign had been turbo-charged by a digital grassroots strategy, dubbed Obama for America, the culmination of innovation within the party since John Kerry lost four years earlier, those outsider voices so closely associated with the turn toward technology were quickly silenced (Han, McKenna, and Oyakawa 2021).

Two million regular users of Obama for America's digital platform, MYBO, helped unseat Hillary Clinton as the Democratic Party's candidate, using new campaign technology to advance new public policies. Christopher Edley, a law professor from UC Berkeley and a close adviser of Obama during the campaign, aimed to institutionalize the apparatus of Obama for America to advance an expansive policy agenda, should Obama be elected (Sifry 2017). Not everyone on the campaign or in the Democratic Party agreed with Edley. Importantly, the pre-election transition team was unconvinced the ambitious plan would work or was even a good idea. Rather than an extensive digital platform to connect the campaign to the transition and later to the White House, the transition team launched change.org, a minimalist site for those seeking a job to upload a resume. Obama for America would be renamed Organizing for America and would be housed in the Democratic National Committee, no longer operating as an independent organizing tool to empower Obama supporters.

Disabling Obama for America at this earlier stage had long-term consequences for the Obama agenda, but in the near term, it was who the president-elect chose to oversee key parts of the transition that made the biggest impact. Though the Center for American Progress was brand-new at the time, it was deeply rooted in the Democratic Party. John Podesta had served in the Clinton White House before helping to establish this new think tank in 2003. In 2007, in addition to running CAP, Podesta was planning a potential Hillary Clinton presidential transition. When Clinton conceded, Podesta and his dozens of CAP policy experts were ready to help Obama prepare to govern. Obama soon chose him to direct the transition.

These links to the Bill and Hillary Clinton insiders had a moderating impact on the Obama transition. Reed Hundt (2019), who had been on the 1992 transition team and then appointed to the Federal Communications Commission (FCC), later joined the Obama transition and wrote an entire book on that experience. He volunteered on the team to address the monumental challenge of the housing and financial crisis of 2008. Obama, a lawyer by training and community organizer by profession, hadn't campaigned on economic issues—it wasn't a core issue for him or a long-standing priority—yet crises have an unpredictable way of dictating the agenda during the transition. Lacking Wall Street connections and a strong resume on economic issues, Hundt (2019, 31) wrote that "Obama turned most of his transition planning over to [Hillary] Clinton's people, picked many of them for powerful posts." Timothy Geithner, Lawrence Summers, and Peter Orszag were all tied to Bill Clinton's treasury secretary Robert Rubin and were driving Obama economic planning. There were exceptions during the transition. Jared Bernstein and Christina Romer were not a part of the "School of Rubin," but they were outnumbered. Even Carol Browner, a founding board member of CAP, who wasn't aligned with the thinking of the Clinton wing of the economic team, had little influence on the economic recovery plan coming out of the transition. As a result, Hundt contended: "[Clinton's] advisers had the inside track on persuading Obama to do what they would have told Hillary Clinton to do: restore Wall Street to profitability and end the recession without spending too much money. . . . Neoliberalism will reign again."

Hundt was not alone in observing the Obama transition team's commitment to past economic policies of the party and derision of unorthodox views. One progressive advocacy group expert on economic issues recalled a meeting held during the Obama transition: "The transition team sent one person to meet with a room of about 100 different progressive stakeholders at the AFL-CIO headquarters."[9] These were the groups that had turned out voters for Obama, that had helped him win, and all they got was access to one person from the team. And, what they heard from that single person was anything but encouraging to hopes to influence policy change. "The attitude in that room was a very condescending tone from the person that was sent over. It was sort of like 'I'm meeting with you all to check a box.'"[10] And what about those campaign pledges? "You all need to know that the things that we promised that we would do in terms of changing [economic] policy during the campaign, we're not going to be able to do [that]."[11]

The Obama administration faced many other barriers to enacting widespread policy change on a variety of issues. Obama as the next FDR was opposed with extreme partisan vigor from Day 1 by nearly every Republican in Congress and a grassroots movement animated by racism and xenophobia (Rudalevige 2012; Skocpol and Jacobs 2012). But, internally, the decisions made within the Democratic coalition during the transition period on organization, staffing, and a policy agenda also directed the Obama presidency toward stability, moderation, and policy orthodoxy (Edwards 2016). This is in part why political scientist Martha Joynt Kumar (2017, 6) wrote, "The preparations for the 2008 transition were more extensive and polished than any preceding one," but not ultimately the most transformational.

One way to make sense of these competing dynamics that tie parties and groups together is to think of the two most important theoretical factors driving access and influence during a transition as *status*—whether a group is a high-status insider or a low-status outsider—and *priority*—whether any given issue is a high or low priority. The consequence of an institutionalized transition period is that status and priority are tightly restricted, creating a closed process in which outsiders with new policy ideas or recommendations of bold personnel choices have few opportunities to influence the incoming administration and major change is greatly limited (Baumgartner and Jones 2015; Baumgartner and Jones 1993).

What determines a group's status in the party is a function of many historic factors, especially the role played by the group during past campaigns and transitions. Likewise, why an issue is a high or low priority for an incoming administration relates to established party commitments as well as the president-elect's long-standing interests and expertise. To be sure, status and priority are hard to define precisely, since they mean different things for different party actors and groups as well as for different types of issues. In practice, most groups likely operate along a continuum of extreme insider to extreme outsider. The same could also be said for a continuum of high to low priority.

Status and priority are largely stable and not prone to change, but they aren't set in stone (Baumgartner et al. 2009). Insider status shifts to outsider status from time to time, as do issue priorities. A group that was a marginal player in voter mobilization in the past might emerge during a campaign as especially effective at getting out the vote or fundraising to contribute to the campaign. This will elevate that group from outsider to insider just as transition planning begins. For example, gay and lesbian rights groups coordinated large donors for the first time to support the Clinton campaign in 1992, leading to wide-ranging access to the transition team never before offered to these groups (Vaid 1995).

Change in issue priority is also especially important to consider during the transition. Since the transition period is fixed in time, an exogenous change in political context may coincide with the eleven weeks of the transition, like the housing crisis in 2008 and the pandemic in 2020. Such unanticipated events will shift an issue from low to high priority, changing the political dynamics of the transition period and the chance for groups to gain (or lose) access and influence.

What these factors suggest is that, in general, insiders have a large amount of status and outsiders have very little, leading insiders to be given access to the new president, such as a seat on the transition, meetings with members of the team, and other opportunities to advise the team. This may lead to influence, especially when the insider group's issue is a high priority for the new president (upper left quadrant of Table 1.1). In Congress, political scientists E. J. Fagan and Zachary McGee (2022) showed that high-priority issues lead legislators to consult experts for information. Something similar happens during the transition, as addressing a high-priority issue requires the transition team to collect and analyze a lot of information.

High-priority issues, though, are likely to attract many groups and are ones transition leaders will be hesitant to delegate, since the president-elect is surely to have made big promises during the campaign (LaPira, Thomas, and Baumgartner 2014). This congested environment compels the transition team leaders to trust a small proportion of groups and prioritize the views of the highest-status insiders, thereby restricting the influence of lesser-status insiders and outsiders, alike.

The converse is the case for outsiders and low-priority issues: an outsider focused on low-priority issues is unlikely to be trusted or given access (lower right quadrant of Table 1.1). As a result, outsiders will have almost no chance to influence the transition team, especially since the low-priority issue will mean the transition team's efforts will be focused elsewhere.

More interesting are the other two possibilities. Insiders focused on low-priority issues are likely to face fewer competing groups jostling for access to the transition team, a situation similar to what political scientist Amy McKay (2022) described as *stealth lobbying* when this happens in Congress. In this case (lower left quadrant of Table 1.1), the transition team has no choice but

Table 1.1: Status and Priority during the Transition

	Expected outcome	
	Party Insider	Party Outsider
High issue priority	high access, low influence, limited chance to advance policy and personnel goals	medium access, uncertain influence, limited chance to advance policy and personnel goals
Low issue priority	high access, high influence, strong chance to advance policy and personnel goals	low access, no influence, no chance to advance policy and personnel goals

to trust that small group of insiders with access to the team, even though the low priority means the transition team won't be centrally concerned with the issue. Insider access will then lead to more influence, especially since the president-elect is unlikely to have locked-in a campaign promise on the low-priority issue, leading the transition team to be more easily influenced by the insiders' ideas.

On the contrary, outsiders focused on high-priority issues face a steep challenge to gaining access, let alone influence (upper right quadrant of Table 1.1). For these outsider groups, access likely depends on fortunate timing to overcome the institutional roadblocks in their way. An unexpected change in the political context of an issue—a natural disaster, national tragedy, or unforeseen event—will increase issue attention and move an issue from low to high priority, such as finance in 2008 and policing in 2020 (Truman 1951; Downs 1972; Birkland 1997). Such a disruption in political context may lead the transition team to grow distrustful of insiders with outdated information and then seek out new outsider groups with novel perspectives and fresh information (Cobb and Elder 1983). This will open a window or present a critical juncture, allowing outsiders to gain surprising access to the transition team, especially if they are in possession of a list of novel staffing recommendations or fluent in new-issue framing that insiders do not yet employ, such as the reframing of public education in 2020 to emphasize health and safety and the move in environmental circles toward highlighting racial justice (Kingdon 1995). Ultimately, though, the institutionalized nature of the transition period will limit the influence that might come from this outside access, especially as the issue inevitably moves from high priority back to low priority.

Some of the examples from this chapter illustrate these expectations. A Republican Party outsider in 1980, the Heritage Foundation took advantage of the high priority of its issues for Ronald Reagan—the core issues of the ascendant conservative movement—to gain access to the transition team and influence over the Reagan personnel decisions and policy agenda. It even used its rising status in the party to block access for other insider groups, like the Center for Strategic and International Studies (CSIS), that were not sufficiently committed to Reagan's priorities, thereby establishing Heritage's extreme insider status and influence over the Reagan administration (Smith 1993).

In 1992 the DLC, though closely tied to Bill Clinton himself during the campaign, also was a party outsider. But once the transition began, the DLC's priority issues waned as health-care reform dominated the agenda resulting in access for the DLC, but only in limited influence over the eventual Clinton staffing plan and policy agenda. The Democratic Party's longer-term concerns for representing identity groups and loyalty to those groups committed to diversity dictated much of the direction of the Clinton transition period and which groups had the greatest amount of influence.

Conversely, party insiders, like the economic experts associated with Hillary Clinton, faced the financial crisis in 2008: a newly high-priority issue. That this pressing issue was not one Obama had a deep familiarity with, nor had focused on during his campaign, meant the group of Clinton insiders had a high degree of access and influence during the transition period and beyond.

In 2016 public health organizations were outsiders in respect to the Trump transition team. Their key issue, a potential pandemic, was a low priority at the time and largely ignored by the transition team. This meant those public health groups had little access and no influence over the Trump policy agenda, a potentially contributing factor to the poor response to the COVID-19 pandemic three years later.

In 2020 Reverend Barber's organization, party outsiders, had a newly high-priority issue—racial and social equity—that resulted in access to the transition team in part due to the novel tactics they used so well, but also unclear influence, a result of the institutionalization of the transition process that mutes the chance for long-term policy change.

Like any parsimonious theory, these two factors explain something about what transpires during the transition period, but not everything. Many other important things transpired in recent years that also explain what happens during the transition period. Differences across presidents, across transition teams, and across policy areas also must be incorporated into a full understanding of what has happened in the past and may happen in the future. Exceptions abound when a political phenomenon happens so infrequently. Nonetheless, throughout the remainder of the book, these two factors—status and priority—arise again and again, suggesting how important it is to understand them.

Given this theory, what would the 2020 transition bring? More of the past, with insiders dominating the agenda and staffing decisions, or something brand-new, as outsiders pushed through major change. Trump, too, promised a radical overhaul of Washington, but he largely failed on fulfilling his ambitious policy plans (Potter et al. 2019). Would Biden's fate be the same?

This is the focus of the book. To set the stage, consider the case of criminal justice policy, an issue in which political context was in great flux, its priority rapidly rising in 2020. Though the origins of the Movement for Black Lives preceded the campaign by several years, national attention shifted to Black Lives Matter (BLM) activists organizing hundreds of protests that spring and summer of 2020 after the murders of George Floyd and several other Black individuals by police. So effective was this organizing that 40 percent of counties in the United States had a protest in 2020, and estimates ranged as high as 26 million Americans participating in at least one of these marches (Buchanan, Bui, and Patel 2020).

Would 2020 be a year when groups would bring protest movements and the Democratic Party together on a common agenda and candidate, unsettling institutionalized patterns (Schlozman 2015, 5)? At the state level, political scientists Jeron Fenton and LaFleur Stephens-Dougan (2022) were surprised to discover no difference between the responsiveness of Black legislators to messages from long-standing civil rights groups, like the NAACP, and newcomer BLM, suggesting that the outsider had quickly achieved a similar level of access. Likewise, sociologist Sidney Tarrow (2022) described the rise of BLM as a *critical juncture* that "had a lateral influence on other movements" by centering racism in the fight against climate change, sexual violence, advocacy for health-care workers, and opposition to the government's response to the pandemic. And, in summing up the 2020 campaign, though the Democratic Party was moving slowly leftward already, political scientists John Sides, Chris Tausanovitch, and Lynn Vavreck (with Michael Tesler) (2022, 165) concluded: "[George] Floyd's murder, and Trump's reaction to it, only helped to push the Democrats further to the left."

If, as this evidence suggests, protests against police violence had changed the national conversation about criminal justice, policymakers were paying attention to BLM, specifically, as well as other outsiders, more generally, in a way they might not have in the past, a window may have opened for access, influence, and a change in personnel and policy during the 2020 presidential transition. Whether that change would be radical, incremental, or just symbolic was hard to predict, but what happened during the formative stage of the Biden-Harris administration—the presidential transition—explained a lot about what came next.

CHAPTER 2

Securing a Seat at the Table

It was December 1992, yet sweat poured down the brow of the chief of the US Border Patrol. He insisted he didn't have time for the meeting, but Linda Yanez had called ahead to the attorney general's office to free his schedule. "Power is an amazing thing," said Yanez, recalling her experience on the Clinton transition team (Gutierrez 1997).

Just weeks earlier, Yanez had been a member of the Harvard Law School faculty, busy operating the school's immigration clinic. She was hardly a political novice, however; she'd come up in local politics in Texas, working closely with civil rights leaders, like Norma Cantu of the Mexican American Legal Defense Fund (MALDEF), to defend the rights of immigrant children to an education. When Yanez volunteered for George McGovern in 1972, she nearly met the presidential candidate's young southern campaign director, Bill Clinton (Gutierrez 1997).

Washington, DC, though, hadn't been one of the stops on her legal journey. By the fall of 1992, Yanez resided in Cambridge, Massachusetts, getting used to academic life.

Meanwhile, the newly elected Clinton team rushed to get ready to govern. Peter Edelman, a long-time friend of the Clintons and husband of the Children's Defense Fund's Marion Wright Edelman, headed up transition planning for the Department of Justice. Things weren't going well. Clinton aimed to appoint the first woman attorney general, but he withdrew the nomination after a public outcry over Zoe Baird's hiring of two undocumented workers at her family's home. At the time, Senator Joe Biden chaired the Judiciary Committee, which would convene Baird's confirmation hearing. When she explained the situation during a closed-door meeting, acknowledging the mistake, Biden raised no red flags (New York Times Editorial Board 1993). This wasn't something that had ever come up before, though no woman had ever had to get through the confirmation process to become attorney general before, either. It was weeks later when Baird's supporters on Capitol Hill and in the incoming administration disappeared. About the same happened to Clinton's next failed nominee, Judge Kimba Wood.

Amid the disarray of the transition, Antonia Hernandez, MALDEF's Washington, DC, representative, and Henry Cisneros, the former mayor of

San Antonio, Texas, met with the transition team in Washington, urging for more representation for Latinos. The last time a Democrat was elected, fourteen years earlier, this was exactly what the transition team didn't do, leaving groups like Mexican American Democrats (MAD, on the outside looking in. MAD had helped get Jimmy Carter elected in Texas but had received few of the spoils of victory. Alicia Chacon, a founder of MAD, said: "The campaign had been easy because [Carter's advisers] were courting us, but then after the election was won, and between November and January . . . we . . . had all the phone numbers and all the phone numbers were disconnected" (Gutierrez 1996a).

The problem, according to another of MAD's founders, Marc Campos, was that even though one of his friends, Rick Hernandez, was on the Carter transition team, MAD had no insights into how the transition worked (Gutierrez 1996b). After the election, the organization was a literal outsider, located nowhere near Washington or Carter's headquarters in Atlanta. Campos later lamented: "Why in the fuck are we meeting in Corpus Christi, Texas?" (Gutierrez 1996b). He had a point: "How in the hell are we going to get our resumes read from Corpus Christi? . . . Nowadays, right after an election, we're going to go down to Washington. . . . We're going to have resumes. And we're going to be taking them to all these executive buildings, the transition office. . . . That was like [what] we didn't know then. So, we meet in Corpus."

A decade and a half later, Latino groups had learned from their mistake, and just in time, because in 1992 Clinton promised the most diverse cabinet in the history of the country. Others were listening to Clinton, too. The boldest-faced insiders in the women's movement converged on Diana Meehan and Gary David Goldberg's (creator of *Family Ties*) estate in Vermont (Noble 1992). Luminaries Bella Abzug and Carol Bellamy were there, as were leaders of the DC-based Institute for Women's Policy Research and the Center for Policy Alternatives. Betty Friedan, who'd been at the table for every big meeting for decades, said to the *New York Times:* "It was the best meeting I've been to in 20 years" (Noble 1992). Sarah Kovner from the transition team also was on hand to take notes to bring back to Clinton in Little Rock.

But just weeks into the transition, Clinton was already chafing at the criticism of interest groups, including insiders, that he wasn't doing enough on diversity. The president-elect complained: these groups are "bean counters" and "they're playing quota games and math games" (Marcus 1992). MALDEF disagreed. It was not persuaded that Clinton was making progress and called Yanez in Cambridge to ask for a copy of her resume to share directly with the transition team.

Days later, Edelman was on the phone to Yanez: "I hear you know a little bit of immigration. . . . How would you like to come and head up the immigration team for the President at the Justice Department?" (Gutierrez 1997).

Edelman didn't have a job to offer or any pay; he was looking for volunteers. But not to worry, he explained to Yanez: "'Well, join the ranks of half of the Harvard faculty that's going to go work . . . on the transition team. . . . I believe that the dean of the law school has already said . . . they're going to pay your salaries to go over there and help Clinton'" (Gutierrez 1997).

If that was the case, Yanez could do it, especially with the help of some of her colleagues she wanted to bring along: Professor Patty Blum from the University of California at Berkeley, Maurice Roberts from Interpreter Releases, and Dan Kesselbrenner from the National Lawyers Guild.

Wilmer Cutler—one of DC's most prestigious law firms and soon to become WilmerHale—hosted Yanez's team. A huge conference room, free long-distance telephone calls, even a fax machine. A partner at the law firm explained to Yanez: "Whatever you need . . . we are donating it. . . . You just pick up this phone here and you speak into it and somebody else is going to transcribe whatever you are saying. . . . If you need to get it to President Clinton in the morning . . . we will have it ready for you to deliver" (Gutierrez 1997).

The *Washington Times* started calling, too. *Times* staff had heard that Yanez was a "radical crazy person" and was now in charge of reviewing the immigration service (Gutierrez 1997). Clinton was supposed to be a centrist, king of the New Democrats. Who were these *radicals* now directing immigration policy?

But the work of the transition team was to be kept quiet; no interviews for now. Wilmer Cutler provided a shredder to take care of all the paper when they were done.

The *Times* wasn't alone. Advocacy groups, MALDEF and others, used their access to lean on Yanez's team to "put their issue on the front burner to tell the President this is what you've got to address" (Gutierrez 1997). The immigration team's work was secretive, but it was also driven by the news of the day. A refugee crisis in Haiti sat atop the agenda, and Bosnia was not far behind. What interested the groups across Washington wasn't necessarily what Yanez and the rest of the transition team were spending fifteen hours a day on.

Fast-forward to 2020. Another Democratic presidential transition, but this time teams of volunteers didn't arrive in Washington, and there was no enormous conference room. They remained at home, huddled behind computers, sifting through many of the same complex issues: deportation, refugees, the border.

Geovette Washington volunteered to help the Biden-Harris transition team. Washington shared some things in common with Yanez: both are women of color lawyers with experience on hot-button issues of the Justice Department, and both were employed by universities at the time, with Washington at the University of Pittsburgh.

The similarities ended there.

Geovette Washington was an insider's insider. A stint at the Department of Justice's Office of Legal Counsel in the 1990s had set her up for a job in the Gore administration. That was not to be, yet future positions at the Department of Commerce in 2010 and the Office of Management and Budget (OMB) in 2014 meant she understood how DC worked as well as the power of the presidency. Her job at the OMB had been to review all of Obama's executive orders! In 2020, Washington knew she didn't want to *go* back but she did want to *give* back.

Leading a twenty-one-person team—some old friends and some who she'd never met—overseeing the transition at the Commerce Department meant 24/7 video calls with people spread out from California to New Mexico. One was based in Canada for a time.

The volunteers hailed from an array of groups as well—among them, the National Audubon Society, the Greater Washington Black Chamber of Commerce, and the Roosevelt Institute. People from Visa, the Pew Charitable Trusts, and Third Way volunteered as well as from a dozen other think tanks, associations, and universities. Together, Washington explained, they aimed to "help get this administration to be well-positioned to hit the ground running" (Baker 2021).

Thirty years separated these two transitions, though Joe Biden had a role to play in both. We see in these two volunteers, Yanez and Washington, how the execution of the transition and the larger politics of the Democratic Party played out. People were central to the chaotic work of the two transition teams: it was primarily volunteers drawn from those sitting under the umbrella of the party who were chosen to hurriedly get the new administration ready, though Yanez was at the outside fringe of the party in 1992 while Washington was an insider in 2020. People also mattered to the day-to-day work of those teams: collecting resumes, vetting candidates, and advising on final personnel decisions was all paramount. As such, representation mattered during and after both transitions.

Yet, DC in 2020 was not the place it was in 1992. For one, the number of women, and women of color, in the Democratic Party and the nation's capital had grown. At the turn of the century, when Clinton left the White House, under a quarter (23%) of senior federal employees (SES) were women; in 2020 that percentage increased to over a third (36%), though African American and Hispanic women still lagged far behind men and white women.[1] And, in 2020, the first woman and first non-white vice president elect awaited her January swearing-in ceremony.

The country also had changed. When Bill Clinton claimed his cabinet was going to "look like America," the United States was nearly 70 percent white and just 12.5 percent Latino or Hispanic (Locin 1992; Frey 2020). When Joe Biden made a similar claim in 2020, the country's demographics had shifted (Hunnicutt 2020). White people made up just 60 percent of the population and less than a majority of those under age sixteen. A quarter of the under-sixteen population was Latino or Hispanic. What it meant to make appointments that reflected the country's demographics was decidedly different in 2020 compared to 1992, as were claims to better descriptive representation of various identity groups that dominate the transition period as well as debates about political empowerment of marginalized groups (Hardy-Fanta et al. 2006; Lowande, Ritchie, and Lauterbach 2019; Reingold, Haynie, and Widner 2021).

The political environment of the capital had shifted as well in important ways during this period. Polarization and animosity between the parties increased; the confirmation process became gridlocked, leaving many positions dangerously unfilled; and the influence of some organizations waned while others waxed (Tenpas 2022; 2018). In 1992 it was how several nominees hired undocumented workers that stirred debate; by 2020 it was old tweets. Unlike during the 1990s, social media now set the DC agenda, large followings reinforcing who held power. These changes resulted in a remarkably different environment for influence, staffing, and advising a new administration. For Biden and Harris, they confronted progressive groups disappointed by the many moderate Obama cabinet picks now with digital bull horns at the ready (Leher 2008).

For example, when Joe Biden named Neera Tanden, the former president of one of the most important think-tank allies of the Democratic Party, the Center for American Progress, to run the Office of Management and Budget, she was to become the first non-white woman director of this important cabinet post. The transition team's vetting, though, could not wipe clean the thousands of tweets Tanden had shared in the past (Associated Press 2021). She had compared Republican senator Ted Cruz to a vampire and called Senator Tom Cotton a fraud, but also criticized Democratic senators Joe Manchin and Bernie Sanders. Deleting the old tweets was not sufficient to smooth things with her conservative, centrist, and progressive detractors, and Biden ultimately had to offer Tanden a position in the White House that didn't face Senate confirmation. Thus, as important as race, ethnicity, and gender, it was the inter- and intra-party dynamics as well as the new interest group and media politics of DC that increasingly shaped who was in and who was out during the presidential transition period.

Furthermore, in both periods, the window for change in the direction of federal policy was wide open, but quickly closing, during the transfer of power. The thousands of personnel, policy, and organizational decisions to make about the White House and federal agencies necessitates delegation of decision-making to those outside the president-elect's small team of advisers. There's simply too much to do and too few hours in each of the seventy or so days to do it. And, over time, as DC became more complex, the need for help had only grown. The transition teams provided that help. In comparison, there were less than four hundred official members of Carter's transition team in 1976, but by 2020 there were well over triple this number helping Joe Biden and Kamala Harris.[2]

The work of the transition team, especially writing transition memos on pressing issues, also matters because it is often done by those who later serve in the White House. One member of the Biden-Harris transition team explained: "If a transition policy team is just limited to what gets thrown down in [transition] memos and then the whole thing turns over, like almost no one goes in, it's very unlikely to be successful." If, in contrast, "we could identify volunteers who, based on our knowledge of people and what seems possible, are people who plausibly could staff the administration . . . a [transition] memo can translate and really serve as preparation for an administration. If the person who wrote the [transition] memo happens to be actually staffing the issue, then it's a whole other thing right there, their head will be into it. . . . You start from a very different space than if someone's coming in cold on day one."[3] Newly elected presidents, then, choose a transition team from those affiliated with the party and the party's agenda, but each volunteer still brings a perspective on policy and personnel, a preference for certain solutions over others, sometimes approaching a conflict of interest with the public spirit of the job. It mattered that Linda Yanez had an expertise on immigration policy drawn from years of work for MALDEF defending the precarious lives of newcomers, just as it mattered that Geovette Washington had a unique understanding of the constitutional limits of unilateral executive action for an incoming president. Transition volunteers (and short-term employees) have interests, and, as with other public officials, some of these interests reflect their professional background, education, and affiliations (Carnes 2013).

Given changes in DC and the importance of who serves, it's worth figuring out: has the composition of transition teams changed over time? Does partisanship make a difference such that certain professional backgrounds or interests are better represented on Republican and Democratic transition teams? And in 2020, did the changing structure of the Democratic Party mean different interests and groups were on the Biden-Harris transition team compared to previous Democratic transitions? This chapter figures this out.

Who Serves on the Transition Team?

In December 1976, Joe Browder wrote to the newly elected President Carter: "It is important, to me and to you, that you understand some things" (Carter Library 1976). Browder had worked on the campaign on environmental issues, sharing the expertise he'd acquired as co-founder of the Environmental Policy Center. After the election, he was chosen to run one of the transition policy groups considering the new administration's approach to energy.

Just a month into the transition, Browder wanted to make sure Carter understood: "I did not quit, I was fired" (Carter Library 1976).

Browder thought he had the president's ear on the right way to proceed on natural resources and the direction of the Interior Department, but he'd grown despondent with what he saw. This was a conflict between the political demands of the campaign staff and the aspirations of the policy people, a classic transition conflict that repeats every four to eight years (Burke 2000).

Browder was especially angry with one of Carter's "Georgia Boys," Frank Moore, who, Browder claimed to the *New York Times*, was in the bag for Big Oil. "When you have to raise $200,000, you'll do anything," Browder said (Hill 1976). He contended that Moore had promised campaign donors in Texas that several environmental experts wouldn't have a seat on the transition team, including Dave Freeman, who headed up the Ford Foundation's Energy Policy Project, and was viewed as a critic of industry. Freeman was fresh off the release of "A Time to Choose," a 340-page report from the foundation that proposed energy consumption be cut in half, conceding: "What is good for business is not always good for the rest of the country" (Cowan 1974). Freeman had sent the report to all fifty governors; then Governor Carter had read his copy (Orsmeth 2020).

Instead of giving Freeman the biggest seat on the transition team, lawyers for Exxon and American Electric Power were now in the mix. Browder fretted that another was the lobbyist for El Paso Natural Gas. And, when he recommended Harris Arthur, a Navajo leader he viewed as unbiased and fair, the campaign preferred Peter McDonald, another Navajo leader with ties to the energy industry (Hill 1976).

There's little to resolve whether Browder was in fact fired for insubordination or quit in protest—the transition team claimed he was put off by not being given enough influence, though both he and Freeman did end up with positions in the Carter administration. Browder was a gadfly, a policy entrepreneur who knew how to play the media and influence game, if not always successfully. His tale illustrates the competition over who gets a seat at the table during critical moments, especially during the transition.

Importantly, in the 1970s, Browder ran a particular type of environmental group, the Environmental Policy Institute, at the very point when there was a boom in the influence of this type of organization (*New York Times* 1976). Memberless and research-focused, these groups are savvy about how policy is made in Washington. Political scientist Theda Skocpol (2001) wrote: "Over the past third of [the twentieth] century, the old civic America has been bypassed and shoved to the side by a gaggle of professionally dominated advocacy groups and nonprofit institutions rarely attached to memberships worthy of the name." Skocpol's revelatory analysis of the emergence of the non-member-based Children's Defense Fund reinforced earlier survey research by Jack Walker (1991) that demonstrated the rise of these memberless, policy-oriented organizations.[4] Browder ran just such an operation.

That these types of groups are useful during the transition period is not surprising. Whereas member-based groups such as unions and trade associations have the power to mobilize large numbers of voters, these new groups invest in legal advocacy, data collection, and policy research.

Illustrative of this, when Carter named his transition team, Barbara Blum, one of the directors of the transition, explained on the nightly television news program *The MacNeil/Lehrer Report*: "This is a nuts-and-bolts think tank type operation" ("Carter Transition" 1976). Unlike the nearly all-male world of past transitions of Eisenhower, Kennedy, and Nixon, women joined the Carter team as well, likely a result of the pressure placed on Carter during the campaign by the Committee of 51.3% and the Coalition for Women's Appointments (Carroll 1986; Weko 1995). Blum reported: "And one other thing is—and I come at this from a rather prejudiced point of view—is that this is the first transition in which women have been, I think, significantly involved" ("Carter Transition" 1976).

Blum was surely right, though the historical record on who exactly worked on past transition teams is patchy. The leaders of the previous full transition, Richard Nixon's team in 1968–1969, included Paul McCracken, George Schultz, Roy Ash, and two dozen others, all men, though the records on this are incomplete (Ford Library Museum 1968). The only woman listed as a member of the Nixon transition team was Linda Underwood, who went on to a job in the White House Personnel Office.

For the Carter transition team, however, it was clear: diversity mattered.

Diversity mattered so much that days after the election, Beth Sullivan, an aide to the director of the transition, Jack Watson, wrote a memorandum with an overview of "Affirmative Action." The memo indicated that 11 percent of

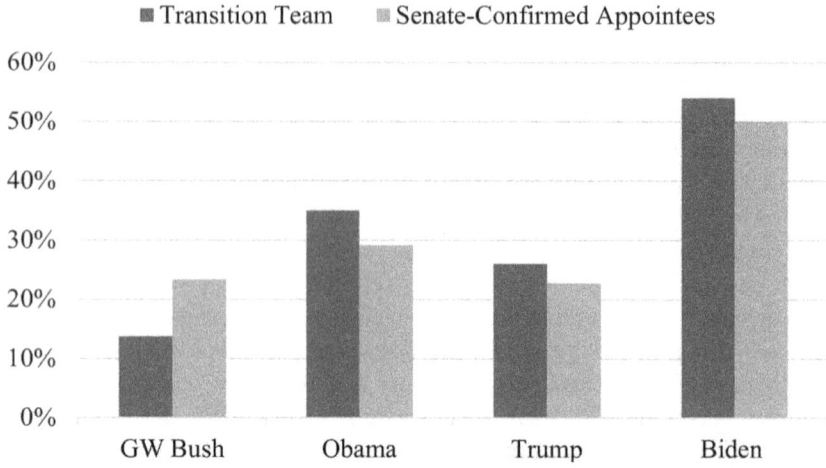

Figure 2.1: Percentage of Women on Transition Teams and of Early Senate-Confirmed Appointments. Each bar in the figure shows the percentage of women on the transition teams of George W. Bush, Barack Obama, Donald Trump, and Joe Biden compared to the percentage of women appointed to Senate-confirmed positions in the first six months in office. Source: Original data collection and analysis by author and data collected by Kathryn Dunn Tenpas.

the transition team members were "Blacks" and 36 percent were "Women," and further broke down each of the eighteen clusters of the team by race and gender (Jimmy Carter Library 1976). Watson wrote back to Sullivan on the memo that he was "extremely pleasured with the competence & character of our entire transition group" but that her figures weren't quite right: there were a couple hundred more people to be added to the transition team, and the percentage of Black people on the team would "round out to 12.7%" (Jimmy Carter Library 1976).

So, on this point, Blum's assertion also was right about the commitment of the Carter transition to gender diversity. Based on the Staff Directory of the Carter-Mondale Transition Group from December 16, 1976, women made up nearly a half (44%) of those identified as members of the Carter transition team. It is clear, however, that the significant role played by women during the Carter transition was not precedent setting, at least not in the sense that it was immediately followed. Four years later, nearly all the major figures on the Reagan transition team were men, over 90 percent; Nancy Clark Reynolds, Anne Armstrong, and Ann Gorsuch were prominent exceptions.

Figure 2.1 presents a best estimate of the historical trend in successive presidential transitions since 1992: Clinton, Bush, Trump, Obama, and Biden. Incoming Democratic presidents have consistently had a larger share of women on their transition teams than Republicans, but not until Joe Biden and Kamala Harris organized their transition in 2020–2021 did women make up a majority (54%) of transition team members whose names were shared publicly. This reflects what Yohannes Abraham, executive director of the Biden-Harris transition team, said about the aim of the team to find "a diverse group of experts" to help prepare for Day 1 (Biden-Harris Transition Team 2020c). Additionally, though women made up a minority of the list of transition co-chairs and of the Biden-Harris transition's advisory council, women served as the team lead of twenty-two of the thirty-eight agency review teams. And, when it came to racial and ethnic representation, much harder to assess historically, people of color made up 41 percent of the senior leaders on the Biden-Harris transition team (Vitali 2020).

However, who was on the official transition team remains murky, even as voluntary public disclosure has become a norm. In early November 2020, the Biden-Harris team named a small group of transition leaders as well as thousands of volunteers (some treated as full-time staff) and paid staff on the agency review portion of the transition team and posted those names on its website.[5] A host of news stories followed with praise from various factions of the Democratic Party on the initial appointments (Derysh 2020). Nevertheless, others joined the transition team after that announcement and were not shared with the public by the transition team with such fanfare. *Politico* reported on several with close ties to the private sector, including former employees of Goldman Sachs, Boston Consulting Group, and McKinsey, that would likely not have been lauded by the progressive wing of the party (Meyer and Thompson 2020). Who was a part of the policy planning, vetting and appointments, and operations groups of the transition team also was never posted on the transition team's website and largely remained a mystery. As with so many aspects of the transition period, any conclusions about the changing compositions of the transition teams must be tempered by the opacity of the process.

With that noted, if we can assume that women served on the Biden-Harris public agency review teams (as well as the previous three transitions) at about the same rate as the non-public operations, legal, policy, and personnel teams, we can examine another aspect about this transition: was the representation of women on the transition team associated with representation of women in the administration? In general, this seems to be the case: there is an association between the share of women on the transition team and the share of women who are ultimately appointed within the administration.

With the exception of George W. Bush's transition, the next three saw a slightly higher rate of gender diversity on the agency review transition team than in appointments (see Figure 2.1).[6] For Biden, there was a 4-point difference between the gender ratio for the transition (54% women) and for

Table 2.1: Percentage of Women on Biden and Trump Transition Teams and Early Senate-Confirmed Appointments by Agency

	Biden		Trump	
	Transition %	Appointments %	Transition %	Appointments %
Agriculture	53	66	0	0
Commerce	72	60	20	30
Defense	65	52	6	15
EPA	58	0	13	NA
Education	70	57	33	50
Energy	43	43	20	0
Health and Human Services	54	57	71	29
Homeland Security	68	50	17	25
Housing and Urban Development	62	67	0	50
Interior	67	63	60	25
Justice	45	38	33	22
Labor	70	67	25	0
State	64	44	40	29
Transportation	28	50	27	17
Treasury	52	57	27	11
Veterans Affairs	64	29	38	17

Source: Original data collection and data on appointments collected and shared by Kathryn Dunn Tenpas.

appointments (50% women). This followed a 6-point difference for Obama and 3-point difference for Trump.

As interesting as these general comparisons are the differences across specific agencies (see Table 2.1).[7] For example, women made up 43 percent of the Biden-Harris transition team reviewing the Energy Department, and the exact same percentage of women were later appointed to the Department of Energy. Conversely, women made up nearly three-quarters of the transition team for the Department of Commerce (72%) but were just less than two-thirds (60%) of the appointments to that agency. The pattern was the reverse for the transition team for the Department of Transportation, where just 28 percent of volunteers were women, but half (50%) of appointees to that agency were women.

Overall, of fifteen agency review teams on the Biden transition, four had more representation for women than the eventual agency appointments (Agriculture, Health and Human Services, Housing and Urban Development, and Transportation). In comparison, not only did the Trump transition have less representation for women (just two agency review teams had an equal or greater percentage of women: Health and Human Services, at 71%), and Interior, at 60%); of the sixteen agency review teams, five had more representation for women in appointments than during the transition (Commerce, Defense, Education, Homeland Security, and Housing and Urban Development).

Organizations Represented on the Transition Team

Blum's other claim about the nuts-and-bolts nature of the transition also was one we can evaluate with data from subsequent transitions. Was she right that this has been a "think tank type operation? The role of Heritage four years later suggests Blum rightly anticipated what was to come, but what about the Carter transition itself?

Using the list preserved by the Carter Presidential Library, the immediate employment backgrounds (the last job held prior to the campaign) of half (45%) of the Carter transition team (176 of the 383) were reconstructed based on newspaper archives, obituaries, oral histories, and other sources. For those members of the Carter transition team, relatively few—just 1 in 5—were associated with a think tank or other nonprofit organization. A larger portion were Georgians who came from the campaign, law firms, or local businesses, and many others were working in the state government or on Capitol Hill. This set made up over two-thirds (69%) of the Carter transition team, though even the ones from Capitol Hill were not by and large longtime Carter supporters.

Think tanks, in comparison, were not nearly as prominent on the Carter transition team. There were exceptions, of course: Donald McHenry from the Carnegie Endowment for International Peace and Edwin Deagle and Heather Ross from the Urban Institute. Several from Brookings, including Fred Bergsten and Paula Stern, were on the official team, and others, Henry Owen and Charles Yost, had advised Carter on policy during the campaign.

Largely absent from the Carter team were university faculty. Just 5 percent of the Carter transition team was employed by universities, such as Al Stern at Wayne State University and Lynn Davis at Columbia University. Also missing were representatives of traditional interest groups, trade associations, or member-based organizations. Matt Coffey, the president of the Association of Public Radio Stations, was an exception, as was Larry Bailey from the US Conference of Mayors and Joseph Duffey from the American Association of University Professors.

Consequently, while there were a record number of women on the transition team, women's organizations did not have a lot of representation or clout. And, though it was true that Jane McMichael, the director of National Women's Political Caucus, had a spot on the transition team, her organization grew frustrated that the telegrams and dozens of phone calls to the transition offices were unanswered. One official from the caucus explained to *The Sun* that "Hamilton Jordan," one of the leads of the transition team and future de facto White House chief of staff "has never returned a call" (Banisky 1976). The same could be said for prominent civil rights organizations like the NAACP, revealing a potential distinction between descriptive and substantive representation that happens during the transition period. Women's groups criticized the eventual appointments made during the transition as disappointing for advancing women's interests. They were all from Yale, class of 1948: "Pete Preppie" calling "Mike Macho" to get a job, was what future senator Barbara Mikulski, just elected to the House from Maryland, surmised (Banisky 1976). And Ralph Nader, who had supported Carter in the campaign but was not on the transition team, even complained to the *New York Times* that key economic policy positions would be "a plantation for bankers, the old-line establishment, money centered people" (Smith 1976).

Much changed in Washington after 1976, and there are more complete data on some subsequent transitions with which to compare the work of the transition teams as well as the role of think tanks and other interest groups. Based on these data, it seems, just as the Biden-Harris team broke records in terms of gender diversity, it also did on the role of various groups on the transition team. As I did earlier, to make the comparisons across transitions clearest, I focus on the professional backgrounds of those serving just on agency review teams.[8] Doing so results in the clearest apples-to-apples comparison, but it does likely underestimate the number of volunteers from law firms on each transition team, because much of the work to vet candidates is done by lawyers in transition counsel teams whose names are not always shared publicly.

Accepting that limitation, nearly 40 percent of the team in 2020–2021 had been working for a think tank, association, or civic group before the transition, a much larger share than any of the previous transitions (see Figure 2.2). Other differences also are apparent from the comparative data. As with the previous two Democratic transitions, Clinton and Obama, the Biden-Harris transition team had a large portion of university-affiliated members, much more so than the previous Republican transitions. To the contrary, the Biden-Harris transition team had relatively few representatives of law firms and the business sector, just 5 and 9 percent, respectively. This differed greatly from the previous two transitions, Obama and Trump, when those two sectors made up around half of each team: 48 percent in 2008–2009 and 50 percent in 2016–2017.

These differences are interesting to the extent that the actual people and groups on each team bring a different perspective based on their affiliations. Broad sectoral categories only suggest differences, but closer inspection is

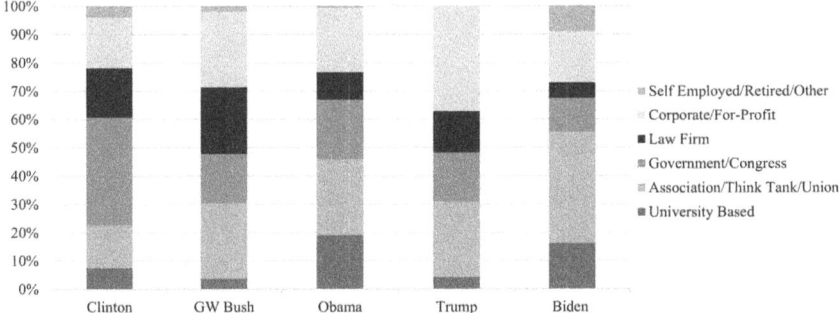

Figure 2.2: Professional Background of Transition Team Members. Each bar in the figure shows the percentage of transition team members drawn from various professional backgrounds for Bill Clinton, George W. Bush, Barack Obama, Donald Trump, and Joe Biden. Source: Original data collection by author.

needed to really understand the composition of each team. For example, the Biden-Harris transition team and the Bush-Cheney transition team both had a large portion of officials from think tanks and associations, but the similarities stop there. Take the two transition teams focused on the Department of Energy. Of the forty-eight members of the Bush-Cheney energy advisory team, ten were people drawn from industry associations, including the Independent Petroleum Association of America, US Oil and Gas Association, and National Association of Manufacturers. Political scientist Shirley Ann Warshaw (2009, 52) concluded: "[Dick] Cheney intended to signal to corporate contributors that their views were welcome in the administration's decision making," leading Warshaw to dismiss the importance of these teams as nothing more than "fluff."

Whether substantial signaling or symbolic fluff, the contrast with the Biden-Harris transition advisers is clear. Of the twenty members of the Biden-Harris energy agency review team, there wasn't a single industry group represented. Instead, volunteers from the AFL-CIO trade union and the Environmental Defense Fund joined the team, along with five university-based individuals and several from grant-making foundations. The differences between the two transitions and the two parties couldn't be starker, though the impact of those differences on the regulation of the sector remained undetermined at the end of the Biden-Harris transition.

Another way to consider this is to compare which think tanks showed up on different transitions. As noted in the previous chapter, the structures of the Republican and Democratic parties differ, leading Republicans to focus on a single, common ideology and Democrats to focus on representing a variety of identity groups. The success of the Heritage Foundation in 1980 to

Table 2.2: Members of Each Transition Team from Top 10 US Think Tanks

	George W. Bush	Obama	Trump	Biden
Brookings Institution	0	10	0	6
Peterson Institute for International Economics	0	0	0	0
Center for Strategic and International Studies	0	3	0	3
Carnegie Endowment for International Peace	0	0	0	0
Urban Institute	0	2	0	7
Center for American Progress	0	13	0	7
Heritage Foundation	2	0	13	0
Wilson Center	0	0	0	0
RAND Corporation	0	0	0	4
Other think tanks with most on the team				
American Enterprise Institute	2	0	0	0
Hoover Institute	2	0	2	0
Center for a New American Security	0	3	0	4

Source: Ranking of think tanks (Think Tank Watch 2022) and original data collection by author.

corner the market on advising the Reagan transition team has never been matched by a single dominant think tank for Democrats. Data from the past four transitions bear this out (see Table 2.2).

If you use the list of what researchers (Think Tank Watch, 2022) deem the top ten think tanks in the United States, two think tanks were best represented among the people on the Obama-Biden transition team: the Center for American Progress (thirteen) and Brookings (ten). This compares to just one, the Heritage Foundation, which had two officials on the Bush-Cheney agency review teams and thirteen officials working on the Trump-Pence agency review transition team. In comparison, five of the top ten most influential think tanks had representation on the Biden-Harris transition team, including at least seven from the Urban Institute and CAP, at least six from Brookings, and at least four from RAND.

These data on who served on the past four transition teams suggest several things. For one, Republicans and Democratic presidents-elect draw transition volunteers from very different think tanks. This is not surprising, nor is the dominant role played by a single think tank, the Heritage Foundation, for Republicans, and an array of groups, CAP, Brookings, Urban Institute, and Center for New American Security, for Democrats. Previous research suggested just these patterns (Brown 2012). Additionally, these data show the consistency over time for both Democrats and Republicans. Despite the outsider status of Donald Trump, the same think tanks, Heritage and the Hoover Institute, played prominent roles in his transition, as they did during the Bush transition in 2000 and the Reagan transition in 1980. The same is true for Democrats: a similar set of think tanks had staffers volunteer on both the Obama and Biden transitions. This also isn't surprising given that Biden was involved in both transitions, but the wave of social justice protests, the rise of Senator Bernie Sanders, and the related set of new policy ideas raised by each did not displace the established, insider think tanks associated with the Democratic Party, just as Donald Trump hadn't dislodged Heritage four years earlier.

Broad patterns, though, may overstate the consistency across transitions in who is asked to serve on the transition team. Despite the regular prominence of Brookings, the Urban Institute, and CSIS across multiple transitions, in 2020 newcomers did emerge. For example, the Roosevelt Institute, a progressive think tank associated with the Franklin Roosevelt Library, had never had a prominent seat on past Democratic transition teams. In 2020 this changed. Dr. Felicia Wong, the think tank's president and CEO, wasn't just given a spot on one of the agency review teams but was chosen to be on the sixteen-person advisory council along with Pete Buttigieg, Susan Rice, and Vivek Murthy, each who soon went on to an appointment in the Biden-Harris administration. Wong wasn't alone. Others who had been on the outside looking in during past Democratic transitions, like the Washington Center for Equitable Growth, now had insider's access to the transition team.

Furthermore, these findings on think-tank affiliations reinforce party differences on staffing from earlier. The gender composition of transition teams over time is not surprising, yet it underscores widely held perceptions about the transition period. Women are more central to the work of incoming Democratic presidents than Republican ones, and this has been the case for a long time. The Biden-Harris transition had considerably more women on the transition team than Donald Trump and George Bush—and even more than Bill Clinton in 1992. What this shows is that, in descriptive terms, the Biden-Harris transition team was in fact different from previous teams.

Nonetheless, descriptive representation is only part of the puzzle of diversity and representation. How the Biden-Harris transition team actually addressed women's issues is another question. Did the rising salience of gender, racial, and social justice issues impact the Biden-Harris transition team and how it dealt with equity and justice issues? And in which ways? Also, what came from the access given to these think tanks and other interest groups, especially newcomers to the transition process? Did the access lead to policy change or influence over key decisions made by the incoming administration?

Quantitative data like these don't provide much to answer these questions. Quantitative data also cannot explain what was actually happening on the Biden transition teams, how they juggled the political changes that seemed to define 2020, and how interactions with the outgoing Trump administration affected the work of the transition. For this, quantitative data is insufficient for the task. Qualitative data drawn from interviews presented in subsequent chapters, then, aim to address these questions.

CHAPTER 3

Inside the Biden-Harris Transition

First question: "What is it about President-elect Biden's agenda that inspires you to want to serve?"[1] Check.

Next question: "Name a time when you had to execute on a project that you felt you weren't prepared for?"[2] Check.

After the scripted interview questions—the same general ones asked of everyone—there was some time left over to freelance on policy and values questions. Then they checked some more boxes and made a recommendation.

That's what one volunteer did fifteen times during the 2020–2021 transition, helping the Biden-Harris team complete the monumental task of filling thousands of open positions across the government. Of course, staffing wasn't the only thing the transition team was charged with addressing. The White House needed to be organized and staffed while federal officials debriefed to figure out what was happening at each agency. Hundreds of campaign promises had to be translated into a governing agenda, some to be ready for a Day 1 announcement. Almost all of this was to be done in secret and at home. New cybersecurity threats, the pandemic, and an uncooperative outgoing administration made the 2020–2021 transition a special challenge for the thousand or more people, mostly volunteers, helping Joe Biden and Kamala Harris get ready to start their jobs.

The work of the transition teams can be understood in one way as entirely bureaucratic and technical, a fast-paced master class in human resource management and organizational change, the prose to the poetry of the campaign. That approach, though surely valuable, would underestimate the role of politics in the transition period. Jill Biden seemed to understand just this when she read aloud a verse of the poem "A House Called Tomorrow," written by Alberto Rios, in a virtual staff meeting during the transition, a metaphor itself for the elusive poetry often absent from popular conceptions of the transition period. As the previous chapter showed, who serves on the transition team has always been political, a demonstration of who has access and influence with the incoming administration. Transitions are a bridge between the campaign and the administration, and thus how they function says a lot about what the incoming president's agenda will be as well as possibly something about that agenda's eventual success.

The 2020–2021 transition was no different. This chapter applies the concepts of access and influence to a case study derived from interviews with seventy-eight individuals, some insiders and others outsiders, serving on the Biden-Harris transition team. How did these insiders and outsiders use their access to influence the direction of the incoming administration? How did they confront the external and internal roadblocks placed in their way to do this? Several curious answers emerge from these interviews in this chapter: first, the uncooperative Trump administration presented a surprising opportunity for the transition team; second, despite efforts to promote collaboration in a virtual work environment, many members of the transition team felt isolated and disconnected; and, third, the formal structure of the transition team helped and harmed the goal of greater social equity and justice.

Answering these questions with an interview-based, qualitative case study allows for a close inspection of the quantitative findings from chapter 2. This is especially useful because so few original documents (e.g., letters/memorandum, meeting notes and minutes, and other internal communications) were preserved by the transition team. Despite the advantages of a qualitative approach, there are several challenges to applying it to the transition period. For one, the secrecy of the Biden-Harris transition team, really of every presidential transition team, poses a methodological challenge. In 2020, after the election, the transition publicly circulated a complete list of the names of those serving on the post-election transition advisory board as well as those serving on the agency review teams—or ARTs. For other functions of the transition, such as personnel and policy issues, no such list ever materialized in public, nor did the names of those serving during the pre-election transition period. Volunteers on the transition were discouraged from sharing their role in public and even to discuss details of the work with friends and family. Over time, the names of some of these individuals emerged, often based on self-identification on social media, but it remained the case that there was not a full public accounting of who served on the Biden-Harris transition team long after the transition ended. Perhaps a Biden Presidential Library will share the list of those names in the future as the Carter and Clinton libraries have.[3]

A second challenge was that, because even the largest agency review team had just a couple dozen volunteers, I had to group teams together into issue areas to maintain the confidentiality of those who agreed to be interviewed for the project. Throughout the remainder of this chapter, I focus on the broad issue area of the economy, which includes interviews with transition team members on several different agency review, personnel, and policy transition teams with a direct or indirect focus on the economy. What I call an "issue area," however, does not align precisely with any unit on the Biden-Harris transition team, though there was a "Domestic and Economic" team for appointments within the personnel function of the team and someone who oversaw "economics" within the Domestic Policy transition team. Given what many transition team members reported about inter-team conversations, meetings, and collaboration, it isn't apparent that this approach exaggerates the importance of economic issues for different parts of the Biden-Harris transition team, including on international economics, intelligence issues, and foreign policy.

Focusing on a broad issue area like the economy comes with a secondary benefit. The breadth of the economy for the incoming administration meant there were a range of priorities, some so important that Biden had made clear promises during the campaign, such as infrastructure spending at the center of the Build Back Better program to revive the economy, and others much less important at the time and barely mentioned on the campaign trail. Consequently, those interviewed for the book focused on issues during the transition related to the economy—including from the perspectives of policy, personnel, and strategy—that spanned high to low priority.

Additionally, interviewees included insiders and outsiders. For example, one person said, "I was not particularly close to the senior leadership team,"[4] and another revealed, "I was surprised to be picked on the Biden transition team. I hadn't worked on the campaign . . . and I'm not a very political person that way to begin with. . . . So, I was very surprised that they asked me."[5] And one more said: "I am not close to the Biden people. . . . He has a big array of people in his orbit who had worked for him or with him, and, in that solar system, I'm probably around Jupiter or Neptune."[6] These three individuals were outsiders. Another outsider said: "I hadn't worked in Democratic politics before, so a lot of people that I was working with [on the transition] had known each other from previous campaigns or even worked for the Bidens. . . . I was very much a kind of an outsider."[7] One final person, who hadn't worked on the campaign, credited experience for their invitation to join the team: "I was chosen because there were very few people who had my specific expertise. . . . That's why, and they really needed it."[8]

Compare this with the individual who explained, "A senior person from the transition team literally sent me a 1-line e-mail with a subject that said: 'come do the transition with me.' That's just it. Literally in the subject line."[9] When a transition leader knows you that well, so well that formalities are set aside, it suggests you are an insider. To this point, the person continued: "I think a lot of it goes on trust. . . . I previously served in the Obama-Biden White House," and the trust that came from working together meant that joining the Biden-Harris transition felt like being a "part of a family that I loved."[10] This person was a clear insider. Another person with the close trusting friendships indicative of an insider reflected: "I knew I was trusted by people who I'd be interacting with on economic and budget policy . . . because it had only been four years since there had been an Obama administration, and we all knew each other pretty well, and it was mostly the same cast of characters involved, so that was probably the main thing."[11]

Others came to the transition as insiders because of the role they played during the campaign. One such person said: "I was pretty plugged into the election process for about seven to ten days after November 3," but then "The transition team reached out to me. . . . It was right before Thanksgiving and they asked me to help."[12] Another person said: "I don't think I'm special, but part of it is relationships," such as past relationships with "a number of people who were connected to the transition, and the Bidens."[13] After doing some volunteer policy work on the campaign during the summer, "the 'ask' came and I was like 'well, I think this makes a lot of sense.'"[14]

As with priorities, there's no clear science to determine how much of an insider or outsider someone was, but the ways interviewees were asked to join the transition suggested a range of relationships, some very close and others more distant to the president-elect and vice president elect as well as to the transition team leaders.

The only thing that really mattered was what Joe Biden said: twenty days earlier during a debate; twenty weeks before that as a part of the nomination campaign; or twenty years ago when he was in the Senate. When the candidate has a forty-year track record, it is not easy to find an issue without an opinion, vote, or platform statement. If you were looking for a mandate to govern, what the candidate has said is where you go to find it (Edwards 2016; Azari 2014).

This was the most important thing for anyone to remember during the transition period, especially for the thousand-plus people on the transition team. Nearly every person interviewed offered some version of *it all came down to the president-elect.* Someone said, "I first met Joe Biden in 1976. I mean this is a man who's had a record."[15] One member of a cross-cutting policy team on the transition shared, "We would always go back as a reference to what Biden's platform was, because that's kind of your constitution."[16] And another person leading a team during the pre-election transition said the job was "keeping people focused on the mission, which is just really to help this guy [Joe Biden] do what he said he would."[17]

This collective understanding stretched from the bottom to the top of the transition team. Former senator Ted Kaufman, who Biden had tapped to set up the transition in the spring of 2020, explained in a public interview: "We got from the campaign all of the policy statements [Biden] made, and we collected them into what we called a 'campaign promises book.' Then, the transition took the book and sliced and diced it so that people [responsible for reviewing] each agency knew what the Biden policies were for that specific agency" (The Transition Lab 2020). The job of the transition team was not to make policy.[18]

To start, this much was clear: what directed the work of the transition team was what the candidate and then president-elect, and to a much lesser extent the vice president elect, had said in the past. The clearer the statement or the higher the priority of the pledge, the more importance it held for directing the transition team's work. The second was the organizational structure established by leaders of the transition team: some of it imposed by federal law; other parts passed down over time from past transitions, Democratic and Republican; and some brand-new in 2020. Several factors that led to the structure are especially worth noting.

It is important to recognize the obvious: the planning for 2020 occurred after the 2016 transition, one defined by a near-total failure of organization, according to many experts on the presidency (Lewis, Bernhard, and You 2018). Political scientists James D. King and James W. Riddlesperger Jr. (2018, 1822, 1831) described the Trump transition as either "flexible" or "chaotic," one marked by scandal, controversy, and a set of nominees for the cabinet that "encountered more opposition than those of any recent president." Instead of the typical approach to staffing, the Trump transition team used enormous "beachhead" teams, a group of a thousand political appointees hired as "special government employees" to fill in temporarily at federal agencies, leading to what political scientist Karen Hult (2022, 92) called "confusion" and "occasional conflict" with the permanent appointees once they were confirmed by the Senate. Likewise, scholar of presidential transitions John Burke (2017, 563) concluded that the Trump national security transition was "a case study on opportunities missed and mistakes made." And journalist Michael Lewis (2018), who'd just written an account of the Trump transition, opined in an interview, "The degree of malice and neglect, there's never been anything like this." Two consequences of this messy run-up to Day 1 were long delays in appointments and remarkable instability in White House personnel; an early Trump presidency that political scientist Kathryn Dunn Tenpas (2018, 503) called "a year of record-setting staff turnover that created an aura of near-constant chaos" (Lewis and Richardson 2021).

In part a response to this failure of transition planning in 2016 was a new round of congressional action to address weaknesses in the transition process. As late as 2019, just a year before the 2020 transition, Congress updated the 1963 Presidential Transition Act to require the GSA to sign formal service agreements with each campaign after the party conventions and to require campaigns to release a transition ethics plan on the role of lobbyists and conflicts of interest (Buble 2020). This was the latest in a string of updates to the law—including two attributed to Senator Ted Kaufman, who later oversaw the Biden transition planning—to mandate and formalize aspects of the transition that had in the past been voluntary or informal.

And, finally, during the 2016 campaign, it was in part emails hacked from Hillary Clinton's campaign director, John Podesta, about transition planning that created headlines and fueled support for Donald Trump (Sullivan 2016). "John Podesta's emails . . . we were haunted by them," said one Biden–Harris transition leader.[19] (Center for Presidential Transition 2022a). Elaborate electronic security precautions hadn't been something to worry about in the past. In 2020, this was central to the transition planners.

All too aware of this recent history, as well as tradition, the transition team leaders started early, during the spring before the 2020 election, adhering to convention by separating the campaign and transition team, and establishing cybersecurity as a new priority (Center for Presidential Transition 2022a). According to top leaders of the transition team, like co-chair Kaufman: "Until Election Day, the campaign [was] by far the most important part of the Biden effort," and Yohannes Abraham, executive director of the transition: "One of our values was to do nothing to distract from the campaign" (Marchick 2021; Transition Lab 2020). This reinforced the transition as a separate and secondary activity through the early fall. "The campaign and the transition were highly separate enterprises. . . . It [was] very structured, very organized," someone described.[20] Another said simply: "We were not allowed to talk to the campaign people."[21]

A pandemic with everyone working from home made this conventional structure even easier to implement in 2020 (Wayne 2023). Another person who served on a pre-election transition team said: "We were totally divorced from the campaign. Totally divorced from it . . . [because of] all the communications and daily conversations, and of course this is during the pandemic, so everything is being done electronically, so security is a huge issue."[22] For many serving in key positions on the transition, they were sent a Google Chromebook with detailed instructions on how to secure this dedicated work computer along with their personal devices and social media accounts, as well.[23] They were also each given an @jbrpt.org email account to use exclusively for transition work. And, if they wanted to make a phone call or send a quick message, they were to use encrypted platforms only, like Signal or FaceTime audio; "no regular phone communications," said one team leader.[24] To the delight of those organizing the transition, when hackers attacked the transition team's accounts in 2020, the cybersecurity protections that they'd worked so hard to establish held strong.[25]

The attention to security also reinforced the secrecy demanded of everyone participating in the transition. Abraham later revealed that he chose people for the transition team specifically because of their discretion, and he called "holding all information closely" a "golden rule" agreed to by everyone who served on the team (Marchick 2021). One person who worked on a policy team before the election explained: "No one wanted to be caught as a leaker, especially if they want a job on the other side."[26]

Taken together, the tradition of separating the campaign and the transition, along with a deep concern about leaks and security, posed problems for some of those on the transition team. Asked why one transition staffer had been chosen for the team, they responded: "[The transition team] never tells you who reached out and puts out your name. . . . I'm not totally sure because they share as little information about the process as possible. I don't know why there's a preference for opacity, but that's how at least these folks seem to work."[27] That person continued: "They were extremely rigorous about [information security], to the point of almost confusion, like you didn't really know who was on the transition."[28] Another person agreed with this, explaining that it "felt a bit stealthy. Very little communication, strict rules. . . . The transition folks were under just such strict guidance, it was something that characterized the campaign's level of attention to cybersecurity, to information protection."[29] For example, that transition staffer working on economic issues chafed at the strict communications rules, saying: "I'd have my former [transition] subcommittee chairs saying to me, 'Can I talk to so and so? . . . Is it alright to have a conference call?' and I said 'yeah, please, go ahead, please, just give them all of your recommendations.' My view was 'hell'—pardon my language—but 'fuck it.'"[30]

Despite new worries about electronic security and the pandemic, the transition used a similar organizational structure in 2020 as it had in the past. In general, this is how Clinton-Gore did it in 1992 and Obama-Biden did it in 2008. The team even circulated binders prepared by the Mitt Romney transition team in 2012, according to one person on the Biden-Harris transition, "not that we're going to repeat this, but 'look at all they did.' We should be as organized or better," said one person on the team.[31] Illustrative of these similarities, in 2008 Obama-Biden had policy working groups for economics, education, energy and the environment, health care, immigration, national security, and technology/innovation/government reform (Kumar 2017). Four years later, perhaps surprisingly, the agency review work during the Trump transition looked the same, with a director, Ron Nicol, overseeing the work of separate teams for Defense (Keith Kellogg), National Security (Mike Rogers), Economic Issues (David Malpass and Bill Walton), Domestic Issues (Ken Blackwell), Management/Budget (Ed Meese and Kay Coles James), and Agency Transportation & Innovation (Beth Kaufman). A separate set of policy teams addressed "immigration reform & building the wall," health-care reform, regulatory reform, and several other cross-cutting policy areas.[32]

In 2020 Biden-Harris set things up in a similar, though not identical, way. One person who had served on both the 2008 and 2020 transitions said, "The big three hold: personnel, policy, and agency review."[33] The personnel work was divided between nominations for Senate-confirmed positions (overseen by Lisa Monaco) and appointments that did not need approval (led by Suzy George), and then within those by issue: domestic cluster, health, national security, energy, economics, and so on (Kumar 2021; Center for Presidential Transition 2022a). Around seventy people, mainly lawyers with degrees from Harvard and Yale, vetted the backgrounds of those considered for positions in the administration.[34]

Despite the strict organization of personnel on the transition, there still was an element of disorder. One person said: "Someone basically took the Plum Book," the master list of all presidentially appointed jobs, "and dropped it into a spreadsheet. . . . You could color code and rank and do all that stuff."[35] But though this made searching and sorting jobs easier, that person confessed they were using old information: "I don't even think the 2020 [Plum Book] had come out by then." On vetting (the process of search-ing through job candidates work and personal background for disqualifying statements or experiences), the team chose a two- or three-year cutoff for social media posts: nothing older than that was given much time by the vet-ting team, what one person thought was "an arbitrary timeline."[36] Even an extremely organized transition team still had elements of informality and a little bit of disorder.

Transition leaders also divided policy and agency review, first across in-ternational (led by Avril Haines) and domestic issues (led by Cecilia Mu-noz), and then for each by cross-cutting policy issues and agencies. Within the realm of economics, the team broke into eleven subcommittees focused on everything from finance and banking to poverty and racial equity to the Federal Reserve.[37] After the election, there were other teams for communica-tions, outreach, congressional relations, fundraising, and operations (Center for Presidential Transition 2022a).

It wasn't just that a similar organizational structure was in place as in the past; the transition was also highly formalized and centralized. Indicative of this formality, during weekly virtual press briefings after the election, Yo-hannes Abraham wore a crisp suit and tie, the exact same light blue and polka dot tie each time.[38] More importantly, transition leaders adopted clear pro-tocols, gave teams specific guidance, and directed team members how to do the work. One transition official with experience in 2008 and again in 2020 said about the Biden-Harris transition: "We were given templates, specific kinds of questions" that the team was required to answer to help get ready for Day 1. "The format of memos, the format of call sheets, people who were allowed in the room and not," all became stricter after the election, explained someone who served before and after the 2020 election.[39] Another described a highly predictable routine: "We met twice a day, every day, in the morning and in the evening . . . new instructions coming down from transition central in terms of templates to fill out, issues to identify. . . . [The transition] was very centrally controlled . . . all of our formats, our instructions."[40] And one final person said: "You had prescribed roles; the assignments and the papers that you're working on were things that were agreed. . . . It [was] very directed and very prescribed."[41]

The templates leaders created for team members included a notice to keep it brief: "Please keep under two pages," the template pleaded for Day 1 actions, with a suggested under four pages for actions in the first one hundred days.[42] The team adopted this rule because of what it had learned from "mini sprints" conducted before the election with people who had been through transitions in the past.[43] "[The transition team leaders] learned immediately that the memos were not very useful. . . . We heard from people writing memos, saying 'I pulled all-nighters and I never even knew if anybody saw what I wrote,'" said one person. And, it wasn't just frustrating for past transition team members: "We heard from cabinet members: 'Yeah, I got a freaking trolley full of binders full of memos and you know what I needed? I needed a 1-pager to help me figure out the negotiation I was going to have the next day with OMB on my agency budget.'"[44] Transition leaders directed team members accordingly: "The stuff that [the transition team] wrote was in the service of making sure that the people in the chairs making the decisions on January 20th and beyond had what they needed, especially for the things that needed to happen in the first 100 to 200 days."[45]

To do this, the Day 1 action template used by the team before the election included a box to briefly summarize a proposed "Policy Change" as well as small boxes for the "Rationale," actions the Trump administration had taken on the policy, and the "Equity Impact." Importantly for what we've learned so far about the mantra of team leaders, the template compelled team members to clarify candidate Biden's views: "Does he have a public position and/or made a campaign promise?"[46] All of the required information in under two pages, please.

This was an area where the vision of those at the top of the transition conflicted with those experiencing it at the bottom. In a media interview, one of the transition leaders, Yohannes Abraham, described one "tweak" the team made to promote collaboration between agency review and policy work.

He explained, without offering many details, the aim to create "connective tissue" and to "break down silos" by putting similar policy and agency review activities under the same departmental leadership of Haines and Munoz (Marchick 2021). One person interviewed opined that this decision "changed everything."[47] And, presidential transition scholar Martha Kumar (2021, 11) concluded that this strategy to link policy and agency review functions served to "make certain the two were connected in order to break down artificial department barriers."

One benefit of this approach was to build camaraderie between those insiders who went on to high-profile positions in the administration. A senior person on the transition team, an insider, compared the work of the policy side of the transition to Model United Nations, the high school club that simulates world events to build knowledge and student relationships: for those who are "going to end up being in the administration, who are going through the exercise of meetings and talking, even if you're not really making decisions, even if the memo that you're specifically working on people may not read a lot on the other side," still "building the muscle memory of what it is to work in an intense policy environment that is not a full replica of an administration, but it is the beginnings of what it would look potentially look like" is worth it.[48]

For those working on the transition, some didn't feel like they'd joined the Model UN and didn't see those silos coming down, because, as with previous transitions, the team was organized in formal tiers, clear hierarchies established across issues.[49] "The transition team was extremely tiered, much like government itself," said one person.[50] Even though there were hundreds, if not thousands, of people involved, it was the insiders who did much of the most consequential work, influencing the direction of the incoming administration. One person said: "There's an inner circle of a few people. Then, outside of that, probably another, and then you have a bigger circle."[51] For this person, some of these insiders were friends, but still that person conceded they themself "[was] not in that inner circle of like six people, like [incoming Secretary of State] Tony Blinken and others, who'd been there with the Vice President since he was 27 years old."[52] This meant that "[I] had windows into [the inner circle], but I did not have visibility."[53] Access, but limited influence.

For someone else low in the hierarchy, an outsider, this meant limits on vertical integration within the transition team: "Our job was basically to suss out issues. . . . Then we would go to the head of our team and say, 'we think this needs elevating.'"[54] To help with this process of elevation up the chain-of-command in the transition, since everyone was working virtually, "there was a regular information collection of a Google Docs spreadsheet. . . . Your team leader would say, 'I think you're right, this needs to be elevated' or 'hey, this is something that needs to go into the briefing book for the incoming secretary.'"[55]

These lines worked vertically, but also horizontally across the transition. One person explained: "You are on a certain team. . . . I wasn't like 'OK, I'm on the transition team and calling anybody I want' and just sort of chatting about it."[56] Another person on an agency review team concurred with this: "The policy teams kept to themselves," this despite the interconnections of issues like reviving the economy, on the domestic level, and trade, on the international level. The person continued: "Both policy and strategy were things that everyone needed to work on . . . but there wasn't a lot of great coordination in that way, and even if you tried to enter the conversation, [members of the policy team] were much more of the old school government folks who, if you're not already in the room, you're not invited to the conversation."[57]

The virtual-only dimension of the 2020 transition exacerbated this problem, but not for everyone. Someone who was a Biden-Harris insider on the team explained: "The virtual nature of the transition did not have much of an impact at the most senior level in terms of their ability to build connection. We were just constantly in meetings with one another and calling one another. . . . I think the junior staff had a harder time with it. It may have been because they were in fewer meetings."[58] Another reason for this was that people working at lower levels of the transition didn't necessarily know who else was on the team; only the names of those on the agency review teams had been revealed. This resulted in some strange encounters. "I figured out one person in my neighborhood was on the transition because I was turning in my COVID test kit and I saw there was already a COVID test kit at the postal drop off and I glanced at it and saw her name on it," one transition volunteer shared.[59] Another person involved in technology issues explained that early in the transition they wanted to "reach out to somebody in industry" to discuss an issue, but once they reached out to that executive for a meeting realized, "Oh wait, they're on the transition."[60] The opposite happened to someone else on the team: "There're definitely meetings where I'm meeting people in real life, not knowing if they're involved. So, I'm like, 'Hey, are you part of the transition? . . . And, more often than not, they're like, 'Oh no, I'm not.' And I'm like, 'Oh, well, God, I guess I just exposed myself as being part.'"[61]

The consequences of this opaque work environment were more than just comedic; there were noticeable effects on collaboration. A person working on an agency review team said: "There were some real constraints on collaboration because it was all virtual, because there were limited opportunities to just casually meet and figure out who was interested in what you were working on."[62] Another person involved in personnel issues agreed that there was "very limited collaboration across departments . . . or if you wanted to make that collaboration, you had to work exceedingly hard."[63] That person gave an example: "There are a number of candidates who were phenomenal. . . . I was like, 'This is an excellent candidate, this is a female, a woman, a person of color, a young person, someone who's differently-able. . . . They should be picked up by the administration somewhere.'"[64] If that excellent job candidate wasn't chosen by your small team, what could you do? Within the transition's electronic records system, the person explained: "You could add a tag to their name . . . to flag it for another agency [review team], and you just have to hope that whoever was my counterpart at any one of those agencies would find it."[65] Rather than just crossing fingers, team members could try to connect with other people on the transition team in order to share the name, but this proved difficult, too, because of the rules set up by the transition team. The person continued: "Then it was trying to figure out who is my equivalent at each of these agencies so I can give them a call or send them an email to recommend these candidates . . . so when I would ask, 'Can you just tell me who is my counterpart?' you really had to provide a justification [to the transition leaders] as to why it was necessary. . . . It really limited collaboration."[66] And, the technology provided to the team didn't help solve the problem: "Even when you were trying to search for someone's name in the Google address book, there wasn't a universal address book. . . . There was never a list of who all was actually on the transition. . . . You couldn't actually even use Zoom: they blocked it so you couldn't see all of whom were on the call."[67]

Not everyone agreed with this critical sentiment. One person said: "I'm a military guy; structure is not a problem for me."[68] Someone else offered a similar assessment, that even though "it was all tracked and was organized . . . I didn't really ever feel really constrained or anything. . . . I thought that I was able to add a completely free hand to give my views and I talked to anybody."[69] This could have been because that person's issues were not priority issues for the incoming administration. They explained that their issues on the transition weren't "political" but "more technical" and stressed that "it was policy" as opposed to something ideologically charged. As a consequence, "A lot of times there would be [background papers] on things and in there [the transition leaders] would mention positions that the Vice President [Biden] had taken. . . . I always felt that it was more just like, 'Be aware of this,' not like 'This is our position.' . . . it was more 'just to inform you.'"[70] This is a subtle difference in tone, yet one that resulted in a very different perception of discretion felt by someone lower down placed by the upper echelons of the transition team. The result, it would seem, was that the low-issue priority—an issue that was more technical than political—meant more discretion and *possibly* influence for this outsider.

Contrast this with the perception of another person on an agency review team whose issue "was definitely needing presidential attention."[71] As a consequence, the person explained: "There is a kind of a central core group of insiders, not just recruits with subject matter expertise, but close to the candidate," who were brought in to talk. They continued: "I spent a lot of time briefing the people" on the "central core group" of the transition.[72] This higher-priority issue area meant a much closer connection to insiders on the team, and possibly less discretion.

Overall, what emerged by the fall of 2020–2021 was a transition structure that resembled the past: an institutionalized arrangement with clearly delineated areas of responsibility, hierarchies, and technology to link it all together. Another implication of this merging of tradition with new solutions to problems, like the pandemic and cyber insecurity, was that the Biden-Harris transition team had a model for how to address social justice and equity, newly salient issues in 2020, and fulfill the commitment Biden made at the announcement of his transition on November 10 to "building an administration that looks like America" (Biden-Harris Transition Team 2020b). Social justice and equity moved to the center of the debate on every aspect of both the campaign and the transition.

On the campaign side, the candidates incorporated the words of protest for justice into the party's platform as well as their speeches and debating points (Viser 2020). The 2020 platform read: "We will never amplify or legitimize the voices of racism, misogyny, anti-Semitism, anti-Muslim bigotry, or white supremacy" (DNC 2020). The word "racism" appeared seventeen times in 2020; it was absent from the 2008 platform.

The Biden team also could draw on the detente established with supporters of Senator Bernie Sanders when he exited the campaign. The so-called Unity Task Force, a team of policy experts chosen by Biden and Sanders, met in June to write a series of reports on important issues, a consensus established at the time across factions of the Democratic Party, long before the party convention agreed on a platform. One member of the transition team surmised, "All of the policy energy was coming from the Left, and [Biden's team] just adopted that. . . . There [were] a number of [Senator Elizabeth] Warren plans that were more or less adopted by the campaign."[73]

This was, in part, because members of the Unity Task Force came from various wings of the party, including some not even willing to endorse

Biden at the time. Take Varshini Prakash, executive director of the Sunrise Movement, the progressive environmental group pushing for a stronger stance on climate change. Selected by Senator Sanders, Prakash joined the Climate Change group of the Unity Task Force along with former Senator John Kerry and a sitting member of Congress, Representative Alexandria Ocasio-Cortez, along with several others. Prakash explained that the task force "will help craft the 2020 agenda for the Biden campaign, inform the DNC policy platform, and have a role in Biden's transition process should he defeat Donald Trump in November" (Prakash 2020). While this was not an endorsement, Biden was the person Prakash believed could move ahead the movement's Green New Deal agenda. And, though Prakash didn't ultimately join the Biden transition team, several others did, including Jared Bernstein, Vivek Murthy, Juan Gonzalez, and Chris Jennings (others from the Unity Task Force also may have volunteered but were not publicly announced by the transition team).

For his part, when the Unity Task Force released a final report, Senator Sanders concluded: "Do I believe that Biden believes that now is the time for bold action to protect the working class and lower-income people in this country? Yes, I do believe that's the case" (Wayne 2021). During the campaign, the impact of the Unity Task Force could be seen in the addition of new progressive policy promises made by Joe Biden and Kamala Harris as well as in a more progressive Democratic platform than 2016 or 2012 (Fagan 2020).

On the transition side, this meant something different: the impact of the Unity Task Force and summer of protest for equity and justice was more institutionalized and implicit. So much so that Wide Eye—the company hired to design digital material for the transition—explained, "Inclusivity, accessibility, and performance were at the heart of the process for creating" the brand for the transition (Wide Eye n.d.). By institutionalizing justice and equity issues as well as many progressive policies—some new to the party and even new to Biden and Harris in 2020—there would be fewer risks that a team of hundreds of volunteers working remotely on the transition would forget these were priorities. For example, one self-identified progressive serving on the transition team explained the impact of the Unity Task Force: "They had this unofficial or task force where they had Bernie and Biden people get together and they hashed it out."[74] But the impact of this work was as much implicit as explicit. "It didn't explicitly play into our work . . . but there was this acknowledgment that we're not going to necessarily put [former Clinton and Obama economic adviser] Larry Summers in charge. . . . A number of people have internalized, even if they haven't said, that 'this transition needed to be different than the 2008 one and needed to be more progressive, more reflective and to kind of balance . . . some of the political enthusiasm from the Bernie campaign,'" the person explained.[75] Another said: "In regular twice-a-day meetings and the feedback with principals and those at senior levels of the transition, the message was that 'Hey, this is different.' This is not the Clinton administration approach or even the Obama administration approach on [economic issues]. . . . We were committed to helping people who are left behind. We're committed to being more forward thinking, and we're going to try new approaches, different approaches."[76]

One way that transition team leaders instilled consensus ideas from the Unity Task Force was through staffing. Felicia Wong, a member of the transition advisory group, said in a public interview the transition team was "trying to bring people together from across the very big tent that is the Democratic coalition" (Roosevelt Institution 2021). As the previous chapter showed, while there was consistency in many parts of the transition between 2008 and 2020, there were also newcomers, especially from parts of the party that hadn't had a seat at the table for past transitions. One person on the transition team explained: "[The transition] looked a little bit more like a parliamentary system of sorts where you have 40 to 50 percent of the people coded as being part of what people either call the 'Warren Wing' or the 'Sanders Wing' of the party, and then you had half of them or a little over half being folks that had served in prior administrations."[77] For instance, the transition team named Josh Orton, an aide to Senator Sanders, to the Labor Department agency review team, and Anne Reid, the chief of staff to Senator Warren, to the Health and Human Services review team.

It wasn't just the legacy of the Unity Task Force that was "internalized" but also the case for the movements for social justice and racial equity. One transition official said: "Coming after the summer of protests after George Floyd's murder, there was a stated, and very serious, level of commitment on the part of Joe Biden, the candidate, and his running mate: his transition would look like America."[78] Someone else said: "Equity and justice and all that was an overriding theme that would be considered on a rigorous basis in almost everything we did."[79] Equity and justice "was a mandate that we all had throughout; every single plan had to have a section explicitly analyzing impact."[80] Another person focused on staffing said: "The issues from the campaign had pretty much permeated everyone's consciousness. . . . The issue of social justice was constant and deep, but it wasn't because 'did you see what they did yesterday?' or because Reverend Sharpton said 'X' or because this police officer did 'Y.'"[81] Another echoed this sentiment: "I can't say that we would have meetings at any point and say, 'the George Floyd murder makes it really clear that [this issue] is one part of a whole social justice movement' . . . that said, that kind of idea sort of develops as you're working."[82]

And one other said: "It affected our vocabulary quite a bit. . . . It definitely affected the way we talked about things."[83]

Nearly everyone shared this same sentiment: diversity, equity, and inclusion (DEI) mattered to the candidates; leaders of the transition reflected this in organizing the teams; and members of the transition team recognized this as a priority. One person on the transition team said: "The senior management could tell you at any given moment, like if you popped up on a Tuesday at 3:00 o'clock and said, 'What's the proportion of our own staff of women to men? of African Americans, Latinos, Asian Americans, Native Americans, veterans?' [the transition team leaders] always knew what the answer was. So, it was constantly visible. Constantly reinforced as everybody's job."[84]

The transition team relied on insider groups to fulfill this goal, too. A good example of this was how the transition team interacted with women's organizations, especially those connected to a national network of state and local organizations. One member of the transition team explained: "If the national headquarters of Planned Parenthood is here [at a transition meeting], they have affiliates across how many states . . . so some of it was also [the transition team] working with the national headquarters and then essentially asking for them to identify the grassroots voices or the local leaders."[85] So, the team would ask Planned Parenthood: "Can you bring us a practitioner from Texas? Can you bring us a practitioner from deep Georgia, from Mississippi? From Alabama?"[86] An established group like Planned Parenthood, a classic insider in the Democratic Party, then served as a one-stop shop of trusted connections to those far from the nation's capital.

Organized labor maintained a similar position. "It wasn't lost on me where the incoming [transition recommendation] was coming from. . . . We tracked that they were endorsed by the AFL-CIO and the Teamsters," one person involved in personnel issues said. And, although the person "didn't feel like I had to hire someone just because the Teamsters had backed them," they concluded, "When you start seeing the same name over and over again, then you're like, 'OK, well, this is probably someone I should look into a little further.'"[87]

Nevertheless, conflicts emerged, sometimes when apparently high-priority goals didn't align. One official on an agency review team explained: "One of the things that I kept pressing for in terms of how we staffed [was] that we have to do everything. We have to walk and chew gum at the same time. And, we can't exclude the oil sector."[88] Recall, climate change was a transition priority, meaning a job candidate's commitment to that issue had to be tested, especially those who'd been working in the energy sector. The team had gone as far as writing into its ethics plan that "leaders of fossil fuel or private prison companies" were not welcome on the team (Biden–Harris Transition Team

2020a). Another member of a personnel team revealed just how difficult it was to square these priorities. They explained that transition leaders did not want anyone considered for positions in the Biden administration from certain industries: "This was a priority in terms of absolutely a hard 'no' on anybody in the oil and gas sector, not a lot of wiggle room."[89] This stance came directly out of the progressive turn in the campaign and principles embedded in the transition's ethics plan, but it had unintended implications for other transition goals. The person continued that many people from these restricted industries "were considered not pure enough and so tens of Black and Brown candidates were automatically excluded from consideration, and it was just shocking because . . . it's limiting by race . . . and so it was just really frustrating to sort of keep bumping up against that."[90] For this person's team, the strong position taken by Biden—the "hard no" on anyone working in certain industries—resulted in less discretion, less "wiggle room," and that had the consequence of making it harder for that team to meet the transition's DEI goal. One advocate for diversity who advised the team backed up this perception: "A largely white good government frame comes in and ends up filtering out and disqualifying a lot of strong Black candidates because they had at one time worked for a particular company."[91]

In other cases, the transition team conflicted over high-priority policy issues, like whether to cancel student debt, a major issue during the Democratic campaign and priority of many progressives in the party. One person on the transition team, an outsider who advocated for cancellation, described the resolution of the issue. "I was privy to some fights over 'should we cancel student debt?'"[92] As an outsider, though, the issue was resolved elsewhere, soon moving up the hierarchy of the transition, into the hands of those insiders, it would seem. The person explained: "Things kind of move up the chain, and it's a little bit unclear whether [recommendations from the transition team] just go into a file somewhere or whether they actually get into the bloodstream of the president's inner circle that's going to be making these decisions."[93] Ultimately, Biden didn't act on this issue with an immediate executive order after the conclusion of the transition nor within the first hundred days in office. It took nearly two years for action on student debt.

With an organizational plan in place, clear lines of authority established, and technology ready to make the transition secure and virtual, the Biden-Harris transition team was ready for the real work after the election. They'd even signed a memorandum of understanding with the White House a month earlier, a shock to leaders of the team who'd expected Trump to comply with none of the new federal transition rules (Whipple 2022).

Election Day came and went, but the votes were too close to name a winner. It took until Saturday after the election, and the counting of thousands of provisional and mail-in ballots, for Joe Biden and Kamala Harris to be declared victorious. On November 9 and 10, the transition publicly released the names of hundreds of people who would serve on the transition, including nearly all of those serving on the thirty-nine agency review teams as well as the five transition co-chairs and fifteen-person advisory council.

Though the announcement of a twelve-person COVID-19 Advisory Board had little precedent in past transitions, it is what happened next that was truly surprising—if not for the transition team leaders, at least for the public. President Donald Trump refused to concede the election, even days after the votes had been tallied. Not since 2000, when a virtual tie in the Electoral College meant the state of Florida had to recount thousands of ballots, had a losing candidate for the presidency not given an immediate concession speech and accepted the results of the election.

This meant that the General Services Administration, the agency with the authority to release post-election public funds and government office space to the transition team, waited to act. In this case, acting meant "ascertaining" the election results, typically viewed as a formality, but in 2020 that formality didn't happen right away. A week later, the GSA administrator, Emily Murphy, still hadn't signed the letter authorizing nearly $10 million in federal funds as well as office space and federal assistance to the Biden-Harris transition, as previous administrators had (Rein, O'Connell, and Dawsey 2020). After Trump tweeted "Great job Emily!" President-elect Biden pinned the delay on outgoing President Trump, calling his failure to concede "an embarrassment," and marking the start of two and a half months of the most difficult political and legal wrangling related to a transition of power in US history (Faulders, Flaherty, and Siegel 2020; Sprunt 2020).

For the transition leaders, knowing a delayed ascertainment had slowed the Bush transition in 2000, they had prepared for what political scientist Stephen Wayne (2021) called "the politics of obstruction." On November 10, the team announced its strategy: "The agency review teams will proceed by meeting with former agency officials and experts who closely follow federal agencies, and with officials from think tanks, labor groups, trade associations, and other NGOs (non-governmental organizations)" (Biden-Harris Transition Team 2020b). Unlike in the recent past, when much of the work of the transition team would be to canvas the federal government to identify pressing problems and meet with *current* political appointees and career bureaucrats, in 2020 that work would have to wait. On November 20, Yohannes Abraham said to the press that "this isn't a game of who gets to talk to whom" and noted that groups as varied as the National Manufacturers Association, the US Chamber

of Commerce, and the American Medical Association had urged for cooperation and ascertainment (Biden-Harris Transition Team 2020d).

Nevertheless, in waiting, some on the transition team believed they had
discovered a surprisingly effective way to get ready to govern. One person
described the impact of delayed ascertainment as "a powerful tool" and that
the Trump administration "sort of handed us something unintentionally that
proved to be very valuable and very unique, which was because they didn't
ascertain us for so long, we were forced to talk to people outside the government."[94] Another said: "Instead of starting with the agency and working our
way out to the stakeholders, we just talked with everybody who was outside
of the agency who could talk to us. That included congressional staff, organized stakeholder groups, former employees, and directors of the agency."[95]
Someone else concurred that "usually what would happen in a transition like
this on an agency review team is I would run into a lot of people just walking
down the halls and they would all want to tell me something," but in 2020,
"The Biden team did not want us to do those kinds of contact."[96]

In at least one case, though, discrete communications with Trump officials did in fact happen, an apparent violation of the stated policy of the GSA
before ascertainment, according to one member of the transition team. That
person said: "There were conversations that took place . . . encrypted phone
conversations that the Trumpies didn't know about; they couldn't stop the
conversations."[97] Sometimes a person in the administration would say, "Call
me when I'm home" or "call me on this encrypted chat," and a conversation
would transpire, sharing information with the transition team weeks before
the GSA had authorized communications.

Such stealthy communication, though, seemed to be an exception. Instead, the transition team turned to former federal officials who had already
left government, some as recently as the summer of 2020. These conversations turned out to be incredibly valuable. "People who have left are a lot
more forthcoming, so that was actually a very good information source. . . .
I don't think I would have worked as hard to get those people if I'd had access to people who were still in government," one person said.[98] Once the
members of the cabinet were nominated, they too began to meet with outside
groups, such as treasury secretary and deputy secretary-nominees Janet Yel-
len and Wally Adeyemo, who met with racial and economic justice groups in
the middle of December (Biden-Harris Transition Team 2020e).

The virtual dimension of the 2020 transition also expanded the impact of
this strategy. One person said: "The fact that we were doing so many virtual
meetings multiplied the number of interviews by a lot."[99] So, when ascertainment finally happened twenty days later, the transition team members were
ready: "We had hours and hours of interviews with these people, and so by

that time we finally were able to speak with the folks inside [the government]; we had done so much work and had so much knowledge."[100] For example, those outside the government could help the team figure out who to retain and who to get rid of: "I gained real views about people, individual people, and who were keepers and who were incompetent," said one person on a personnel team.[101]

Since the transition team anticipated a delayed ascertainment, it could prepare the contingency plan that, arguably, worked even better than tradition. Waiting to meet with current federal officials until after a full briefing with those outside of the government gave the transition team insights, sharpened the questions they could ask, and allowed them to discern who in government to keep and who to let go.

This did not mean, however, that the delayed ascertainment resulted in the transition team knowing exactly who to recommend for key positions. One person involved in the transition explained their goal was "to identify at least three people for every position that we're going to interview. . . . The interview process itself helps winnow that down, because you're asking questions about 'What would you do in this circumstance? How do you handle this?' . . . Pass that, then you end up saying, 'OK, we've got three really good candidates here.'"[102] And, the work didn't stop there: "If you've got three people" then you ask "what's the diversity? And that diversity may not have anything to do with race or ethnicity. That's diversity of gender, that diversity may have been . . . about skill sets or philosophy."[103]

Divisions within the party also remained an issue, even as the transition leaders sought to mend those fences through a team that represented all parts of the party and established tight controls over coordination across teams. For example, one agency review team member who participated in hiring interviews said: "They would choose three different people . . . someone that was totally corporate . . . and then you have folks who would be really moderate in their presentation and very measured, not ready to get outside the bounds."[104] This person concluded, "It seemed [the transition team was] seeking out a kind of 'a team of rivals'. . . . Pick people who had very different perspectives on basic policy questions deriving from really different sets of values about the role of the government and the role of the private sector."[105] For this volunteer, a self-professed progressive, this presented an opportunity, and they used that opportunity to seek influence over personnel decisions made by the transition team. They explained that there was a clique of progressive members of the transition who would ask each other: "Should we be heading folks off?" who they feared would get jobs. This group of progressives "would strategize and communicate outside of the official channels to see 'OK, do you need something to help bolster your case?'" against job candidates they opposed.[106] They would help by communicating to each other: "'Let me get that for you' to share information about potentially problematic people who were more traditional in their thinking."[107] It is unclear whether this strategy worked as intended or even how common this was, but it reveals a lot about the disconnect between the goal of the transition team leaders for order and consensus and the ways some volunteers pursued different and competing priorities.

Appointments also faced an even bigger challenge outside the transition team: Republican control of the Senate and the confirmation process. The day after the election, not only was the outcome of the presidential contest unclear, the two Senate races in the state of Georgia were too close to call and headed for mandatory January runoffs. Though the Democratic Party later won these two elections and secured the slightest of control of the Senate, in November the prospects looked bleak. One Biden-Harris campaign staffer who later joined the transition team said: "[The transition team] made it very clear that this is a shift from the work we did on the campaign: the work that we're doing as a transition team is bipartisan and inclusive."[108] That person continued: "This was about everyone, not just Democrats, and making sure that Republican elected officials had a seat at the table, were also included and informed about the plans and intentions of the administration."[109] To do this, the team held closed-door meetings, no press invited, with the president-elect and state and local officials, many Republicans, to "have a dialogue with the president[-elect]."[110]

The transition team also lined up Republicans to endorse Biden cabinet nominees, such as Tony Blinken for secretary of state.[111] One advocate who watched the transition from the outside surmised: "Biden's sitting there thinking 'I gotta get this cabinet through a hostile Senate.' And, nobody thought the Democrats would win Georgia, so his cabinet picks were not progressive. He picked people from the center of the party. He consciously avoided people who would have trouble getting confirmed."[112] As much as progressives within the transition team might push favored candidates, some of that had to occur below the cabinet-level positions and in non–Senate confirmed slots.

Others disagreed with this assessment. One person working on appointments within the transition said: "Confirmability is always a consideration in the nomination process. . . . That said, it would be a mistake to assume that this led to more 'centrist' nominees. . . . I think President Biden's choices speak for themselves . . . reflecting his priorities, the policies, and programs he spelled out in the campaign."[113]

This balancing act, though, didn't involve Republicans chosen for the cabinet or other key agency positions. Another person involved in personnel issues, an outsider on the team, said: "I put a lot of [Republican] names and resumes into that [human resource] system, and I don't think any of them actually ended up being called. You just don't hear back; you'd get an auto-mated response: 'We've received your information. Thank you for your inter-est. We'll be in touch.'"[114] In the end, the transition team didn't get back in touch; the interest of Republicans willing to serve was not a part of the plan.

That control of the Senate altered the personnel strategy of the transition team ultimately mattered little to speed the confirmation process. Even once the Democrats gained majority control of the Senate, Biden's confirmations were the slowest in a generation. Political scientist Kathryn Dunn Tenpas (2022) found, three hundred days into the administration, that the Senate had confirmed half the number of Biden nominees as it had for George W. Bush and a hundred fewer than Barack Obama. Knowing this possibility, the transition team had a plan: "Given the very real possibility that there could be major delays in the confirmation process given some of the partisan di-vide, [the transition team] spent a great amount of time focusing on selecting appointees who could effectively serve in acting capacities and/or effectively lead the departments/offices in the absence of a confirmed nominee," said one person on the team.[115] This meant finding people with past agency ex-perience to fill in until the Senate confirmed the top officials, as well as a willingness to step back once the appointees were in place.

Balancing various interests played out on the policy side as well, but those interviewed on the transition team, including progressives, explained a dif-ferent way that they absorbed new ideas to moderate conflicts. Recall, the Biden-Harris transition team established a clear approach to policy accord-ing to one person involved on that side of the transition: "We are not making policy; we are figuring out how to implement what the policy that [Biden's] made."[116] Yet, since the transition team had brought in a diverse group of volunteers with different interpretations of Biden's policy promises during the campaign, team leaders had to devise plans to bring everyone together, though not necessarily change everyone's mind. One team leader explained, "With such ideological diversity" on the team, they told everyone: "anything you want to recommend to the Biden administration is fine, but, unless it's something that he's already committed to, this needs to be in the form of different options, and we need to canvas all of the options and not make it a specific recommendation."[117] This point gets to the centrality of the pres-ident-elect's priorities as well as how the team could manage internal policy disagreements in a constructive way. Another volunteer explained something similar about how the team took advice from outsider progressives. "There were definitely new voices at the big kids table . . . but by the same token, there were just tons of people misreading where the American people were in their everyday lives and how we could meet them there and describe things in a relatable way," they explained.[118] That person concluded: "Almost anything can be at least talked about, even if some things are quickly rethought and right-sized a bit."[119] As with the balancing act on personnel, the transition team moderated rapid policy change to adjust to a country that might not agree with every bold campaign promise.

The long days of the transition stretched through the holidays and into the New Year. Then the unthinkable happened. Rioters attacked the Capitol at the very moment Congress would make official what the country had known since early November: Joe Biden was the next president. Congress prevailed over the insurrectionists, ultimately voting to certify the election late on January 6. Meanwhile, outgoing President Trump continued to defy convention, discouraging cooperation with the Biden transition team, especially within several key departments, including the OMB and Defense Department, according to media reports (Lesniewski 2020).

While Trump's intransigence drew outrage and headlines, many involved in the day-to-day work of the Biden transition interacted with Trump appointees and federal bureaucrats who fully complied with the transition law. One person working on an agency review team said that, though the agency's secretary was "pretty checked out at that point," the "under-secretaries and other people were very forthcoming; they arranged meetings. . . . They were very constructive and they were very professional."[120] Another person working on a different agency review team concurred: "We had heard rumors the [Trump] political appointees had instructed the career staff to not be very forthcoming with us," yet when the meetings occurred "[the career staff] were generally pretty collegial."[121] A third person also agreed: "My personal experience was people were largely cooperative." And, one final person said: "There was nothing poisonous or nothing vindictive. It was all very straightforward. . . . I would say it exceeded my expectations, how cooperative people were."[122] This was, in part, a function of the "unglamorous, mission-oriented work" of the civil servants they spoke to. And, when "there were differences of opinion on how things are going or specific technologies and how they're about to bear," the conflicts didn't amount to much because they were "mundane, in-the-weeds disagreements or differences of opinion."[123]

While this may have characterized the work of some on the transition team, for certain issues the lack of cooperation from the Trump administration was real and consequential. One person working on international business issues said: "We'd get bits and pieces from different people, and not everyone was on 'Team Obfuscation': some people were just federal employees who've seen every transition and were just giving us the answers from what they knew best."[124] For others, though, the person said "it was so clear just how much they were hiding in every answer. We knew we weren't getting honest answers."[125] That person had done their own research and knew the outgoing Trump appointees they were meeting with were obfuscating the truth. They concluded: "My guess is [the Trump] strategy was just wasting time . . . so that no progress can occur."[126]

The obfuscation, hiding, and time wasting was especially harmful in high-priority issue areas. International economics and national security policy were such cases: high priorities for the incoming administration where cooperation was important for the safety and security of the nation. For those working on this broad area on the transition, the Trump administration's response varied greatly. "The administration was incredibly obstructionist, and much more so than it was ever reported in the media. . . . They impeded the process," said one person focused on international issues.[127] "They had a political minder in every single meeting, and that person would interrupt and stop the government employees from saying things. . . . Those meetings ended up being a lot less forthright than they should have been." But that person clarified, "This wasn't because any of the political appointees themselves wanted to be obstructionist. . . . They all cared about the mission and the nation and what they were doing. But there was definite intervention from the White House that stifled the conversation."

Another person on the 2020 transition team who focused on similar issues witnessed differences: "With the CIA, [cooperation] was very good because [Director] Gina Haspel, your career professional, had done what career professionals had done in prior administrations: prepare a vast number of briefing books, to make people available for discussion. . . . The level of cooperation with CIA was very good."[128] Haspel had been at the CIA for thirty years when Trump appointed her director in 2018. On the contrary, others in this area were less supportive of the transition. "With the director of National Intelligence, it was not as great. . . . [John Ratcliffe] was making it difficult." Unlike Haspel, Ratcliffe hadn't been a career civil servant; instead he had served as a Republican member of Congress for five years prior to his selection by Trump in 2020. "Still, cooperation did occur . . . [but] it was more grudging," said that member of the transition team.

One final person involved in immigration issues corroborated the variation in cooperation across the Trump administration. "One of the transition team interlocutors from the Trump administration, that guy was fantastic," helping to coordinate meetings with the Biden-Harris team.[129] Others, however, were "the complete opposite." For example, the immigration team member explained the way a rare in-person meeting transpired, the Biden-

Harris representatives all masked and PCR-tested, including a required rapid COVID-19 test just three hours before the meeting. Once in the secure Sensitive Compartmented Information Facility, or SCIF, "not all the Trump team wore masks. . . . Most of the Trump team came in as if there was no problem at all," and none was ready to share the requested information. The Trump official explained at the conclusion of one such meeting: "We don't care. . . . You guys aren't legitimate, so we aren't going to share this information." Consequently, the Biden-Harris team member concluded: "We were unable to provide a complete picture of the current intelligence threat environment. . . . Had there been something similar to [9/11] we wouldn't have had the information."

The budget also was a high-priority area during the transition. An incoming administration is under intense pressure to prepare its first presidential budget, which is due to Congress shortly after inauguration and is typically over two thousand pages long. This massive undertaking involving complex statistical modeling depends on financial data held by only a few people at each agency and the OMB. As a result, those involved in preparing this first budget coming out of the transition had previously relied on existing budget staff for help integrating current budget numbers with campaign promises. "The practice of helping with the budget dates back to Eisenhower," said one person involved in the Biden-Harris transition.[130] This was not the case in 2020. Another person on an agency review team recalled that, unlike in the past, Trump political appointees had to approve all requests from the Biden transition team for budget information.[131] Several times the transition team received "push back" from Trump appointees who deemed the requests "inappropriate," leading to, what the person called, a "blinking red light that they're not going to play ball."[132]

The head of the OMB at the time, Russell Vought (2020), explained as much to the Biden-Harris team in a New Year's Eve letter to Ted Kaufman: "Any work to develop Biden Administration policies should be done by that team. . . . Redirecting staff and resources to draft your team's budget proposals is not an OMB transition responsibility." The result: Biden's first budget was delivered much later than normal, "an acute consequence of not being able to work as closely as they would have" with federal budget staff, said one transition team official.[133] Another person on the team concluded: "We did a lot of dialogue with the [budget] staff. It's not like no transitioning happened . . . but a lot of the serious work that we would have been doing, like working together on the budget . . . we just couldn't do. We couldn't work together in the traditional way."[134]

These comments reinforce the different levels of the transition and the differences between priority transition issues and the rest of the work of the transition team. For some high-priority issues, like preparing the first budget or enacting certain campaign promises, cooperation matters a lot, and an outgoing administration uninterested in helping can do harm to the incoming administration. For many other issues, those that generate little attention, especially from the White House, cooperation is much more the norm, and even a hostile outgoing administration will acquiesce to helping the transition team.

Throughout, members of the transition team continued their work from home. Cabinet nominations were made—the final one a few days after the New Year—and the work of many on the transition team shifted from planning to execution.[135] Appointees had to be prepared for confirmation hearings and informed on who were the best candidates for subcabinet appointments. And those campaign promises, especially the most time-sensitive ones, had to be turned into action. One person on the policy side of the transition explained that over the course of the fall, "It went anywhere from conceptual to pen-to-paper to refinement."[136] Early on they "had put together the memorandum, the present presidential order," but then they "all had to discuss what this was going to look like, and that became more intense the closer we came to January 20. The head of domestic policy on the transition team and the secretary who had just been nominated had to be called in, as did the incoming White House staffer focused on the issue."[137] "Meetings after meetings," the person lamented. "You come back with a memo, and then they think it through again, and then you go up a level and then it would come back."[138] All of this drafting, meeting, and revising resulted in what another transition team member concluded: "On Day 1, everything is written already, all the executive orders are written, they just have to be signed."[139]

And then, at the end of the eleven weeks, with the inauguration planning completed and Joe Biden and Kamala Harris ready to be sworn in, one transition team member said: "We just disappeared at midnight."[140]

All this transition planning meant Joe Biden was ready to be sworn into office on January 20. He signed more than a dozen executive orders that day, all finalized during the previous eleven weeks of the transition. By that point, he'd also named his entire cabinet, organized a White House, and had made more nominations for Senate-confirmed positions (thirty-six) than the past four presidents (Center for Presidential Transitions 2022b).

The pandemic, the obstruction from the Trump White House, and a deepening economic recession were roadblocks that Joe Biden's transition team had overcome, some predictable in a deeply divided country and others unexpected. As they did so, some volunteers on the transition team also confronted internal roadblocks—strict hierarchies, intricate procedures to limit cybersecurity concerns, and competing ways to implement priorities around equity and justice—to translate their access into influence over the new administration. These internal challenges show how the transition team manages intra-party conflicts, juggles new priorities, and welcomes newcomers to the decision-making table.

That's how it looked from the inside, but what did it look like from the outside? What did it look like from the perspective of the tens of thousands of lobbyists, think tankers, and advocates in Washington nervously waiting for the new administration to begin governing? The next chapter addresses these questions.

CHAPTER 4

The Biden-Harris Transition
from the Outside

During the Jimmy Carter presidential transition in 1976, the national director of Americans for Democratic Action (ADA), Leon Shull, said to *New York* magazine that because they hoped "to be able to influence [Carter]," they'd "ask for a meeting" (Auletta 1976). The ADA, the voice of the liberal wing of the Democratic Party, were outsiders at the time and couldn't guarantee the meeting or that the influence would happen with Carter, who'd run as a centrist.

The insider group with one of the most prominent roles in 1976 was the AFL-CIO, lending the Carter transition team staff and offering prized advice. Days after the inauguration, White House aide Landon Butler wrote to the president that "it would be appropriate for you to thank Mr. Meany for the AFL-CIO's assistance during the transition" (Jimmy Carter Library 1977). Meany, who'd been president of the union since 1955, had detailed his "very able lobbyist" Ken Young to the transition as well as Mary Zon to provide research assistance; both worked full-time and at no expense to the transition team. Butler also relayed to the president: "I met regularly with both Lane Kirkland and Tom Donohue [advisers to Meany]. All of these people were extremely helpful to us on a range of matters that went far beyond labor liaison" (Jimmy Carter Library 1977).

The AFL-CIO had been integral to Carter's victory, endorsing the Carter-Mondale ticket in July of the campaign after not endorsing the Democrat four years earlier. The insider role the union played on the transition, as well as other unions like the United Auto Workers, represented on the team by national political director Hank Lacaya, was part of the spoils of its campaign work and an indication of its prominence as an intense-policy demander within the Democratic Party.

Joe Biden had even deeper connections to labor unions during the 2020 transition than Jimmy Carter did in 1976: the Teamsters, the United Auto Workers, and AFL-CIO all endorsed Biden. The historical linkage between Democrats and unions could have meant that unions would have extensive access and influence with the Biden transition team. One member of the transition team expressed this view: "Labor, labor, labor, we're talking about the manufacturing workforce, labor, labor, labor, talking about apprenticeship, labor, labor, labor."[1] What we have learned from this book so far, however, is that despite the well-established patterns of transitions, 2020 was not simply a rehashing of the past. New groups emerged. New frames entered the lexicon. And new issues moved to the center of debate. Unions were just one of the important groups making intense policy demands of the Biden-Harris team in 2020.

For those interested in US schools, the protests and marches for change during the summer of 2020 raised questions for federal education policymakers to address, such as calls for greater concern for racial, gender, and social equity problems in the school-to-prison pipeline; for sexual violence in schools; and for the distribution of educational resources. The pandemic also introduced major new issues for schools to address, raising the stakes for the new administration to prioritize education in its policy agenda. In the fall of 2020, many schools remained closed for in-person instruction, resulting in parental frustration and learning loss, especially for vulnerable students.

Joe Biden, however, was hardly going to be the "Education President." During his decades in the Senate and eight years as vice president, Biden could claim many areas of expertise; schools were never one of them. Few, though, could compare with the new president's resume on international affairs: twice chairing the Senate Foreign Relations Committee and, as vice president, clocking over a million miles traveled to fifty-seven countries aboard Air Force II (Obama White House Archive n.d.). This meant that not only did Joe Biden, and to a lesser extent Kamala Harris, have a well-established vision for foreign policy, they also had a gaggle of trusted experts, loyal Hill staffers, and former White House officials in their inner circle. Much more so than in education, Biden was well-positioned going into the transition to be a "Foreign Policy President."

Take, for example, these two cabinet choices: Antony Blinken for the State Department and Miguel Cardona for Education. When he accepted the nomination, Blinken had been by Biden's side for two decades, having served as foreign affairs aide in the Senate and then as the vice president's national security advisor. Blinken was a Washington insider and well-positioned on the inner circle of Biden's team. He was one of the first named to the Biden cabinet.

Miguel Cardona, on the contrary, was a Washington newcomer. His parents moved to Connecticut from Puerto Rico when he was a child, and he'd come up the ranks as a teacher and leader in state education policy, most recently serving as Connecticut's commissioner of education. The head of the Education Department transition team, Linda Darling-Hammond, had met him just a couple of years before he got the cabinet slot, one of the last to be named and nearly a month after Blinken (Thomas and Watson 2021).

Cardona was anything but an insider. To be sure, both Blinken and Cardona were highly qualified for these cabinet positions, but their connections to the new president and the transition team were markedly different, reflecting priorities of the new administration and the familiarity of the new president with each policy area.

The implications of this difference between education policy and foreign policy, between the transition at the Department of Education and the Department of State, are considerable, especially for those groups interested in influence. Interviews with group leaders from each area reveal just how these differences affected their work during the transition period, leading to different strategies, access, and influence.

The two dimensions that have run through the book so far—insider/outsider status and high-/low-policy priority—show up again in this chapter. Group leaders revealed that their relative status in the Democratic Party and the importance of their policy area to the new administration were two of the most important factors directing their work during the transition. Sometimes these factors aligned to open a door to the transition team, while in others they meant the door remained shut. Insiders sometimes used their status to block access to outsider groups, thereby reinforcing the institutionalization and closed nature of pluralism during the transition period. Other factors also mattered, especially the state of the group's issues coming out of Trump's four years in office as well as relationships to members of Congress and to other interest groups, but status and priority emerged as the central drivers of the transition period for a variety of types of interest groups.

These two issues, however, were not highly salient issues during the campaign: neither was in great flux because of an unexpected international conflict or an event that just impacted schools. Pew polling, for example, showed foreign policy was the sixth most important issue for American voters; a little over half (59%) of respondents chose it as their most important issue, far behind the 79 percent who listed the economy and 68 percent who listed health care (Pew Research Center 2020). Another poll from 2020 showed education and foreign policy tied at just 6 percent of adults who listed each as their most important problem, less than half the percent that listed the economy (20%) and health care (26%) (*The Economist*/YouGov Poll 2020).

The remainder of this chapter draws on interviews with group leaders to show the various ways they interacted with the Biden-Harris transition team within these two stable policy domains. Interviews align with the themes established up to this point in the book, but surprises abound. These unexpected findings demonstrate that transition politics are not perfectly predictable, even in stable policy domains. Outsider groups that faced great hurdles combined novel tactics and new opportunities that arose in 2020 to gain ac-

Table 4.1: Insiders and Outsiders Advising the Biden–Harris Transition Team

	Insider	Outsider
High Priority Foreign Policy	DC-based foreign policy think tank international exchange organization	humanitarian organization global intelligence trade association diplomacy association
Low Priority Education Policy	international student and scholar organization teacher organization DC-based equity-focused organization high school transition organization school violence prevention organization education reform organization	state-based educational equity organization college student-focused organization STEM student-focused organization

Source: Original data collection and analysis by author.

cess and advance their interests, sometimes in unexpected ways. On some occasions, groups also used their insider status as leverage to provide access to outsider groups, demonstrating ways insider and outsider groups sometimes worked together during the transition.

Everyone interviewed for the book was offered anonymity, so in describing these various perspectives, identities have been intentionally masked. For clarity, I focus on nineteen interviews with officials at fifteen groups conducted after the transition ended (see Table 4.1). One interviewee worked for a DC-based think tank with the good fortune to have a colleague chosen for the Biden-Harris State Department agency review team. They were insiders in 2020. Two other groups advocating for international exchanges also were insiders in 2020, because they each had friends on the transition team. In contrast, others were outsiders. One foreign policy expert led a small humanitarian organization but was relatively new to the job in fall 2020 and had built few contacts in Foggy Bottom, the home of the State Department. That organization was an outsider in 2020. Also watching from the outside were two other groups: a global intelligence trade association led by a former appointee in a Republican administration, and an association focused on international diplomacy with limited connections to the Biden-Harris team.

A different set of education groups spanned the insider-outsider divide. Two outsiders in 2020 included a state-based educational equity organization and a brand-new student-focused group. These groups were outsiders, the former because its work was not centrally focused on DC and the latter because it was too young to have built deep connections with the party or the candidates. Another group that advocated for disability rights was also an outsider. Conversely, several education groups were insiders, including an equity-focused group that had a former employee join the transition team and another group representing teachers that had a former official join the Biden-Harris administration. One education reform group even had one of each: someone on the transition team and another who eventually joined the administration. Two more, one group focused on high-school-to-college connections and another that advocated against school violence, also were insiders. Overall, these are a small sample of all the groups involved in the 2020 transition, yet the interviews showed clear patterns of access and influence.

One foreign policy organization focused on international exchanges had the experience to know it had an insider's position in 2020. Though it didn't have the great luck to have someone from the organization serving on the transition team, it realized it had the next best thing. "Typically, in an organization like ours, with someone like me who's been around for a while, the expectation is that you'll know people on that [transition team] list. And, for the State Department that was true. I knew somebody who was assigned to [the Department of] State. . . . So, in that respect, we were insiders," the person explained.[2]

Another group focused generally on international issues had come off a disastrous 2016 transition in which it had prepared transition documents but, as one member of that group shared, didn't "recall having a single engagement with the [Trump] transition team."[3] The Biden-Harris transition was different: "I am very lucky to have a critical mass of friends spread across all the different agency [review teams]," said that respondent.[4] And so this group also was an insider in 2020.

One final organization, though small in staff compared to the big names, like the Center for Strategic and International Studies (CSIS) and the Council on Foreign Relations (CFR), started the transition with what every group most desires: *access*. One of its senior employees landed a spot on the team, and that meant the door was wide open for prized meetings and phone calls. Though that employee wasn't coming back to the organization anytime soon—they were heading in for a job in the administration come January—the organization was another insider in 2020.

That insider position, however, meant the group knew something important: "It was clear what the policy was going to be."[5] It was obvious: "He sat on the floor and on the Senate Foreign Affairs Committee. . . . He's a foreign policy guy so he knows these issues."[6] For this expert, the transition was going to be an extension of the campaign, which itself was an extension of what they'd all known for years. Joe Biden was Joe Biden; they knew what they were getting.

This impression of Biden's priorities stood in stark contrast to 2016 and even 2008, when the incoming presidents hadn't been so entangled in international affairs. One person said: "It's not like . . . with Obama. [Obama] was much more domestic focused and didn't have strong opinions on foreign policy. . . . There was a lot more wiggle room under Obama, for example, or even Trump, because there were a lot of unknowns."[7] This distinction between the Biden *knowns* and his predecessors' *unknowns* raises a surprising point for interest groups: just because the president-elect cares deeply about the issues doesn't mean that it is good for advocates, whether insiders or outsiders. Strongly held positions can mean that the transition team needs little input from interest groups, and with little input comes limited influence. Interest groups thrive when there's room to wiggle.

Not all foreign policy groups could take advantage of the access offered by the change in administration. Unlike these three organizations, other groups were outsiders. A leader of one humanitarian group explained: "We are very small," and also "being new to the NGO space . . . I didn't have as strong a Rolodex."[8] The consequence for this group was limited access to the transition team. They wrote a transition memo, but no meeting invite arrived from the transition team. Interestingly, as the insiders realized, it may not have been the outsider status, but instead Biden's long-standing commitments, that ultimately explained the limited influence on his foreign policy positions. The humanitarian outsider group leader opined: "If you have someone with policy expertise and experience, that's helpful. However, it could be unhelpful if they're rigid in their views."[9] For example, this outsider group cared deeply about the harmful effects of foreign policy sanctions. Sanctions, though, were something Biden had long supported, and the utility of sanctions had been the status quo policy position across Washington for decades, especially for Democrats (Brown 2015; Hufbauer 2007). Even insiders, who had regular access to the transition team, wouldn't disabuse the new president of this stance. An outsider had no chance at all.

Other foreign policy groups also were outsiders in 2020, not because of the newness of their leaders but because of long-standing relationships to Republicans. A global intelligence trade association was in that position when Biden won. One of its leaders had served in Republican administrations in the past and even had been vetted for a position by Donald Trump. Four years later, the association considered itself an "outsider . . . not part of the in crowd."[10]

In practical terms, this meant: "It was kind of a one-way [street] where we were trying to reach [the Biden transition team] all the time. A written letter may be sent by email or [sent] in regular mail to the senior leaders. . . . [When] the Biden administration came in, [communication] was really non-existent for a year or so."[11]

While foreign policy groups approached the 2020 transition with a clear-minded sense of Biden's agenda, education groups had no such clarity. "It was a different feeling when you talk about education for [Biden]. . . . It wasn't presented to us as 'this is a priority for him,'" explained an education expert from an organization focused on disability policy.[12] Just as the foreign policy leader pointed to Biden's record in Congress, so too did this expert: "When [Biden] was in Congress, he really never touched education. . . . He wasn't on the HELP (Health Education Labor and Pensions) committee. That's not his thing."[13] Another representative of a coalition of K–12 organizations said something similar: "Obviously, [education] is not something that the president himself is super into."[14]

There were several practical consequences of this for education groups during the transition, especially for outsiders. For one, there were fewer opportunities to engage the transition team. "We didn't have as many meetings. . . . there wasn't that much . . . communications about who he was going to appoint for those positions because I don't think he knew," said one person with an outsider group.[15] And, when meetings happened, the person continued, the transition team spoke in generalities, avoiding policy specifics: "They did not want to talk about [education] in detail."[16] This was partially because of Biden's lack of expertise on education issues, but also about the way the Biden-Harris team approached the pandemic. One outsider said: "They did not want to talk about strategy about the pandemic; the pandemic for them was not important in the education policy that they were going to help implement."[17]

For others, particularly insiders, this element of Biden's background was a plus. An insider education reform group said: "Because [Biden] had somewhat of a blank slate, in some ways it made things easier for us, that we didn't have to maneuver our agenda around his."[18]

Not every education advocate perceived Biden as uninterested in education. Several pointed to Dr. Jill Biden as the reason: "Education actually is more elevated than you otherwise would think just looking at the president himself because of the first lady," said one insider.[19] The role of spouses in White House policy activities had been on the rise recently, so this was not unusual in 2020 (Wright 2016). Jill Biden was a community college professor at the time, and she intended to remain in that job, even while playing a prominent role in the White House, leading someone else to say: "If you want to go higher than the Secretary of Education in the education world, you're probably not going after presidential involvement. You're going after the involvement of the first lady."[20] One member of the transition team focused on education confirmed this perception of advocates: "Someone very, very savvy said to me, 'don't worry . . . you're not playing in the big leagues; these aren't the decisions where you're going to see a lot of sharp elbows. [Education]'s not going to be one of those,' but people shouldn't forget that Doctor Biden is a teacher, and it is a priority for her."[21]

Jill Biden was strongly interested in education, but other groups could see specific education issues that had drawn Joe Biden's attention in the past. Another expert from the education division of a legal rights group said about federal protections against sex discrimination offered by Title IX, "That's always been a priority of Biden's. . . . When he was vice president this was an issue. . . . It definitely was something that [the transition team] identified as a priority."[22] So, while some saw education as low on the Biden agenda, this insider group saw an opportunity: "We definitely took advantage of that because we wanted to make sure they were going to move quickly and . . . did it the right way."[23]

The different perspectives on Biden's interest in education policy seemed to be associated with the relative position of each of these experts and their organizations as insiders or outsiders. The member of education reform group, the one with a former colleague on the transition team, explained: "We were as well connected as possible."[24] What this meant was that they "had fairly substantial contacts with this transition team."[25] And when it came time to talk about its issues, "They would ask us for meetings."[26] This included two types of meetings: coalition meetings, when a group of representatives convenes with the transition team, and one-on-one meetings. The education reform group member continued: "The more important conversations are really the one-off conversations. . . . They need expertise . . . and then you provide that."[27] Those were the meetings where insiders shined, what are sometimes called the "I'm working on this" meetings, because that insider connection leads one key person on the transition to contact you directly for assistance, sending a message that says: "'I'm working on this, can you help?' Of course, everyone said 'yes.'"[28]

Similarly, for the legal rights group that had been around for decades and had deep connections to Biden's team, this meant that "[Biden's transition team] would know our organization, they would know of our leaders. Maybe they've worked with us in other capacities . . . and come to us as a trusted source on some of these issues."[29] This was the crux of access and what insiders enjoyed: trust resulted in access. And, access had its privileges, including frequent meetings with the transition team, so many that they may be taken for granted. "I should have realized they're probably hard to come by. . . . I'm not sure you know how hard it's been for other organizations," said the organization's representative, an admission of the different stakes for insiders and outsiders.[30]

For another group representing teachers, a former employee joined the transition team, but that didn't mean the door to the transition office was wide open. This was because another barrier to influence was the set of ethics rules placed to protect the transition team from accusations of favoritism. These rules, initially adopted by George H. W. Bush in 1988, were standardized over subsequent transitions, becoming a feature of the institutionalization of the transition process and required by Congress in 2019 (Biden-Harris Transition Team 2020a; Brown 2012). In 2020 the education group explained: "There were very strict rules about how [our former employee] could interact with our organization as it pertained to the transition. There was a real firewall."[31] Ethics rules enacted by the Biden-Harris team limited such self-interested interactions. Nevertheless, these connections did bring obvious benefits to that organization. "We were able to connect with other people in the transition so that we could ensure our teachers had a say in the transition even though [the former employee] had to be walled-off from us in regards to the transition . . . had to be separate."[32]

This type of access, however walled-off it may have been, was not afforded to all groups. Another education group representing high school students was just a couple of years old in 2020. In September, during the campaign, people started asking: "'What are you going to do about the presidential transition?' . . . And we're like, 'Well, what presidential transition? isn't it September?'"[33] This group, though they were inexperienced, did have one thing on their side: a close connection to insiders. "We're lucky to be kind of proximate to those sorts of people, and so have that kind of access that makes getting knowledge about the transition and how important it is."[34]

The strength of relationships to insiders going into the transition was incredibly important for groups at the margins—that is, to outsiders. Strong relationships informed the new group of when to begin planning for the transition, and after Election Day, of who to contact on the transition team. For older groups, they already knew when to start, even if they weren't insiders. The leader of the outsider disability rights group, who'd been through several previous transitions, explained when some groups begin their work: "August before an election is when we start talking about writing transition papers because that's the down time. . . . People started gathering as we do to talk about 'what are we going to put in the transition documents to go to the next president?'"[35] They had the experience to know when to begin as well as what to write. Other groups didn't, especially new groups that had been formed on intersectional issues after Obama's transition, such as those defending immigrant and transgender student rights. The disability rights leader said: "[Those groups] had never been through a transition before because they didn't get started until 2010, 2011, 2012, so they were in shock in 2016 when [Hillary] Clinton didn't win and they didn't know how to handle talking to a Republican White House."[36]

The advocate for a coalition of K–12 schools described this another way: "It's just sort of like 'OK, who's going in this time' . . . and [people on the transition team] will eventually self-identify and say, 'Hey, if you have ideas to send, you know here's the place to send it to,' and then that starts getting passed around. . . . I'm going to email this person at the email address I know and be like, 'Hey, can you send me your transition email so that I can send some stuff over to you?'"[37]

This differed from what many education group leaders said about the Trump transition. One advocate said: "It was not like the Trump [transition,] where you really had to scrimp and push and ask a bunch of people to try and get one email. . . . The 2016 experience was one of putting a lot of effort into writing a memo and sort of shooting it into a black hole and hoping that something happened from it. . . . There probably is still some inbox out there that has a thousand messages, probably with 990 of them being unread."[38] Another recalled about 2016: "You do that relationship indexing to figure out: 'OK, how do we start to talk to folks about what their priorities are?' There was a tremendous amount of uncertainty [in 2016], probably more than any other transition in recent history."[39]

Across groups, the Biden transition was perceived differently: organized, coordinated, planned, just as the Biden-Harris team intended it. Groups also described it as opaque, close-mouthed, and secretive, like what many members of the transition team said in chapter 3. The leader of a state-based education group coordinated a letter sent to the transition team and received a "thank you" but nothing more. Given their outsider status, this was not a surprise. Another leader of a large DC-based group, a true insider with a former employee headed into the administration and another on the transition team, described a similar interaction: "I would send [our transition letter] to people that I know and said, 'Just want to make sure that you saw this again.' And I might get a 'thanks.'"[40] No meetings for this group, either, which was more surprising, given that the organization had such close connections to the transition team.

The same thing happened to some foreign policy groups that were insiders in 2020. The member of the organization advocating for international exchanges knew someone on the transition, but this didn't lead to a meeting. They explained: "We communicated to those people, but those people were inundated with people like us requesting meetings."[41] No meeting during the transition ever happened: "We never connected directly with the formal transition people between whenever they were named, December 1 and January 20."[42] In this case, it appeared to have been the speed and enormity of the transition period that limited access to interest groups, even those that considered themselves insiders. It also reflected Biden's long-standing positions on issues that already reflected the views of insider foreign policy groups. One member of the transition team focused on foreign affairs issues concluded: "I have friends who are at the centers of those sorts of [transition] letters"; nevertheless, the transition team "didn't see any of that. . . . It is possible that those external views and opinions had already been baked into the [internal transition] memo that was sent to me."[43]

Another education advocate related an interaction that illustrated an additional dimension of the transition: the opacity of the process. "I did have one colleague who was on the transition team who would email me cryptic questions, [and she] never provided me any context around why she was asking the specific question," the person said.[44] Not to be bothered by the oddness of the request, the response was an easy one: "Of course, I would give as detailed an answer as I could, because you want to be helpful. However, you can suspect that if they're asking questions in areas that I'm interested about, you know that's probably good."[45]

Groups that were lucky got more than a "thank you" or a follow-up email. They received an invite to a meeting; in 2020, all virtual. The education agency review team section of the transition team organized thematic meetings: "There were four members of the transition team, and there were maybe seven or eight of us from different organizations. . . . All of the education associations that have interests in that [theme] were at that table," said one person.[46] This meant, at the very least, that "you knew someone had read that [transition letter]; at least someone had logged the existence of the transition memo [and] hopefully then had read it."[47] A member of another group, also an insider group, expressed something similar: "It was done on Zoom, and then they were collecting, you know, there was a lot of conversation happening in the chat which they were collecting, and I felt that they were very much truly interested in hearing what we had to say."[48]

As the previous chapter showed, the pandemic drove the policy agenda of the Biden-Harris transition team as well as the mode of the work: all Google docs and virtual meetings. Another feature of the 2020 transition, perhaps the one that any casual observer knew, was the response of the Trump administration. While it refused to concede the election and the GSA waited to ascertain the results, the Biden-Harris team was not permitted to meet with those in government, political appointees and career bureaucrats alike.

Instead, as we learned in chapter 3, many transition teams devoted much of their schedule in November to meeting with retired federal officials and interest groups. According to one foreign policy insider: "This is kind of a good thing, because the transition teams were stalled from going in because Trump wouldn't authorize the money. They weren't allowed to talk to folks in the administration." Instead, "They were reaching out much more to civil society, think tanks, policy people. So, that was actually a good thing that happened."[49] That was, good for those groups that the transition team knew. Good for groups with access.

Many of the barriers to greater access to the transition team were a function of the rapid pace of the transition and, in 2020, the impact of the pandemic on scheduling meetings. Another factor to consider was the relationship between organizations and the interorganizational competition for attention and access. In some cases, groups lifted each other up, insiders opening doors for outsiders. In other cases, insiders fiercely protected their access.

Within education, no organization was as much of an insider with the Democratic Party as the two powerful teacher unions: the American Federation of Teachers (AFT) and the National Education Association (NEA). This had long been the case, at least since Jimmy Carter's transition in 1976. As chapter 2 showed, each union has had sufficient access to gain seats for key officials on the Democratic transition teams.

In 2020 this was again the case. Donna Harris-Aikens from the NEA had a seat, as did Shital Shah and Marla Ucelli-Kashyap from the AFT. For some groups, this meant trouble. A member of one education reform organization, an insider in 2020, related a rumor circulating in education circles during the transition: "I've heard that the transition team members weren't supposed to be meeting with people without a representative of the union at the meetings."[50] Washington is a rumor-ridden town, especially when the political process is concealed, so people hear a lot of things. Nonetheless, given that teacher union representatives made up a sizable portion of the education agency review transition team, this may not have been a hard rule to follow. In practice, this may have been nothing more than a rumor, but the education reform group official said at the very least: "It was a message that [Biden] needed to send."[51]

Or, consider the disability rights group described earlier. It was an outsider in 2020—experienced in DC but linked with a policy agenda that was at the fringe of the party establishment. In particular, this group, and several others it was associated with, maintained strong ties with Black Lives Matter and the calls for racial and social justice. When it came to education, that meant closing the school-to-prison pipeline and limiting police presence in schools that disproportionately impacted students of color. It also meant supporting policies to remove police from schools, a position with only limited support among teacher unions. According to that disability rights group leader, "I tell [AFT President Randy] Weingarten every time I can, 'they can't continue to support police in schools.'. . . . Weingarten's going to sit here and talk about 'I'm for Black Lives Matter,' but you will not say that police should not be in schools or that you don't want to talk about law enforcement in schools?"[52]

This mattered during the transition because it was the teacher unions that were the insiders, closer to the party than any other education group: "The unions have this in with the DNC," said one expert.[53] And that insider status meant some groups perceived that they could try to block access: "[The unions] tried to block us from having our conversations with [the Biden transition team]. . . . They try to block any kind of policies that we push."[54]

In the end, this didn't work. This disability rights group got the access it was pushing for; its years of experience had paid off: "The reason groups like ours get in is because we have been around."[55]

But many of its allies outside of DC didn't get such favorable treatment. Black Lives Matter co-founder Patrisse Cullors sent a letter on November 7 that read: "We would like to be actively engaged in your Transition Team's planning and policy work" (Black Lives Matter 2020). Despite helping turnout voters for Joe Biden, two weeks later Cullors continued to wait for a call from the transition team.[56] "[BLM groups] sent their [transition letters] and didn't get a response," believed one education leader.[57] That person continued, "Groups like Black Lives Matter and the Movement for Black Lives couldn't get those [transition] meetings, because they are not in DC. . . . Their power base comes from doing state work . . . and so that's why they don't get that [transition team] invitation."[58] Despite the global attention to these social movements and the virtual nature of the 2020 transition, location still mattered. "They are not very heavily invested in DC Beltway work. At least not yet," explained the education advocate.[59] Even in 2020, in some cases, outsiders remained outsiders.

It seems clear that where you sat determined much of the access to the transition team. If you sat on the inside, you knew who to contact and to whom to send your letter. You were more likely to get a "thank you," and even an invite to a transition meeting, if you were an insider.

If that was the case, why did groups that knew well that they were outsiders do anything at all during the transition? And, what explained why, when even insiders acknowledged that access still may not guarantee influence, they still put in so much work? The outcomes seemed unpredictable at best and an apparent waste of time for many.

The answer is that the transition team is only one of the important audiences for the efforts. Groups have many constituencies. Some groups have dues-paying affiliates; others have valued board members. Some groups have donors and financial supporters while others have close relationships to journalists. One insider education organization explained that its federal transition activities could aid in its state policy work: "We have a number of states where we physically had people on the ground, and so they were very happy about the transition document and were able to use it in different ways . . . talking with state policy leaders."[60] Additionally, for this group, "Our funders, even when they were not funding us to do any of this work, were very happy to see that we had engaged at such a high level."[61] Keeping donors happy is always a good idea, as are relationships with state policymakers, who often have more authority over schools than federal officials.

A foreign policy group looked at this another way. For that group, external audiences mattered a lot, especially when the transition might lead to a hostile incoming administration. In that case, the transition recommendations have a different purpose: "You're trying to win the narrative."[62] They sent their recommendations to the transition team, of course, "but they're not necessarily the audience."[63] Who is the audience, if it's not the transition team? "The audience is the media, the audience is the American public, the audience is the people that we want to rally in the public opinion, that we want to rally in order to support those [transition] recommendations," said the organization's leader.[64] So the transition recommendations all go up on the organization's website, shared on social media, and delivered to media contacts.

For groups that have an internal and external strategy, another justification is related to how they view influence (Kollman 1998). Sometimes, making sure the worst doesn't happen was enough. One foreign policy group member said: "We didn't get exactly what we wanted out of the first three months, but it wasn't the bad things that could have happened."[65]

Other groups were more fortunate. For these groups, positive outcomes happened quickly. An education group had recommended specific reform to the structure of high schools in the United States. A leader of this group said: "And lo and behold, there was a program proposed in [Biden's] first budget requests on high school redesign."[66] That leader didn't take all the credit for this decision by the Biden administration but did see the connection: "I wouldn't draw necessarily a straight line to that, 'we asked for this and they gave us that,' but perhaps a dotted line would be appropriate."[67]

For others, the line of influence was not only dotted but also very long.

The long game of influence may start with the transition, but it ends long after—sometimes too long after to even anticipate. "You don't make changes overnight. . . . And you have to know sometimes . . . there's a drip, drip, drip, drip, drip," said one foreign policy group leader, an insider in 2020.[68] Another education insider explained: "If Biden could wave a wand, we would have the Build Back Better Act. We would have voting rights legislation. We would have police reform. There's a ton of stuff that we don't have because we do not have a monarchy. We have a democracy."[69]

By thinking beyond the first three months, or the infamous first one hundred days of the administration, groups can see longer-term outcomes of their transition strategy. One foreign policy group leader said: "The reality is we don't know [the transition letter's] impact. . . . Another reason to be doing it is you plant seeds. And it may be that somehow somebody on the transition team got it, glanced at it, set it aside, and maybe three months later something comes up and some kind of little light bulb is ticked and it had some impact."[70]

This is exactly what happened to another foreign policy group. One of its leaders had sent advice on creating a new position at the State Department: "I sent this [transition] letter in mid-January to Secretary Blinken. . . . No answer, no answer, no answer."[71] If that was the end, the advice was rejected and transition work might have been viewed as a failure. But over a year later: "I picked up the phone and called one of them [at the State Department] . . . and she said, 'Oh yeah, yeah, I was just about to call you about this [transition] letter.'"[72] Patience paid off: "I don't know if it's from us, but they hired a senior person there," the very advice that the group had offered one year earlier.[73]

Pick your metaphor: A dotted line. Planting seeds. Drip, drip, drip. Interest groups care about the transition period; many care so much that they plan for months to get ready. But when they plan, nearly all have realistic expectations for influence and impact. They all play the long game.

For insiders, planning pays off because it is done in such close consultation with the transition team. These groups know their time is worth it because they've got friends on the inside: former bosses, colleagues, and friends. These ties that bind groups to parties tighten during the transition period, when so much is on the line.

The experience of outsiders is quite different. With fewer friends around, many groups wait for a phone that never rings, an email left unread. These outsiders confront enormous uncertainty for their interests, potentially losing out on gains made over the previous four years. Anticipating these losses, some turn elsewhere, pursuing a transition strategy focused on the media and the general public.

It would seem these losses would be magnified when the incoming administration cares deeply about the issues, possibly even campaigning on policy change. The interviews suggest something a bit more complicated. Sometimes with attention comes inflexibility. As in 2020, with a new president steeped in foreign policy, what use would the transition team have for advice? They knew it all already. Insiders explained that Biden's expertise in foreign policy sometimes limited, rather than expanded, their influence. These groups had plenty of access, but that didn't necessarily translate to the desired impact.

For other issues, like education, insider groups were truly needed. The advice they provided could redirect the Department of Education from the path of outgoing Secretary Betsy DeVos and Donald Trump. But even these groups, including insiders and outsiders, reported not always knowing what was going on. The opacity of the transition process, the secretive nature of the transition teams, fearful of their work getting out, meant even those with friends on the team waited for a meeting invite. And even when one of those invites came, the transition team sat sphynx-like, asking questions, taking notes, but committing to nothing.

The secretive nature of the transition period also magnifies the insider/outsider dynamic of the transition. In 2020 the social movements that drew global attention to racial justice, as well as gender equity and the environment, pushed for access to the transition team. Access, though, was not always granted. This reflected many factors, especially the sustained power of the Democratic Party to patrol access, despite an era of declining party control. That power may have waned during the open and fully democratic campaign phase of the presidency, but the peculiar dimensions of the transition phase, when the public's attention is elsewhere and limited transparency renders the process opaque, allows for continued party power.

Nevertheless, what we learned here about foreign policy and education are from too stable policy domains. What happens when there's a great disruption to the political context of a specific public policy? How do groups reposition for influencing an incoming administration when the political context is in disarray? The next chapter answers that question.

CHAPTER 5

Healing the Nation in 2020

"I give you my word. If I'm elected president, I will marshal the ingenuity and goodwill of this nation to turn division into unity and bring us together because I think people are looking for that," Joe Biden said in Gettysburg, Pennsylvania, with one month remaining in the 2020 campaign (Biden 2020). He noted that he'd recently met with George Floyd's young daughter and Jacob Blake's mother, each the victims of police brutality earlier that year. From those meetings, Biden concluded that the country needed leaders that aimed to "de-escalate tensions, to open lines of communications, to bring us together, to heal, to hope." He promised, "As president, that's precisely what I will do." One activist later said: "I still am inspired by his Gettysburg speech."[1]

Other groups heard in Biden's words an invitation to push for change once he won the election. The Grassroots Law Project—a six-month-old education and legal advocacy organization—did just that when its leaders met with the Biden-Harris transition team in November 2020. For such a new group—newer even than Reverend Barber's—to have been given a meeting was a surprise, but it was their approach to the meeting that was most novel, much more drawn from the tool kit of outsider movement organizers than insider interest groups and think tanks. Unlike past years when most grassroots groups focused almost exclusively on the campaign and left the transition to others, this time it was going to be different (Milkis and Tichenor 2019).

The facts the Grassroots Law Project supplied came by way of a policy paper prepared in advance of the transition meeting as well as four recently elected district attorneys on hand to explain why these were the right ways to address police violence and systemic racism. Two grieving families, the sister of Botham Jean and two sisters of Sean Monterrosa, provided the emotion. In 2018 Jean had been killed in his Dallas, Texas, apartment when an off-duty police officer mistakenly entered his residence and shot him in the chest. Two years later, Monterrosa was shot and killed by a police officer in Vallejo, California, who mistook a hammer Monterrosa was holding for a gun. Both cases drew protest and anger in local communities toward police violence and the failure of the criminal justice system to hold law enforcement accountable.

Shaun King, one of the founders of the Grassroots Law Project with a million followers on Twitter, an early promoter of the Black Lives Matter movement, and a highly controversial figure in Black politics, recounted the meeting on the 366th episode of his daily podcast, The Breakdown (King 2020; Adams 2020; Grove 2022). Referring to Monterrosa's sisters, Ashley and Michelle, he said: "We wanted the two of them to be there for the Biden-Harris transition team to see the human consequences of police violence and what it feels like. . . . I could tell it touched many of the Biden-Harris transition team; they were emotional." King also explained that the virtual meeting with nine members of the transition team itself was the result of another movement strategy. "We were told, quite frankly, that it was our petitions, phone calls, emails, we sent millions of emails to the transition team [that] got their attention and showed them how important this topic is. . . . It got us a foot in the door." Again, these are not the conventional ways interest groups gain access to a transition team; typically access is based on long-standing relationships and an established position in the DC policy ecosystem. But things had changed, and movement leaders, like King and his new group, recognized: "If you wait until they are inaugurated you are way too late."

As November ended, the Biden-Harris team wasn't waiting either as it saw impediments to the transition removed. The GSA was now providing the delayed federal funding, and state court after state court rejected claims of electoral fraud by Trump's allies. Progressive groups like King's, many ready for a fight, surprisingly applauded the initial decisions made by the transition team. Clear road ahead.

But the Grassroots Law Project wasn't alone in worrying about what direction the new administration would take on civil rights issues and police reform. Long-standing civil rights organizations, those that had lived through past transitions and knew how this all worked, also sought to influence the Biden-Harris team (Minta 2021). Yet, as of early December, it was Shaun King as well as another upstart, Color of Change, and not the old-timers, that had lined up a meeting and held regular phone calls with the transition team. None of the old guard seemed happy with this.

In public, Derrick Johnson, president and CEO of the century-old National Association for the Advancement of Colored People (NAACP), complained to NBC News: "We haven't had a meeting with (Joe Biden). . . . Civil rights leaders in this country should be on par if not more than other constituency groups he has met with" (Pettypiece and Bennett 2020). Marc Morial, head of the equally venerable Urban League, echoed these concerns.

Within a week, a meeting was arranged, and this one was with Biden and Harris, not merely members of the transition's domestic policy team. In addition to Johnson and Morial, invitations went out to leaders from the Lawyers' Committee for Civil Rights Under the Law, the NAACP Legal Defense Fund, the National Action Network, and the National Coalition on Black Civic Participation.

The video call began on December 8 as you'd expect: "We lost you Marc [Morial]." President-elect Biden said to the camera: "You are muted Marc." The vice president elect added "You're muted."[2] From there, things went downhill.

The heads of several groups spoke, sharing congratulations as well as their hopes for the next four years: listen to Black farmers when you consider appointments to the Department of Agriculture; rename the Office of Management and Budget the Office of Management, Budget, *and Equity*; and, add *Equity* to the Domestic Economic Council, too. When it was his turn, the NAACP's Derrick Johnson cautioned: "A lot of people in our community are getting a little anxious because they are not seeing a lot of the progress they thought they would've seen at this point; let's not disappoint them."

Much like Bill Clinton thirty years earlier, this criticism enraged Joe Biden. The president-elect jabbed his finger on the desk repeatedly: "Ok, let me respond. . . . Let's get something straight, you shouldn't be disappointed, what I've done at this point is more than anyone else has done thus far." He then pointed his finger at the camera, "All I'm saying to you guys . . . and ladies [is] . . . we are on the exact same page."

Biden fumed about his recent appointment of Cecilia Rouse to head the Council of Economic Advisers, the first African American woman to get that job: "[Cecilia], she is a significant player, that's a serious position. . . . Well, if it doesn't count for y'all well then the hell with y'all because it's real." He then pleaded with the group: "The reason I'm not telling you who the Black, maybe, cabinet positions I'm going to appoint are is: it is going to get out, and I can't defend them. . . . I promise, you will have access to us on a regular basis, and any emergency you'll have access."

Biden ended with a joke that he would "Turn it over to Kamala who's saying 'what the hell am I doing with this guy right now?'" A few on the call laughed; Johnson did not.

There are stark differences in the style, access, and influence suggested by the meeting reported by Shaun King and the video call with the civil rights leaders. To his credit, Biden's assurances on the call were not just posturing; he had more appointments coming soon, likely already known to several on the call. That's because for two of the people who spoke at the virtual meeting, Vanita Gupta and Kristen Clarke, were the ones Biden would soon nominate to key positions at the Department of Justice: Gupta for associate attorney general and Clarke to lead the Department of Justice's Civil Rights Division. For all Biden's bluster, this was a sign that these groups were going to have real sway with the new administration.

It is, of course, easy to read too much into these anecdotes. Much of the transition is private, and even these glimpses behind closed doors reveal just snapshots of several of the hundreds of other interactions between advocacy groups and the transition team. But these stories lead to questions, such as: Did Shaun King's new group's access to the transition team indicate it had influence, or was he taking credit for a meeting that amounted to little more than just that? Were the old-guard civil rights organizations ignored during the early transition period, or were their policy arguments and personnel recommendations already so familiar to members of the transition team that a meeting was unnecessary?

To answer these questions, the political context of civil rights policy in 2020 must be understood. A lot happened during the campaign, but little altered the political context of the election and subsequent Democratic transition like the brutal police violence and resulting racial reckoning that preceded Biden's Gettysburg speech. Millions of Americans marched for justice in US towns and cities, the most substantial set of protests since the 1960s. Public opinion soon reflected the sentiments of this mass movement. Gallup found that concern about race relations reached a twenty-year high in 2022 after George Floyd's death: nearly a majority (48%) of all Americans worried a great deal about race relations in 2021, up from under 30 percent two decades earlier (Saad 2022). Furthermore, a majority (57%) of Americans in summer 2020 believed the police were more likely to use excessive force against Black people, up from just a third (33%) four years earlier (Monmouth University Polling Institute 2020).

These issues were especially salient for Democrats and liberals (Sides, Tausanovitch, and Vavreck 2022). Between 2017—when the Black Lives Matter movement started—and the summer of 2020, Pew found support among Democrats for BLM increased 12 points, from 55 to 67 percent (Horowitz 2021). Additionally, during this period ideological liberals rapidly decreased their support for police and increased perceptions of racism against Black people, according to political scientists Tyler Reny and Benjamin Newman (2021).

For groups with a stake in the protests and associated civil rights–related public policies, this altered political context stood in contrast to what groups faced in the previous chapter. Recall, chapter 4 compared the experience of insiders and outsiders advocating for a high- and low-priority issue with the Biden-Harris transition team. The theory presented in chapter 1 suggested how access and influence might transpire for groups in these various circumstances, some leveraging their insider access to influence the incoming administration and others frustratingly seeking just a returned phone call with no luck.

Importantly, these were interactions within relatively stable policy domains in 2020. Even though the pandemic, and to some extent the George Floyd protests, did impact schools and education, many saw Biden's attention elsewhere, focused on other dimensions of the response to COVID-19. And in foreign policy, the transition transpired without an unexpected international conflict to address, so Biden's favored policy domain also wasn't in flux.

Not every policy area was so stable in 2020. As has been mentioned throughout this book, the summer of protests following the murders of George Floyd as well as Ahmaud Arbery and Breonna Taylor rapidly elevated national attention to racial justice and equity. Political scientist Sanford Schram (2022) described this period as "undoubtedly a racial inflection point for American politics." In chapter 3, we saw just how much of an impact this had on the priorities of the Biden–Harris transition team and the way it incorporated themes of justice as well as diversity, equity, and inclusion into personnel and policy planning.

Though alluded to several times in the previous chapter, what consequence this shock to the national system had on groups advocating with the transition team remains unclear. In chapter 1, I speculated that such an unexpected change in political context might elevate the role of outsider groups with new ideas and creative issue framing, leading to additional access, and possibly even influence with, the transition team. We also know that while prominent Movement for Black Lives groups were rebuffed, Shaun King's outsider group had a meeting with the transition team on policing and criminal justice issues, and insider civil rights groups grew frustrated that their meeting was long delayed.

Police reform, however, was only one of the paths advocates pursued in the wake of protests. A coalition of groups also organized to advocate for a national commission focused on racial healing and transformation, building on years of similar state and local initiatives (Posthumus and Zvobgo 2022). Another coalition pushed for a commission to consider reparations for slavery. One activist who'd been involved with both coalitions said: "There's a commission to find out if there are aliens in outer space, there's a commission to find out if there's life on Mars, there's a commission to find out if dogs have four paws. . . . This country stands up commissions all the time."[3] Whether the Biden transition team agreed depended a lot on the access and influence of these two coalitions. How racial justice groups and coalitions, some in their infancy, others long-established, confronted the 2020 Biden–

Harris transition reveals much about what happens when political context changes rapidly and in unanticipated ways during a transition.

A Window for Change Opens

With several days remaining in the Biden-Harris transition, fifteen-time Grammy Award–winning singer Alicia Keys lamented in a video posted online: "I can't believe I'm back 4 years later with '17 More Ways You Can be Killed."[4] Keys recalled the video she and other celebrities had produced in 2016 in conjunction with the Black Music Action Coalition: "23 Ways You Could Be Killed by Being Black in America." Black people continued to be killed, so the group was back in 2021.

"Leaving a party, Jordan Edwards," the singer Khalid said to the camera. The rapper Asian Doll continued next: "Sleeping in your home, Dominique Clayton." Mary J. Blige, A$AP Ferg, Offset, and others followed. Once the list of those killed was over, they called for the incoming Biden-Harris administration to create a commission to "address and correct racial injustices" leading to "restorative and reparative action within the first 100 days of taking office." Keys was the last of a group to say: "Breathe with me," invoking the #BreatheWithMe Revolution with which they intended to pressure the new administration into action.

As Keys suggested, this move to form a commission didn't start during the Biden-Harris transition. On Capitol Hill, Rep. Barbara Lee from California had been pushing the idea in Congress for several years, based, in part, on the work of Dr. Gail Christopher of the Kellogg Foundation. Christopher had pioneered a comprehensive approach to racial healing, officially launched in 2016. She'd been spreading the idea as a way for local communities in the United States to be transformed through conversations about the country's true history of slavery and ongoing racial injustice as well as ways to overcome racism in the future (Christopher 2021). Three years later, in 2019, the 400th anniversary of the arrival of enslaved people from Africa in the colony of Virginia, Representative Lee reached out to activists to gather the momentum needed to convince Congress to create a national commission to implement many of Christopher's ideas. A year delayed, Lee introduced the resolution to form a Truth, Racial Healing, and Transformation (TRHT) commission in June 2020, a week after George Floyd's murder.

Representative Lee's wish for a movement to back the resolution was soon fulfilled.[5] Coordinated by the US Truth, Racial Healing, and Transformation Movement, the TRHT coalition included groups like the Black Music Action Coalition, the Religious Action Center, and the March for Our Lives as well as dozens of other activists, scholars, and organizations. One person involved in the planning explained: "We began a campaign of advocacy . . .

to get co-sponsorship for the Truth, Racial, Healing and Transformation resolution."[6] By the fall of 2020, they'd lined up 170 members of Congress to co-sponsor Lee's resolution. Nevertheless, this was a new coalition with limited resources, and much of its work was completed by volunteers. One TRHT advocate said, "We were like newbies. . . . We were new kids on the block."[7] Another bragged about their informality: "We were a bit rock 'n' roll."[8] In these ways, the TRHT coalition was an outsider in 2020.

The TRHT coalition was not alone in organizing to adopt new policies to address the country's history of racism and ongoing harm caused by systemic racism. Another coalition had been advocating for decades for a different commission to develop a national plan for slavery reparations, in its earliest days championed by Raymond Jenkins, a Detroit real estate broker known to his fellow advocates as "Reparations Ray" (Jenkins and Harris 2002).[9] That coalition of hundreds of organizations, led by the National Coalition of Blacks for Reparations in America (N'COBRA) and the National African American Reparations Commission (NAARC), backed House Resolution (HR) 40—so-called to commemorate the unfulfilled promise of forty acres and a mule to formerly enslaved people.

HR 40 was originally proposed in 1989 by Congressman John Conyers from Michigan to create a commission to study reparations for African American descendants of enslaved people (Flemming-Hunter 2016). One long-time activist for HR 40 explained that the commission strategy was a way to "mainstream this movement" and "a way in which we could talk about the issue [of reparations] and reel in support without people actually having to say 'I support reparations.'"[10] This strategic sleight-of-hand meant, "There's no way they could *not* say 'I support a commission to study the issue.'"[11] Conyers reintroduced the bill without successful passage each successive session of Congress, always waiting for it to be the 40th new bill and thus awarded the HR 40 moniker. Because of its long history and strong relationships to important figures on Capitol Hill, like Conyers, the HR 40 coalition would be considered insiders in 2020, fortified by the experience of years of advocacy and litigation on this issue and the resulting connections to the Democratic Party.

Despite its repeated failures, momentum slowly grew for a national study of reparations. What had once been a "political third rail" according to political scientist Melissa Michelson (2002), by the turn of the twentieth century the idea of a reparations commission had started to accumulate more support in Congress and was backed for the first time by the Democratic Party in its 2000 platform. At the international level, US activists had connected with a global movement committed to reparative justice as integral to international human rights, such as at the Conference Against Racism in Durban, South

Africa, in 2001.[12] After Conyers's retirement from Congress in 2017, Rep. Sheila Jackson-Lee from Texas took up sponsorship of the updated resolution to create a commission to "Study and Develop Reparation Proposals for African Americans." The revised resolution now sought remedies to the problem, not merely a study.

In 2020, with national attention drawn to the murder of George Floyd, as well as once-in-a-generation protests against police brutality, the two coalitions—one an outsider and the other an insider—had overlapping motivations to form a commission, but each centered on a different dimension of the problem of historic and ongoing racism. Each foresaw a commission focused on different solutions as well: healing and transformation through acknowledgment of, and dialogue about, the true legacy of slavery and racism, in the outsider TRHT coalition case, and redressing the crime of slavery and its pernicious lasting effects on African Americans, in the insider case of the HR 40 coalition (Lee 2020; Jackson-Lee 2019). The TRHT coalition convened every Tuesday to coordinate its plans; the HR 40 coalition, every Thursday.[13]

Leaders of each coalition acknowledged these differences and the strains between them. Someone in the HR 40 coalition said: "There's communication between both of the groups and there's also tension, because it's also 2020: HR 40 has lived at this point for thirty-something years."[14] Another HR 40 activist conceded, "There might be some areas of tension there, particularly because 'how many commissions can [Biden] do?'"[15] Nevertheless, that person concluded: "I don't see [the two coalitions] as necessarily competitive."[16]

Meanwhile, someone involved in the TRHT coalition reflected something similar: "There's this weird animosity."[17] Word began to circulate that the TRHT coalition was "usurping HR 40 in the interest space."[18] That person explained: "We're only six months old, so [the HR 40 coalition] feels like they need to clear the field. . . . What they can do is make it difficult for us to go forward, so they start to occupy multiple strategies. What they start doing is saying, 'We're going to have an executive and legislative strategy' that in many ways crowds us out."[19] Despite this conflict, that TRHT coalition activist concluded: "What we kept emphasizing is that it's a both/and strategy. . . . We're not competing. We're instead cooperating and collaborating."[20] Another person involved in the TRHT coalition reiterated this point: "HR 40, of course, [has] been around for decades, and they are laser focused on reparations, and so we have always envisioned the two as complementary efforts."[21] A leader of the HR 40 coalition shared a similar assessment: "There was a merging of efforts between that [TRHT] group and the group pushing for HR 40."[22]

A Presidential Opportunity to Advance TRHT

Whether these two coalitions were cooperating or in competition, each had been supporting a legislative path to creating a commission made up of members of Congress, stakeholders, and other experts. The presidential transition offered an executive branch solution. One member of the TRHT coalition concluded: "A lot of bills don't become law; that's just the reality. So, an executive order isn't ideal, but it was a path for us. And, I also felt like 'why not?' when [Joe Biden's] about to do this whole racial justice [plan]."[23]

With Biden at the helm of the Democratic ticket, publicly proclaiming support for many of the same ideals of addressing racism and recognizing the history of slavery, an eminent transition could lead to a quick resolution of the issue and a win for each coalition (Smith 2022). The new president would have the authority to make this happen with an executive order creating a presidential advisory commission on Day 1 or at least within the first hundred days. And, though a presidential advisory commission might not have the same sway with members of Congress as a congressional commission, the ultimate goal of studying the issue, and offering specific policy recommendations for the future, could be met in either case.

This possibility meant the presidential campaign became a priority, at least for one of the coalitions. A member of the TRHT coalition explained how they advanced the alternate strategy, while not abandoning the legislative route altogether. "I don't think [the executive approach] was in lieu of or instead of the co-sponsorship for the congressional resolution. It wasn't tabled," the person said.[24] Instead, they explained: "We were invited to have conversations with the administration transitional folks about our work."[25] Another advocate said: "We wouldn't describe this as a shift in strategy. This was actually an approach where we'd have options available because we know how Congress is and we understand how volatile Congress is in terms of polarization."[26]

Whether a change or an expansion of strategy, a leader advocating for the TRHT commission acknowledged that "the George Floyd explosion of interest in this zone" drew public attention, resulting in Biden talking about the issue on the campaign trail.[27] With the problem on the candidate's agenda, the campaign needed a solution: "[The Biden campaign] had to figure out how they were going to manifest it."[28] In other words, the campaign needed a solution to the problems of racial injustice, and the TRHT coalition believed it had just that.

The coalition also had connections. The person involved in the TRHT coalition continued: "It was the personal relationships that Shelly Marc had with that [Biden] team," that made a big difference.[29] Marc was a part of the leadership team of the TRHT coalition and was its best-connected member.

Marc had been Representative Lee's deputy chief of staff since 2019 and had worked in the Obama White House before that. As the campaign was ending, she'd taken a new job in private industry, but these connections don't end when someone leaves the government. What this meant, explained someone involved in the coalition, was that "some of the folks that were on the racial justice team within the Biden campaign, and then transition, were colleagues of [Marc's] who she worked with and had a good, strong relationship."[30] Another person agreed: "The [Biden campaign] staff overlapped from the Obama years to the point where Shelly knew a lot of the people."[31] Shelly Marc's relationships elevated this upstart TRHT coalition, just a couple of years old at the time, to a position of insider during the late stages of the Biden campaign. Consequently: "We had meetings with that [campaign] and we sent them a memo," said one member of the coalition.[32]

Once Joe Biden won the election, the TRHT coalition moved on to the transition. One advocate explained: "We reached out to the transition team and we had two or three meetings a week coordinated by Ashley Allison. . . . She was the point person on matters of racial equity for the transition team."[33] At a public event hosted by the Harvard Institute of Politics during the transition, Allison said the work of the team was "being done through a racial equity lens, because that will allow for people's lives to be truly impacted" (Harvard Institute of Politics 2020). Connecting with Allison, a former Obama White House official and a senior adviser on the Biden-Harris transition team, demonstrated the access granted to the TRHT coalition. Another coalition leader who had attended those meetings with Allison explained: "We go into those [transition] meetings prepared to give information. . . . We talked about background. We talked about the [TRHT] resolution. We talked about the movement around the country. . . . You just make your case, almost a pitch, but not."[34] In response, "people on the transition team say: 'great idea, we'll work on it, we'll try to set up another meeting,'" according to another person in attendance.[35]

These meetings with the Biden transition team, especially with Allison's transition colleague Jamie Keene, who was directly involved with domestic policy planning, allowed for the coalition to make its pitch and share information, but it also resulted in new insights—insights that only insiders who had been meeting with the transition team would possess.[36] Importantly, a member of the coalition said: "We knew that there was a racial justice memo."[37] Recall from chapter 3 that leaders of the Biden-Harris transition directed team members to write brief, one-page memos on key issues. Racial justice was to be one of those.

Informed that the transition team was going to write a memorandum specifically on racial justice meant the coalition knew exactly what type of advice it would submit. Even better, though, was a specific invitation to submit something on which the team was working, since the transition would be receiving hundreds of unsolicited memos of advice on a variety of other topics. A coalition member explained: "It's a tactic of advocates that you try to get the policymaker to ask you for something."[38] The TRHT coalition tried exactly this, and it worked: "I was on one of the calls where we created the conversation where [the transition team member] asked us for an input memo and we were like 'thank you for asking for that.' That's our dream," described the coalition member.[39]

These insights also signaled to the coalition that the transition team wanted more information than just the idea of a TRHT commission. One person explained that they "developed briefing documents that detailed what a commission would look like, but also it detailed specific recommendations and remedies that we felt [Biden's] administration should do to really begin to help this country heal. And, so, it wasn't all just about the commission."[40] Another activist said, "We were definitely calling for interagency action, a whole of government" approach that depended on "looking at the data between the inter agencies."[41] But it wasn't just that either. Another activist believed that "we had the right rhythm or tone or something, and we also were providing documents, so we had a draft executive order, we had memos, we sent [the transition] legislation."[42] That person continued: "We brainstormed over many days and many Zoom calls the different components that we could present that [the transition team] could perhaps get behind, so we had our concentration on cultural healing," as well as "the commission, the digital library [of documents, images, materials, and articles that help to work toward racial and cultural healing], the racial equity fund, the idea of an interdepartmental agency or some kind of watchdog."[43] After presenting these ideas, the transition team asked for even more information and help: "We had another meeting with [the transition team] where we were then asked to maybe work with individual agencies and help them figure out how to do the racial equity component."[44]

The coalition's access to the transition team had resulted in prized information few others had as well as an invitation, also likely offered to very few others. Critically, the transition team indicated they might even take the coalition's advice. The coalition leader concluded: "[The transition team] was like: 'We're writing a memo and we want to consider [your input memo] as part of it.'"[45] An advocate's dream fulfilled.

The Push for HR 40
While the TRHT coalition was busy meeting with members of the campaign, and then the transition, the HR 40 coalition also was advocating for

its reparations commission. With a several-decades lead on the TRHT coalition, the HR 40 coalition had a different focus as well. Time had told its leaders that a legislative route was the best bet. Early attempts to pursue reparations through the courts had largely failed.[46] And more recently, the last Democratic president, Barack Obama, had shown little interest in forming a commission, let alone the idea of reparations, even after Ta-Nehisi Coates published "The Case for Reparations" in *The Atlantic* in 2014 (Scott 2019b). One HR 40 coalition leader recalled: "We were always told that during the eight years President Obama was in office, the word from House leadership was that there would be no discussion of HR 40 and reparations because it would be an embarrassment to the president because he was not someone who had supported reparations."[47] Another said: "We did push for an executive order. . . . We thought that [President Obama] would do it in his last two years, and he just refused to do it."[48] Understanding this political reality, and with a Republican uninterested in reparations winning the next presidential election, the coalition gave up hope for a White House solution to the problem and instead "spent time educating the masses."[49]

Twelve years later, things had changed in the political context of the issue, though not in the underlying legislative strategy of the HR 40 coalition. Said one advocate for reparations, "2020 turned the clock," noting the "groundswell" of public awareness of the many dimensions of racism following George Floyd's murder and the disparate impact of the pandemic on Black communities. In the past, there were few groups advocating for HR 40, but "in 2020, that all changed and all of the legacy groups began to not just say 'hey, I believe in reparations,' they began to 'walk the walk and talk the talk.'"[50] Those legacy groups, like the ones Biden hectored on the video call during the transition, saw the political opportunity that the original groups advocating for HR 40 had seen since the 1990s. Even groups with little track record on the issue endorsed reparations. "We are somewhat the unusual suspects on that front," explained one public health advocate, "but maybe that makes it potentially more powerful because you don't expect a bunch of [doctors and researchers] necessarily to be pushing this. But if we care about children, if we care about families, we have to care about [reparations]."[51]

In the end, the 350 organizations in the HR 40 coalition launched the "Why We Can't Wait" campaign to make sure it didn't miss its moment (Human Rights Watch 2022). In many ways, the strategy to mainstream the reparations movement had worked; it had even convinced conservative *New York Times* columnist David Brooks (2019) of the wisdom of reparations.[52]

Support for HR 40 had grown so widespread that the Biden-Sanders Unity Task Force focused on the economy endorsed the resolution in its final report, writing: "Enact H.R. 40 as the building block to begin to redress the harms committed against African Americans, including slavery, sharecropping, Jim Crow, redlining, and the deliberate exclusion of Black Americans" (Biden-Sanders Unity Task Force 2020). Several candidates in the Democratic primaries, including Senators Elizabeth Warren and Kamala Harris, even voiced support for reparations (Scott 2019a). This was fortunate for the HR 40 coalition since they'd worked closely with Harris in the past. One advocate said, given "our legislative relationship with Madam Vice President Harris, when we learned she was the eminent choice for VP, we had meetings with her staff and we were very clear with her what we needed from her in her new role."[53]

Other good news for the reparations coalition came by way of the staffing of the transition team. One of the leading groups in the HR 40 coalition lauded the appointment of law professor Mehrsa Baradaran to the agency review team addressing financial regulation agencies such as the Federal Reserve and the Security and Exchange Commission. Baradaran had argued for reparations in a *New York University Law Review* article as well as on Twitter (Baradaran 2020). The transition also chose Lisa Cook, an economist from Michigan State University who had endorsed reparations in the past, to serve on the agency review team (Roberts n.d.).

Despite the apparent openness of certain members of the team to reparations, as well as some access to the Biden-Harris transition team, the HR 40 coalition remained committed to a legislative path. One person said, "The executive ask was always a secondary recommendation of ours."[54] Another said, "At the end of the day, which way the movement" wanted to go "wasn't clear."[55] Shared one more, "The focus has been on Capitol Hill because, first of all, it's a federal piece of legislation and we have to get the support of our elected officials on Capitol Hill in order to be able to move forward with this again."[56]

While interviewing those involved in the HR 40 coalition, the transition team seldom came up as a priority. It wasn't that a White House solution wasn't considered; it had been. Several members of the HR 40 coalition had shared a letter with the transition team advising on how to turn HR 40 into an executive order.[57] Notably, "Black Lives Matter came on board with this whole issue of reparations. They included [reparations] as part of their whole platform for the new administration," explained one HR 40 coalition leader.[58] Another HR 40 leader had even met with the transition team, but they'd only been given a minute and a half to make their case.[59]

Despite these efforts, members of the HR 40 coalition consistently expressed pessimism about the possibility of success with the Biden-Harris transition team. One advocate said, "Behind the scenes, there was always talk of executive action," and in 2020 advocates turned to the television personality Judge Greg Mathis for help.[60] "An [executive order] approach was sent to Biden by Judge Mathis," said one activist, not identical to HR 40 but reflecting similar priorities.[61] Nevertheless, the access granted to Mathis didn't lead to much traction with the transition. Though it had a connection to Vice President–Elect Harris, the coalition's access to the team, especially the part of the team focused on racial justice, appeared limited and not the coalition's priority.

One reason for this resonates with a lesson from chapter 3 about the pre-eminence of what the candidate has promised during the campaign for the transition team. One advocate for HR 40 recalled that Joe Biden never voiced clear support for the resolution or reparations. That advocate said, "It was concerning that the president himself did not articulate strong support for HR 40, although it was encouraging to see the people on this transition team who were supportive."[62] Thus, despite some past support by members, the actual work of the transition team seemed to reflect Biden's ambivalence toward reparations and the wish of leaders of the transition for Biden's words to be followed closely. Consequently, one activist reported that "we had people at the table," but "the reports that came back were unimpressive, symbolic, not substantive. . . . The Racial Justice transition team was trying to take a path of least resistance."[63] Someone else said the transition team was "really being nonresponsive, other than mouthing support for HR 40."[64]

Another explanation for the coalition's reliance on the legislative approach is what someone else explained about the liability of pursuing an executive order: "We could get the commission stood up, but depending on when it's stood up, the next administration could come in and if it's not in favor of the commission, its very first executive order could be to overturn the executive order on HR 40."[65] Another member of the HR 40 coalition agreed: "Executive actions are always not as preferred . . . because of the way that they could easily be revoked by or ignored by future presidencies."[66] A congressional commission authorized by a vote of both houses of Congress would be insulated from such quick action following a future transition, even if the new party in the majority was unsupportive of studying reparations.

Nonetheless, a primarily legislative approach came with some disadvantages. Even if congressional sponsors, like Representative Jackson-Lee, held steadfastly to the dream of John Conyers to pass the bill, many others in Congress saw it as a non-starter; too controversial to pursue. "Those of us who have been in the trenches . . . what we hear all the time [is], 'well, how do I go back to my constituents in the Corn Belt or the Rust Belt and try to explain to them that I signed onto a bill that will give away their money to your people?' and 'your people don't deserve it,'" related one activist.[67] That resistance, according to many activists, was rooted in racism, justified by political infeasibility.

Those doubtful members of Congress also likely read the dire polling numbers on financial reparations. In June of 2020 one poll showed just 20 percent of Americans supported reparatory action that involved cash payments to descendants of slavery (Johnson 2020). Though over 80 percent of African Americans voiced support, another poll from a year later showed that two-thirds of Americans overall opposed financial reparations, including 90 percent of Republicans (Sharpe 2021). In particular, political scientists Ashley Reichelmann and Matthew Hunt (2022) found white Americans were the least supportive of financial reparations for Black people—nearly 70 percent opposed cash payouts, though somewhat fewer were opposed to other symbolic forms of reparation like statues and monuments to draw attention to the history of slavery in the country.

Though the HR 40 coalition was committed to reparations, its immediate policy agenda centered just on a commission to study the issue. One activist said, "The ask was very much minimal because HR 40 just creates a commission to study the question of reparations."[68] Another stressed, "It is a piece of legislation for a *commission*, it isn't reparations . . . and over and over and over again, we continue to have to say that every time. . . . This is very focused, it is a commission . . . and this country stands up commissions all the time."[69] And that person was right; Congress alone authorized 166 commissions between the 101st and 117th Congresses, including the "Commission on the Abolition of the Transatlantic Slave Trade" in 2008 and the "400 Years of African-American History Commission" in 2018. Nevertheless, those unconvinced by the specific idea of reparations, including many Democrats, had trouble seeing the formation of a commission to study the issue as distinct from an endorsement of reparations itself, especially the financial variety. Perhaps, the mainstreaming of the movement strategy hadn't worked well enough.

The Fall for Two Coalitions

In comparison to the HR 40 coalition, the TRHT coalition seemed to face much smaller obstacles to its hopes for a truth and transformation commission. This was, in part, because the idea awakened less of the organized opposition as reparations did: opposition had solidified against reparations over the previous decades among an increasingly conservative Republican Party at the same time support among Democrats for reparations had increased.

Additionally, in advocating for the truth commission, one advocate for the TRHT coalition believed that it presented a multiracial movement in sharp contrast to how many had been convinced to view reparations as serving the interests of the Black community only: "Barbara Lee's bill was designed to be a multiracial approach. . . . If you look at the original press release that she put out, it included Asian Americans, Native Americans, Hispanic support, and it was centered in the Black experience. But, it was definitely framed as a multiracial movement."[70] Another said, "We had all of this representation from a diverse group of people and constituents that had a kind of United Colors of Benetton factor going on."[71] One final person said, "We talk about being a 'movement of movements,' because not only is it interracial, but it's also interfaith as well, so that was a major element of the big-tent approach."[72] In actuality, the HR 40 coalition had grown its support over the years to include Japanese American and Jewish organizations as well as many other faith-based groups, suggesting just how widespread the support for reparations had grown. Nevertheless, one TRHT advocate surmised: "It seemed like if there was anything that [the Biden transition team] could executively enact that would be around racial equity, this would be it, because we had a bigger umbrella."[73]

During the transition, this meant getting the idea of the truth and reconciliation commission, as well as all the other recommendations, into the one-pager the racial equity team was preparing. That would insure it would travel up to higher levels of the transition team and maybe even to the president-elect for enactment. According to one TRHT advocate, for the transition team, "the documents that we provided became a resource. Even if they weren't going to do what we asked for in that executive order [creating a TRHT commission], they clearly read it and used the piece of it that worked for their agenda."[74] That person continued that the transition team "indicated that it was going to be included in the memo."[75] Another advocate for the TRHT said, "We had a series of meetings with the folks [on the transition,] and we know that they included our agenda in an options memo . . . whatever that meant. So, we were like, 'that's all you can ask for.' You know, that you get into the policy sausage-making. So, we were successful in being able to do that."[76]

Precisely identifying the influence on any particular outcome from the transition, of course, is hard to attribute to any single individual or group pushing a policy proposal. Sometimes you have to read between the lines or actually read the written words closely. Though the one-page report written by the Racial Equity transition team was never shared publicly, what President Biden wrote on this issue immediately after the transition ended is known. On January 20, 2021—Inauguration Day—Joe Biden, now president, issued an executive order on "Advancing Racial Equity and Support for Underserved Communities Through the Federal Government." The president ordered several things to advance equity for people of color and other underserved communities, including an equity assessment of federal agencies, more resources to advance fairness, and the creation of an equitable data working group. One advocate for the TRHT commission celebrated that "in the first one hundred days of his administration, in day two or three, [Biden] actually borrows from our meeting and enacts some component of something we advised. We were all like, 'Oh yeah, we suggested that they do that part.'"[77] At least on this front, the TRHT coalition seemed to have wielded its access to influence the transition team.

The president didn't, however, order the creation of a presidential commission to study truth and transformation. One TRHT advocate conceded: "We're still working on the truth commission thing."[78] Another activist reflected that "[the transition team members] were focused on other issues, and I think they just didn't want to touch this."[79] The failure to successfully influence the Biden decision on a TRHT commission reflected the frantic pace of the transition period, which limited the number of issues the team could focus on, but also the hierarchical structure of the team. That person continued: "I'm not aware of anybody who did meet with Susan Rice [who was serving on the transition's sixteen-person advisory board and was heading for the job of White House domestic policy director]. But people down the chain said: 'I think we're interested in this,' and they kept thinking 'maybe we should pursue this.' We could have probably had a dozen meetings, but it was pretty clear to me, and I think to other members of the coalition as well, that this was not going to happen anytime soon."[80] The access used to line-up the meetings didn't lead to the influence needed to convince soon-to-be White House leaders of the wisdom of this novel idea, even while those serving lower down on the transition team indicated support.

Another advocate was more sanguine: "I am thrilled with the progress that was indicated in the power behind those executive orders and the work that they have brought forth from the agencies."[81] They explained, "We proposed that there should be an assessment at every federal agency . . . and to some measure that has happened. Now, success has many parents, so I'm sure we may not have been the only ones that suggested that. But, we look back on those conversations and feel like we had an influence."[82]

Biden's executive order also did not create a presidential reparations commission. An advocate who had been pushing for HR 40 since the 1990s concluded, "It's great that [Biden] came out of the gate with these executive orders to address different things. That was wonderful, but it should not have stopped there."[83] Another leading activist went further, saying that this decision showed "disrespect" and that it was a "great let down, great disappointment" and left advocates for HR 40 "feeling used, not honored."[84] That person continued: "[Biden] didn't feel he had to do it. . . . He was not afraid of the consequences."[85] Someone else agreed that "we know from history that a lot of people depend on the Black vote who don't necessarily turn around and reciprocate once they get in office."[86]

The window of opportunity closed once the transition ended, as racial justice and reparations moved from the center of the national conversation to the periphery. This was, in part, because public attention had shifted, leading the policy to shift from high priority back to low priority. News coverage of protests disappeared by the time Joe Biden was elected, and Americans worried less about the country's problems with race relations (Sides et al. 2022). One advocate for HR 40 said, "The Ukrainian war, issues like COVID, issues like the economy have surpassed issues like reparations in the eyes of many."[87] Though several racial justice initiatives later emerged from the Biden administration, including the creation of the national holiday for Juneteenth, the two racial justice commissions did not materialize.

Taken from one perspective, these stories tell a tale of missed opportunities and unfulfilled promises. The changing political context of 2020 seemed to signal the chance for great policy change to remediate racial injustice and heal the country after centuries of violence committed against Black people. Candidate Joe Biden promised to do just that during his speech in Gettysburg. In this new political context stood these two commissions, each offering a solution to a well-recognized problem, but only one possessing the access to do something about it.

That access, though, was not the conventional sort, based on deep connections, large resources, and a solid position in the Democratic Party. Instead, the timing was right for a newcomer to be given a seat at the table during the planning for the incoming administration. As anticipated in chapter 1, the TRHT coalition benefited from the transition occurring just as the country had shifted its attention to racial justice and a transition team that was eager for fresh ideas.

The other coalition saw the same changes in political context but interpreted them differently. Rather than shift strategies and move to a White House–centered approach, the HR 40 coalition kept its eyes trained on Congress. Its leaders feared a candidate who wasn't committed to reparations and a presidential commission that could be undone too easily in the future. So, despite a transition team that may have been responsive to the idea, the HR 40 coalition didn't entirely pivot to the transition. Though it had some access, it didn't seek more. And, consequently, it had *a* seat, but it didn't get a *prominent* seat at the Biden-Harris table, regular phone calls with the transition team, and the same opportunity to influence the new administration.

In the end, neither strategy had the immediate outcome the two coalitions had hoped for. Access led to minimal influence for the TRHT coalition, but Alicia Keys's wishes were not met with quick executive action. So too for the HR 40 coalition. Despite the Unity Task Force pushing for a reparations commission, Biden did not create a presidential commission—a great disappointment, even for experienced activists.

These stories, though, can also be read in a different way. Perhaps they do not just show how ambiguous campaign promises are short-lived and flimsy. They also show the longer-term difficulty of policy change and the steep hill faced by organizations. This likely comes as no surprise to seasoned advocates, like those pushing for HR 40. For decades they fought for, but never won, the legislative victory Conyers or Jackson-Lee wanted. This is in part because, even when political context changes, even when a new president wins a dramatic election, the policy process remains sticky, gummed up by wide acceptance of the status quo.

In this case, deep-seated racism reinforced the status quo—racism that pitted the claims of Black people against the interests of others. So strong were these racist sentiments that even the murder of Black people by police caught on video and millions of people marching in the street didn't convince enough members of Congress to view reparations as anything other than harmful to the Rust Belt and a prize for the undeserving.

And, more to the point of this book, these factors didn't convince an incoming administration, largely supportive of the racial justice principles of each coalition, to use its new authority to create a commission to study these issues. In the end, Joe Biden's unwillingness to clearly endorse the idea during the campaign signaled that the transition wasn't going to be the chance to realize the policy change hoped for by a variety of racial justice advocates nor the adoption of an administrative structure of a commission that could lead to these same outcomes.

So, advocates moved on from the fury of the transition to the next period of policymaking. With a new Congress in place at the start of 2021, advocates shifted back to pushing for more sponsors for the two resolutions, though with an understanding of which should be the priority as well as a recognition of the tensions between the two coalitions. One advocate involved in the HR 40 coalition reflected on the inter-coalitional politics and outcomes of the Biden-Harris transition: "N'COBRA was really the primary organization for so long, and it's great that we have all of these newer organizations that have organized. But all of these organizations, instead of being in competition, really need to work together to keep up the fight because the bills, as they're drafted, they're not sufficient; even the executive order, it was not sufficient to really go far enough. There wasn't any teeth."[88] And a leader of the TRHT coalition concurred with this sentiment: "Clearly, we've always said, given the history, the longevity, the preeminence of those who stood behind HR 40, we've always said 'that goes first' and the energy goes into that."[89] That person continued: "And, if there was going to be an executive office strategy, those were going to be primarily HR 40 that would lead."[90]

By spring 2021 Congress had in fact taken the next step on HR 40. In April the House Judiciary Committee voted to send the resolution to the full Congress for consideration. Twenty-five Democrats supported that decision and seventeen Republicans said no. Nevertheless, this didn't mean a commission was much closer to its formation. The resolution again waited with no clear signs of a vote of the full House and even steeper obstacles for the companion resolution in the Senate. The long game that these racial justice coalitions were playing would continue, possibly into the next transition and beyond, the progress of its advocacy work measured in decades and the tiny steps toward real and sustained racial justice.

CHAPTER 6
What to Advise the New President

"Here's a draft letter to Biden/Harris [education transition team]," was how the December 4, 2020, email began—really, how so many emails began during the 2020 transition.[1] It concluded: "Please review and edit. Let me know what you think. I'd like to send it out by Monday."

The email and attached letter went out to a small group of state-based education advocates who were working together on a campaign to advance school equity and education finance policy. They had little time to reach an agreement on what to write, since they'd just discovered on a conference call that the incoming administration wanted to hear from them. This had never happened before; definitely not in 2016, and maybe not ever. They had a real chance to influence the new administration. But a joint letter that normally takes weeks or even months to reach an agreement on—the essence of what scholars call a collective action problem—had to be finished in just a few days.

The computer beeped: "I like the letter," someone responded, but "I made one adjustment." A small adjustment, of course, just moving some words around. Right. The mechanics of compromise within a coalition concerned with fairness allowed for this type of wordsmithing; it may even have depended on it.

The computer beeped again: "This is great! A couple of small suggestions below. . . . I'd be happy to send language if that would be useful."[2] This message came from someone with extensive experience in Washington. The precise words mattered, and sometimes only those insiders working within the Beltway know the right ones to use. State-based advocates, even those with decades of experience, were unlikely to know these words. They depended on relationships with those in DC to get the words right.

The final letter was ready four days later, on December 8. The education transition team, led by Stanford University professor Linda Darling-Hammond, received it that morning. "Don't hesitate to reach out to us if you have any questions or would like to discuss these recommendations," concluded the email.

The computer beeped one last time: "Thank you. . . . This is very helpful." Then, nothing more from the transition team. No questions, no discussion, no meeting with Dr. Darling-Hammond. No more beeps.

For many interest groups, this is an apt illustration of activities in the fall of 2020. Unlike the headline-grabbing issues addressed by the two coalitions in the previous chapter, the roadblocks to influence for many other groups were mundane—predictable, even.

Groups often struggle to get together on what to say, even when they are the closest of allies (Hula 1999). Research backs this up: during the course of normal business, coalitions—particularly diverse coalitions—are hard to manage and often result in compromise, moderating ambitious advocacy for bold policy change in favor of consensus (Dwidar 2022). This is also the case for the transition period. And even when consensus emerges, such as on reparations, the rapid pace of past transitions constrains access, often limiting influence to those with pre-existing relationships to the new president and their close advisers (Brown 2012).

The result of wordsmithing within an organization or across organizations in a coalition is a letter, memo, or report sent to the transition team. We know from chapters 4 and 5 how much effort this letter-writing takes and the various reactions of a transition team to a letter from an insider versus an outsider. One person on the 2020 transition team involved in personnel summarized it this way: "There are a lot of groups inside the Beltway that knew people that were on [the] transition . . . who were submitting memos to us as the transition team, identifying list of candidates that they wanted us to consider. It was anything from 'here's just a stack of resumes' to some organizations we're putting together briefing books with photos and bios."[3] Given the interest in 2020, sometimes even a "thank you" was too much to ask for all this work, even for insiders.

Left unresolved from the past two chapters is what groups *actually* wrote and what explains why one group might have focused on personnel and staffing issues and another on policy and organization. To understand the extent of change in 2020, it would be helpful to know whether there was a shift in the tone and framing of issues by groups compared to previous transitions. Also helpful would be to know whether the national movement for racial justice and social equity—guiding principles of the Biden-Harris transition and the focus of several coalitions—was, in general, reflected in the advice given to the transition team, or if past priorities and historic themes remained the same. This chapter answers these questions and others.

To answer these questions, it would be nice to have the universe of all letters sent to each transition team, much like scholars of federal regulations have with the recent help of the website regulations.gov to map all the comments sent as a part of the official federal rule-making process (Potter 2019; Costa, Desmarais, and Hird 2019). Unfortunately, there are almost no public records maintained by transition teams or transcripts of transition meetings— federal law largely exempts transition teams from record-keeping rules. A second-best option are the letters and memoranda shared by groups in 2008, 2016, and 2020 through a press release, social media account, or posted on a website. These *public* letters, largely lost prior to the advent of the internet, provide insights into the ways groups framed their arguments, offered advice, and made demands of these three incoming administrations. Though public letters do not reveal everything about the private and confidential advice shared by groups, by comparing them across transition and policy areas we can discover many suggestive answers about group priorities and which issue frames groups chose.

There are clear limitations to using letters that groups share voluntarily; these are anything other than a random sample, meaning the findings must be viewed with an eye toward potential bias. Nevertheless, for a political process so veiled in secrecy, public letters offer much that no other source of information about the transition period can compare. For that reason, they are the focus of this chapter.

Why Write a Transition Letter?

As the election approached, one education interest group did as it always did: it talked to its partners.[4] The group was just a decade old, its time spent on a range of education issues, often the jurisdiction of state governments. In 2020 federal policy was something new, and it relied on other education groups for help with understanding how Washington operated.

Despite being unprepared for what would transpire, the group went to work. It staff drafted two reports: one for a Joe Biden victory and another in the case of a second term for Donald Trump. Once Biden won, the group used the remainder of November to poll its members and convene stakeholder listening sessions, focus groups, and brainstorming meetings. "We engaged over 200 students directly in the process, meaning they had a hand in drafting the report or they contributed an idea that went directly into the report," one person said.[5] The group submitted a letter summarizing the final recommendations and the report to the transition committee by the end of December.

As this anecdote highlights, letter writing is one of the few tactics an interest group has full control over. You can't make an elected official or member of the transition meet with you if they don't want to or give testimony to a committee if the chair never sends you an invitation.

In some cases, like in 1992, because an issue is high on the incoming administration's agenda, meetings come by invitation. Chris Jennings and Steve Edelstein, in charge of the health transition staff for Bill Clinton and Al Gore, noted meetings with thirty-seven health-related associations and three co-alitions representing hundreds of other organizations, everything from the National Council on the Aging to the National Association of Chain Drug Stores to the US Chamber of Commerce (Clinton Presidential Records 1993). Whether these meetings shaped the Clinton health-care plan is not alto-gether clear, but the stated purpose—to inform groups of the new president's positions—also included an invitation to write to the transition team. If a group shared a concern with the team, it was asked to "provide their posi-tion and any alternative policy recommendation, in writing, to the Transition Team"(Clinton Presidential Records 1993).

In most cases, though, groups don't need to wait for an invitation to put their advice down on paper. Groups have full command over writing letters in one form or another, including amicus briefs sent to the Supreme Court, comments on proposed rules and regulations, and endorsements support-ing a nominee during a confirmation hearing. And, though it is not always easy to observe, writing seems to have some limited influence, especially if the writer's views align with the recipient of the letter (Box-Steffensmeier, Christenson, and Hitt 2013). Political scientist Kayla Canelo (2022) showed, for instance, that Supreme Court justices borrow the language of amicus briefs, but mainly when those briefs were written by groups with a shared ideology. The transition period is no different, which is why so many groups express their views in the written form and send it to the transition team.

That groups send letters to the transition team is one thing; knowing what those letters say is another. Unlike other times when groups write, like during the public comment period of rulemaking or during Supreme Court deliberations, groups are under no mandate to publicly disclose the letters. In 2008, in an effort to promote more transparency during the transition period, the Obama-Biden team adopted a practice of requiring groups to up-load their letter to a public website if they were going to meet with the team. Waivers were given if specific personnel advice was included in a letter, and the requirement was not backed by federal law or enforceable in any way. Subsequent transitions in 2016 and 2020 abandoned this practice, meaning what we know about letters sent by interest groups comes from those groups voluntarily disclosing them, often through a press release or uploaded to the organization's website.

This raises a methodological puzzle for studying the transition, and also a political one: why would a group share a letter with the public if it wasn't required? The answer to this question lies in the two audiences for letter writing: external and internal. For the *external* audience, in this case the transition team, the purpose of a letter is to advise, suggest, and cajole. The letter serves as a part of a process of influence. Publicly releasing the letter may lead to influence with the team, directly or indirectly through media coverage of the group's advice. For example, the *Huffington Post* wrote in 2020: "The 2-million-member Service Employees International Union (SEIU) sent a memo to President-elect Joe Biden's transition team in late December making the legal and moral case for sacking [the National Labor Relations general counsel Peter] Robb, calling him an 'extreme, anti-union ideologue' and a 'uniquely destructive figure' in labor relations, according to a copy of the memo provided to HuffPost" (Jamieson 2021). If the transition team hadn't read the original SEIU memo, it might do so after its members came across this reference in a message the *Huffington Post* writer shared on Twitter.

For the *internal* audience—the members of the interest group, financial backers, and others the group purports to represent—influence matters, too, but in a different way. Publicly releasing a letter is a way for an interest group to claim influence, demonstrate access, and show that despite a change in administration, the group remains a player. Other scholars have shown a similar dynamic for the use of social media by interest groups to claim credit for influencing litigation or Supreme Court decisions (Hansford 2004; Gunderson 2021). A transition letter may be emailed to members or referenced in an organization's newsletter or social media account to make clear that it's ready for the next four years.

For example, in the past this was done through an organization's printed newsletter. In 1976 the Council for American Private Education (CAPE) sent to subscribers of its $6 monthly newsletter, *The Private Elementary Secondary Education Outlook*, an update on how it responded to a request from Sharlene Hirsch, the coordinator of the Carter transition team's Education and Human Development Group (CAPE 1976). CAPE recommended that the transition team consider tax aid to parents who sent their children to private schools and the appointment of specialists on private school issues in the White House and the Department of Housing, Education, and Welfare.

Once we understand these dual audiences for a transition letter, it makes sense that groups engage in memorandum, letter, and report writing during the transition period. Given the opacity of the process demonstrated throughout this book, letters are one of the clearest ways for any group to express its views with those outside as well as inside the organization. This also raises an interesting paradox: as the transition team eschews "going public" to a great extent in favor of discretion, especially compared to once the president-elect is in office, interest groups—especially outsiders—have few reasons not to turn to the public during the transition period.

What to Write?

That letter writing is available to groups also doesn't explain what goes into a letter. What does a group write during the transition, when nearly everything is on the table? This is so much different than other times when a group writes a letter. For example, when interest groups submit formal letters on a pending case before the Supreme Court, in support of or opposition to a nominee for the cabinet, or on a proposed regulation, it is clear what the focus of letters will be. During the transition, however, there are a nearly infinite number of decisions being made, big and small, so an interest group has a wider array of possible issues to address. Of course, as this book has shown, there are a limited number of people to submit the letter to—just a dozen or so per agency and a couple of handfuls more on cross-cutting policy teams—and only eleven weeks for the transition team members to read them.

The first, and most obvious, factor that groups consider in writing the transition letter is who is going to be the new president. Because letter writing usually starts long before the election, some groups write two letters: one for the Democrat and one for the Republican. But do the letters typically say the same thing, a simple act of copy and paste? Groups vary in how much they tailor their message to the candidate or engage in what scholars call "problem definition" or "issue framing" (Weiss 1989). A member of one group explained: "If we were writing a Biden letter, it's hard on the equity piece. If we're writing a Trump letter, it's hard-in on the choice space, and if we were writing to Obama, it would probably be fairly well-balanced between choice and equity."[6]

How could it be that the same group, with the same interests, can change how it frames its issues so greatly? The respondent continued: "From the transition perspective, the issues and the ideologies evolve over time, and it is really important if you want the transition memo to hit [that] you have to be really responsive: 'What is the moment in time that we're in?' 'What is it that the people who are reading this are going to think about it?' And, 'how do we pitch this in a way that is ultimately going to get them excited about it?' Fail to do that, and 'It's going to go into the recycle bin.'"[7]

There's a mixed bag of research to support this assertion. Take the case of education. Political scientist Tiina Itkonen's (2009, 101) book on lobbying and Congress argued that "groups present their messages in ways that appeal to the values of the party in control of the chamber" and that, when it comes to education, "A chamber controlled by Democrats might be more open to issues framed around equity" whereas a "Republican-controlled legislature likely would be more responsive to values of efficiency and self-reliance." If this logic holds for presidential transitions, then we would expect groups focused on education and other social policies to use equity framing during Democratic transitions and efficiency framing during Republican ones. However, political scientists Christina Wolbrecht and Michael Hartney (2014) showed that the two parties converged to a similar view on education policy starting in the 2000s. Political scientists Jonathan Supovitz and Patrick McGuinn (2019, 13) studied lobbying on the Common Core State Standards during the Obama presidency and found that interest groups focused on quality, economic competitiveness, and accountability much more often than equity issues, suggesting that Itkonen's conclusions about party differences might not extend beyond the case of lobbying on special education.

Moreover, though it is true the Black Lives Matter movement started before 2020, large-scale protests occurring in most cities didn't happen until 2020, leading to a national reckoning about equity after the Obama administration ended. If this changed how groups approached the fall 2020 transition, groups would be more likely to use the language of equity during the Biden transition compared to both the Trump and Obama transitions, each of which preceded the protests of 2020.

If this is true, then we would expect to see rhetorical differences across transitions as issues and priorities change. The College in High School Alliance, a coalition of state and local groups interested in high-school-to-college connections, presented an interesting example. The organization sent a transition letter in 2016 and again in 2020 addressing its major issues, including reorganizing the US Department of Education, creating a new grant program, and improving federal data collection. The bulk of the issues in each letter were the same during both transitions. What differed was the language and framing. For instance, in order to advocate for these same issues, in 2016 the organization used the word "efficiency" ten times and "competition" six times in a four-page letter (see Table 6.1). Four years later, the group didn't use the word "efficiency" at all and used "competition" just once in a five-page letter. In 2020, it mentioned "low-income" students eleven times, compared to just four times in 2016. We can draw from this that if you want to remain out of the recycling bin, make sure your letter gets the reader excited with the words they love to hear.

Other groups disagree with this approach. A leader of a disability rights group said, "It doesn't matter who is in that White House. . . . I'm going to write to Biden the same way I write to Trump, the same way I write to Obama: 'You're doing wrong, and this is where I need you to change.'"[8] One of the reasons for this is the legal status of many advocacy groups as 501(c)(3) nonprofit organizations, which limits them to strictly nonpartisan activities. The leader explained the problem with what some groups were doing before the 2016 election: "They wrote the documents geared towards Hillary [Clinton]; [the transition letters] might as well, even though it didn't say, 'Dear Hill-

Table 6.1: Comparison of College in High School Alliance Transition Letters in 2016 and 2020

First Paragraph of 2016 Letter Shared with Trump-Pence Team	First Paragraph of 2020 Letter Shared with Biden-Harris Team
Dual enrollment, concurrent enrollment, and early college high schools are proven, innovative models that allow students the opportunity to take credit-bearing college courses while still in high school. These effective educational options improve the efficiency of the education system by smoothing the transition from secondary to postsecondary education and decreasing the time needed to complete degrees, while increasing college and career readiness and success and saving money for students and taxpayers. Dual enrollment, concurrent enrollment, and schools with an early college design address several of the most significant higher education challenges facing the country, including, most critically, students' ability to affordably complete their studies and secure the degrees or credentials they need to pursue rewarding careers and thrive in the modern economy. This document outlines key opportunities the Trump Administration can leverage to help these models scale and to create a more cost-effective and efficient grade 9–16 education system that improves outcomes for students, employers, and the economy.	In America's public education system, opportunity gaps exist that disadvantage students based on race, family income, and zip code, among other factors. In today's economy, where jobs increasingly require higher levels of education, this opportunity gap presents a gulf between disadvantaged communities and the middle class. The economic impacts of COVID-19 illustrate this disparity well—in April 2020, the unemployment rate rose to 21.2 percent for those with less than a high school degree, more than twice the 8.4 percent unemployment rate for those with a bachelor's degree or higher, with Black, Latinx, and Native American communities being disproportionately affected. This is both a moment of crisis and opportunity. For a strong recovery, it is critical that policymakers invest in seamless pathways for students, especially those from low-income and underrepresented backgrounds, to postsecondary education and the workforce. We believe that college in high school programs—dual enrollment, concurrent enrollment, and early college high schools—are among the most effective solutions for achieving this goal. These programs allow students the opportunity to take credit-bearing college courses while still in high school, thereby creating a smooth transition from high school to postsecondary degrees in a range of fields.

Sources: 2016: https://collegeinhighschool.org/wp-content/uploads/2023/08/CHSA-R1.pdf; 2020: https://bhsec.bard.edu/wp-content/uploads/2021/01/transition-memo-1.pdf.

ary Clinton.'"[9] Looking back at this, they bemoaned, "Y'all are 501(C)(3)'s. What are y'all doing? You shouldn't be doing this."[10]

For some groups, remaining consistent is not primarily about legal rules; instead, it's all about principles. The leader of a humanitarian group recalled a board meeting during the 2016 Trump transition when the organization had to decide, "Should we resist or assist?"[11] They debated the merits of each alternative and decided to resist: "From the point of view of engaging with the administration or the transition team [we said,] stick to your principles and say things in writing and in dialogue [such as] . . . 'this is the policy we see as the right one for the country,' and understand that they're probably going to have a different point of view."[12] If the letter ends up in the recycling bin, so be it; at least you know what you stand for.

Another group agreed with this sentiment, but it was, in part, because its values aligned with the incoming administration in 2020. The group leader said: "[We] definitely hung our equity shingle out. That was where we stood, and we reminded [the Biden-Harris transition team] that if they were going to join us in a partnership to advance equity for students of color then they should be thinking about some things that we're talking about."[13]

Party differences are a factor to consider, yet they are not the only one. Preceding the 2020 transition was a summer of movements and protest, so the incoming Democratic president in 2020, unlike in 2008, faced a different political context—a conversation about police violence, racism, and social equity that was largely absent from 2016 or 2008. One group focused on foreign policy and immigration shared that the protests "informed our [transition] recommendations; we acknowledged race, and [the relationship to] Black countries. Our recommendations were informed by the racial aspect of BLM."[14] For other groups, this new political context aligned so closely with their mission that it had no impact on their rhetoric: "Our message hasn't changed that much in light of either the pandemic or the racial reckoning, other than to say these are the policies we know will advance education for people, students of color, and students from low-income communities. And these situations of racial reckoning and murder have just made the calling even more pronounced, like we need to make these things happen. So, [it] really does not change how we approach things."[15]

Other groups saw the way the movements for social change shifted the Democratic Party's policy agenda. One advocate explained that during the 2008 Obama-Biden transition, "School choice and that sort of concept was much more popular in the Democratic Party than it was going into the 2020 election, where even over the course of 2020 there's been some hardening partisanship." On the issue of charter schools, where the Democratic Party had been largely supportive for decades, in 2020 "there are still big charter school advocates within the Democratic Party, like Senator Cory Booker, but they're much quieter about those issues today than they used to be."[16]

All this suggests that the rhetoric used by groups during the 2020 transition might be different from 2016 and 2008, possibly a greater emphasis on equity and fairness to reflect the social movements that arose in the summer of 2020 or the safety concerns related to COVID-19. Conversely, it could be that party matters most during the transition period, suggesting the greater difference would be between the issue framing of letters sent to the Trump 2016 transition compared to 2020 and 2008. Finally, it also may be the case that the greatest differences are across policy domains such that organizations interested in certain domains, like education and other social policies, would be the most likely to use the framing of equity and fairness compared to nonsocial policies, such as transportation and policies in which private businesses are prevalent, where efficiency and competitiveness would be favored.

To figure this out, I collected 598 public letters across policy domains in all three transitions. With a group of graduate students, we read each letter, paying close attention to the words and phrases that suggested a particular framing or an emphasis on a value, such as equity and fairness, efficiency and competition, security and safety, and freedom and liberty. We also coded each letter for a series of other variables, including the topic of the letter (policy, personnel, budget issues, and administrative issues), whether the letter was written by a single organization or a coalition of organizations, whether the letter was written by a business-oriented organization (or set of organizations), and the primary or secondary policy focus of the letter.

Worth emphasizing is that this is not a random sample and there is evidence that some types of groups were more prevalent in some transitions than others. For example, nearly half of groups sharing a letter publicly during the 2016 Trump transition were affiliated with the private business sector, compared to just 16 percent in 2008 and 27 percent in 2020. Groups focused on social policy issues were more prevalent in 2008 and 2020, but not as much in 2016. However, in other ways, the transitions were similar: a large majority of letters were written by member-based groups during all three transitions: 69 percent, 88 percent, and 64 percent, respectively. These similarities and differences are not surprising given the findings of this book on who is given access to each transition team, and not especially worrisome for the analysis, since what is of interest here is a better understanding of the overall issue framing of groups during each transition, not a count of which groups wrote letters. Given that focus, the nonrandom nature of the sample of letters is important to note, but I do not consider it to be a problematic limitation.

With that noted, across the letters from the three transitions, groups focused on similar topics (see Table 6.2). Close to half of the groups advised each incoming administration on policy change and executive action: 48 percent in 2008, 54 percent in 2016, and 77 percent in 2020. For example, in 2008 the Coalition for an Airline Passenger Bill of Rights urged new rules on extended tarmac strandings, such as working lavatories, acceptable cabin temperatures, and the option to deplane after three hours. In 2016 a couple dozen organizations, including Common Cause and Citizens for Responsibility and Ethics in Washington, recommended President-elect Trump place his business assets into a blind trust. Many other groups also advised on federal spending and budget issues, such as the American Nuclear Society, which pushed for "increased support for US nuclear education programs" in 2008, and the National Hydropower Association, which supported "reinvestment in the federal hydropower system" in 2016. Though some groups may have kept personnel recommendations private, a quarter addressed staffing in some fashion, like the organization Justice in Aging, which recommended the Biden administration "include individuals whose primary expertise is in aging and disability on all COVID-related boards and taskforces."

Though there are some differences in the topics of advice, such as more groups focused on policy and administrative issues, like reorganizing a federal agency or creating a new unit in a department, in 2020, in comparison to previous transitions, a little more than half of the letters focused on budget each time and a similar percentage focused on personnel issues, especially between 2020 and 2016.

The real difference comes down to issue framing (see Table 6.3). Take the case of equity. Less than half of the letters referenced equity in 2008 and in 2016, but this jumps to over three-quarters in 2020. Conversely, nearly half of the letters in 2016 used the language of efficiency, compared to just a third in 2008 and less than a quarter in 2020. There also were some differences in the framing category of security, with the largest portion of letters using this

Table 6.2: Percentage of Letters Mentioning Each Type of Issue by Transition

	Personnel %	Budget %	Policy %	Administration %
2008	16	55	48	12
2016	28	56	54	15
2020	28	55	77	38

Source: Original data collection and analysis by author.

Table 6.3: Percentage of Letters Mentioning Each Frame by Transition

	Equity %	Efficiency %	Security %	Liberty %
2008	45	37	17	1
2016	41	49	16	5
2020	78	22	25	4

Source: Original data collection and analysis by author.

issue frame in 2020, while a small portion of letters during each transition used the frame of liberty.

These letters suggest real differences emerged in issue framing in 2020—differences that were not just because a Democrat had won the election, since the issue framing in Obama's 2008 transition was quite different. It could be, however, that other factors explain these patterns, especially the chance that letters written about specific policy issues or by certain types of organizations would favor one issue frame over another. And this is true, to some extent. For example, eight in ten letters that were focused on social policy, including health, education, and criminal justice policy, mentioned equity, compared to just three in ten for letters focused on nonsocial policies, such as transportation, foreign, and energy policy. Conversely, just two in ten letters focused on social policy mentioned efficiency, compared to four in ten for nonsocial policy.

Though this is not a perfect test of the high- and low-priority theory presented earlier in this book, these findings do align with others from chapter 4 on Biden's interests in foreign policy versus education policy. Recall that interest groups perceived that Biden's long-standing expertise in foreign policy rendered his team less responsive to advice than on education policy. Some attributed this to a rigidity about foreign policy; a qualitative finding that links nicely to these quantitative findings. It is in letters focused on social policy, where education policy fits, that we see a change in issue framing in 2020 to emphasize equity. It is in nonsocial policy letters, where foreign policy sits, that we see more consistency across transitions, perhaps a reflection of the awareness groups in that domain have that Biden's team would be most responsive to a consistent message, not one reflecting the upswing in attention to equity.

These aren't the only conclusions that can be drawn from these data. For example, four in ten letters written by groups in the business sector, especially trade associations, mentioned equity, compared to six in ten letters from non–business sector groups. The reverse was true for efficiency: six in

Table 6.4: Statistical Models of Framing in Letters of Advice (Logit with Odds Ratios and Standard Errors in Parentheses)

	Equity Frame	Efficiency Frame	Safety Frame	Liberty Frame
Obama transition (compared	.17***	2.43***	.60*	.14*
to Biden transition)	(.05)	(.69)	(.18)	(.16)
Trump transition (compared	.24***	2.47***	.49**	1.40
to Biden transition)	(.07)	(.69)	(.15)	(.85)
Social policy (compared to	8.10***	.47***	.75	.51
other policy)	(1.99)	(.11)	(.18)	(.30)
Letter written by coalition	.99	1.00	1.01	.91
(compared to single group)	(.26)	(.25)	(.27)	(.88)
Letter written by business	.58**	3.88***	1.08	.25*
sector (compared to other)	(.15)	(.94)	(.30)	(.20)
Constant	1.62*	.27***	.39***	.07***
	(.44)	(.07)	(.11)	(.04)
Pseudo R^2	.25	.14	.02	.08
Number of observations	436	436	436	436

* p-value<.10 ; ** p-value<.05 ; *** p-value <.01
Source: Original data collection and analysis by author.

ten letters from business groups mention efficiency, compared to just two in ten letters written by non-business groups.

To isolate the relationship between these factors, I analyzed a series of statistical models using binomial logistic regression, each with a different dependent variable and the same set of independent variables (see Table 6.4). This approach means I can compare the probability of a letter written during each transition using each issue frame, holding other variables constant. What these models show is that letters written during the 2020 transition were different: they were statistically more likely to mention equity and safety and less likely to mention efficiency, compared to both the Trump and Obama transitions. For example, there was a 79 percent probability of a letter written during the Biden transition mentioning the equity frame, compared to 35 percent for Trump and 31 percent for Obama.

The opposite was the case for the efficiency frame. There was a 22 percent probability of a letter written during the Biden transition mentioning efficiency, compared to 48 percent for Trump and 47 percent for Obama.

These differences also hold up when other factors are considered. For example, there was a 92 percent probability that a letter focused on social policy written during the Biden transition used the equity frame, compared to 61 percent for Trump and 56 percent for Obama. In comparison, there was just a 16 percent probability that a letter focused on social policy used the efficiency framing during the Biden transition, compared to 39 percent for Trump and 38 percent for Obama. This more rigorous statistical test supports the theory of high and low priority as well as the bivariate evidence on this point from earlier in the chapter.

The rise of the equity frame is clear, but this wasn't the only thing happening in 2020. The pandemic also shifted the national conversation across many policy domains, everything from education and transportation to labor, safety, and security. The evidence from these letters also shows this dynamic at play. For one, there was no difference in references to safety and security for letters written about social policy compared to other policies. The only significant relationship with safety and security was the transition variable. In 2020 there was a 26 percent probability of a letter referencing safety and security, compared to just 14 percent in 2008 and 12 percent in 2016. This evidence suggests the pandemic had an impact on the framing of advice during the Biden-Harris transition.

These findings show several aggregate changes across the three transitions. What these data cannot explain is whether any given organization changed its rhetoric. Too few organizational letters could be found in all three transitions to compare them as a panel. However, a few organizations did, and we can compare what they wrote to observe some different strategies.

Take the National Low Income Housing Coalition (NLIHC), as an example. Founded in 1974, the NLIHC educates, organizes, and advocates for affordable housing. In 2008 the organization's president and CEO, Sheila Crowley, addressed its letter to "Mr. Podesta, Ms. Jarrett, and Mr. Rouse," the co-chairs of the Obama-Biden transition team (NLIHC 2008). The letter began by recognizing the relationship of the economic downturn to failures in housing markets, one of the most pressing issues of that transition. Next, the NLIHC offered several recommendations to "ameliorate the adverse consequences of the recession on those who are suffering the most and to stimulate the economy." It made no mention of the impact of the economy or housing markets on any specific group of people; instead, it focused on "the consequences for the American people." In 2016, with the winner of the election steeped in housing policy, though with a checkered past on affordable housing issues and accused of violating the civil rights of tenants, the organization's new president and CEO, Diane Yentel, wrote to the Trump transition team: "The NLIHC is committed to working with President-elect Trump and his administration to address one of the most critical issues facing extremely low income families today: the lack of decent, accessible, and affordable housing" (Mahler and Eder 2016).

Four years later, Yentel began the letter in the exact same way, using the identical opening sentence. From there, though, the 2016 and 2020 letters diverged greatly. In 2016 the NLIHC used an economic framing of the problem: "We must work towards ending homelessness and housing poverty once and for all, giving everyone the opportunity to break through the cycle of poverty and climb the ladder of economic success." The letter continued with references to Trump's populist promise to invest in infrastructure in order to "spur economic growth, create millions of new jobs, and increase wages for American workers" (NLIHC 2016) This letter resembled much of the tone and framing as 2008. In 2020, however, the NLIHC shifted its framing from an economic argument to an equity argument by linking affordable housing to "the systemic racism that has resulted in the pandemic and housing crisis disproportionately harming Black, Latino, and Native people." The letter mentioned "Black, Latino, and Native people" eight more times, and the LGBTQ community nine times (NLIHC 2020). The letter continued by highlighting the ways Biden's "build back better" promises could "undo generations of discriminatory and racist housing policies" and, later in the letter, that stronger "anti-discriminational laws" would help Biden fulfill his agenda. In line with the statistical finding from earlier, this shows the way a single group changed its framing from primarily economic efficiency to equity.

Not all organizations changed their tone and framing like the NLIHC. The Financial Accountability and Corporate Transparency Coalition, or FACT Coalition, not even founded until after the Obama transition, shared a memorandum publicly in 2016 and again in 2020. As opposed to the sharp changes made by the NLIHC, the FACT Coalition memos remained the same. In the summary to its 2016 memo, FACT used a law-and-order framing to advocate for new legislation to address "shell companies" that were a "vehicle of choice for criminals, terrorists, and kleptocrats" (FACT Coalition 2016). Most of the rest of the letter centered on criminals and terrorists, though FACT also addressed government fraud, all themes of the Trump campaign in 2016. In 2020 the tone of the letter changed somewhat, but much remained the same. In the summary section, FACT highlighted the Biden campaign's promise to build a "stronger and fairer American economy" as well as to addressing "the existential threat of climate change" (FACT Coalition 2020). From there, the letter returned to many of the same themes and framing as 2016, repeatedly addressing criminals and terrorists, and mentioning "dirty money" several times. Despite a different incoming administration, FACT, unlike NLIHC, maintained a consistent approach to advising the transition team.

———

To consider the transition period from the outside in, rather than the inside out, flips the typical approach to transitions on its head. Rather than a primarily bureaucratic process, concerned with order and stability, the transition is revealed as a time of politics, change, and bold ideas. But this change is not the conventional sort: budgets doubled, programs eliminated, and policies launched. Instead, as we learned in chapter 4, groups advising the incoming administration pursue multipronged strategies for change. When they write letters of advice, submit policy briefs, and send memoranda of recommendations, they do so to influence the transition team, of course, but they have other objectives in mind—sometimes, long-term plans for the federal government or goals for state policymaking or even just hopes for their own members. This is, in part, why groups sometimes vary their language, adopt new issue frames, and align with the priorities of the incoming administration. Other times, the stakes are too grave, and a steady course, focused on a group's core values and beliefs, means the same message, worded in the same way, is the best way to advise the incoming transition team.

Conclusion

Jeanette Vizguerra traveled 1,700 miles to Wilmington, Delaware, during the 2020–2021 transition to say: "The Biden administration needs to understand I am a Department of Homeland Security target."[1] In spite of this, she continued: "I want to be here for my family. . . . Mothers and fathers and every parent deserves the opportunity to be safe." Though she'd resided in the country for twenty-four years, since 2015 Vizguerra had been living in Denver, Colorado, at a Unitarian church that provided sanctuary for those undocumented Americans at risk of deportation.

Just days after violent insurrectionists stormed the Capitol in Washington, DC, Vizguerra was at the Biden-Harris transition headquarters in Wilmington to demand a different type of action. "In this moment, the incoming Biden administration has a huge responsibility to fulfill what past administrations have failed to do," she explained. To each of her sides fellow activists held signs: "#moratoriumDay1"; "No Human being is illegal"; "Close the camps!"; and "End all detention and deportation."

Like hundreds of others, Vizguerra had written a letter to the transition team asking for a meeting. Though the team acknowledged receiving it, she was sent no meeting invitation. "So, I will continue to wait for a response and an opportunity to meet with the Biden administration in person. I hope it happens as I am here in Wilmington at great risk," Vizguerra said.

There's little precedent for such direct action during a presidential transition. As this book has demonstrated, transitions rarely confront the protest politics of social movements during the transfer of power. The year 2020 was something different. While the Proud Boys and Oath Keepers swung baseball bats and sprayed mace, Vizguerra used the moral outrage of the sanctuary movement and the opportunity presented by the change of administration to call for help. Yet she knew, even though the Trump administration's anti-immigrant and anti-immigration agenda had recently drawn the ire of activists, many had been organizing for much longer than four years. An incoming Democratic administration, even one that expressed solidarity and pledged change, was still no guarantee to provide Vizguerra and her allies with the protection they needed.

Nevertheless, just a week later, on his first day in office, Joe Biden signed a series of immediate immigration actions, including one that placed a moratorium on deportation. Though it was not permanent, for the first one hundred days of the new administration, final orders of removal would not proceed. Vizguerra was safe for now.

Was this decision the result of Vizguerra's direct action, the promises Biden made during the campaign, or the work of the transition team? As with any policy change, the story is complicated, a series of interrelated factors coming together to produce an outcome, often short-lived and incomplete. This conclusion uses the case of immigration to offer a final answer to the question at the center of this book: Was 2020–2021 more of the same, or something very different? To be sure, despite his ascension to the White House and the most powerful job in the world, Joe Biden could do little to truly provide Vizguerra and her family with the safety they deserved. Transitions of presidential authority are blocked by many factors, robbing those wishing for meaningful change of fulfillment.

Four Years Later

To understand Joe Biden's first action as president coming out of the transition period, we have to roll the clock back exactly four years. During the waning days of the 2016 campaign, candidate Donald Trump was clear about his priorities during a speech in Phoenix, Arizona: "There are at least two million . . . criminal aliens now inside of our country. . . . We will begin moving them out day one. As soon as I take office. Day one" (Trump 2016). In order to do this, Trump proposed a change in national policy: "We will end the sanctuary cities that have resulted in so many needless deaths. . . . Within ICE (Immigration and Customs Enforcement) I am going to create a new special Deportation Task Force focused on identifying and quickly removing the most dangerous criminal illegal immigrants in America who have evaded justice" (Trump 2016). Two months later, Trump was elected based on these far-reaching promises.

To quickly enact this agenda, Trump chose a transition team filled with supporters of his vision for immigration. Heading up transition planning for "Immigration Reform and Building the Wall" was Danielle Cutrona, counsel to the incoming attorney general Senator Jeff Sessions, a leading opponent of immigration in the Senate (Caldwell 2016). Also on the team was Kris Kobach, secretary of state in Kansas, another well-known national anti-immigration advocate. But at the center of planning was a lesser-known name at the time, Stephen Miller, who Trump appointed national policy director for the transition team (Politico Staff 2016). Miller also had been on Senator Sessions's staff and authored many of the senator's virulently anti-immigrant speeches (Ioffe 2016). Miller went on to the White House, helping to enact Trump's campaign promises.

And, true to his word, days after the conclusion of his transition, and with the aid of Miller, President Trump issued Executive Order 13768. After campaigning on a fiercely anti-immigrant agenda, Trump went even further once in office, ordering the secretary of Homeland Security to "prioritize the removal" of a broad range of unauthorized immigrants, including those that "otherwise pose a risk to public safety or national security," a catchall category that granted wide latitude to federal immigration officials (Trump 2017; American Immigration Council 2017). This reversed the Obama administration's 2014 policy to prioritize just the deportation of convicted criminals, much narrower and focused guidance to the Department of Homeland Security (Chisthti, Pierce, and Bolter 2017). The Trump executive order went much further.

It also targeted the type of sanctuaries in which Vizguerra was residing at the time by authorizing the attorney general to refuse funds to any locality that did not comply with a strict implementation of the deportation rules or did not cooperate with federal immigration enforcement.

Days later, Trump issued the so-called Muslim Ban restricting entry to the United States from seven countries with majority Muslim populations for 90 days and banning entry to refugees from any country for 120 days. These actions to rapidly overhaul US immigration policy from the White House were all derived from the work of the transition team Trump had chosen after the election.

Mass protests began immediately, and several of Trump's orders were struck down by the courts. Activists—some drawn from the new sanctuary movement that pushed religious institutions and cities to protect those at risk of immediate deportation—organized a national "Day without Immigrants" leading to employees of hundreds of restaurants and other businesses striking in opposition to the new immigration rules (Yukich 2013).

Preparing for the Next Transition

As Trump, Sessions, and Miller regrouped to rewrite restrictions on immigrants, activists continued to protest, and they also began preparing for the chance of a new administration in four years (Eshbaugh Soha and Barnes 2021). One strategy was to create a new, state-based coalition to share insights with a future administration. "Advocates, attorneys, [and] immigration practitioners wanted to make sure that a new administration was well informed about what's happening on the ground and not just hearing from excellent policy experts in Washington, DC," one state-based advocate shared. They explained: "The idea was to create these task forces to make sure that the voices of those who were practicing on the ground would be heard directly and in combination with policy experts in DC."[2] A series of "Welcoming" task forces formed across border states and Mexico to offer a collective voice.

Another strategy was to write a playbook to overturn the Trump agenda. What eventually became the "Big Book"—a collaboration between immigrant rights organizations—resulted from work that started shortly after the Trump inauguration with the incubation of the Immigration Hub at philanthropist Laurene Powell Jobs's organization, the Emerson Collective. Formed to be a national convener, Immigration Hub coordinated hundreds of groups working to oppose the Trump immigration agenda in a variety of ways.

Immigration Hub was an insider's insider: the co-founder, Tyler Moran, had served in the Obama White House working on immigration policy. Moran, along with several others connected to the Immigration Hub, later went on to the Biden White House after the 2020 transition.

The report that came out from this collaborative work was dubbed the "Big Book," because it included a whopping five hundred policy recommendations for a new administration (Kopan 2021). One immigration advocate explained how central this was to their organization's transition planning: "The first [step] is joining this coalition-wide Big Book effort, which was all these immigration coalitions that came on to develop this huge, comprehensive memo on immigration."[3] Long before election day 2020, the work had already begun.

Each chapter of the Big Book had two lead editors overseeing authors writing subchapters on issues like detention and enforcement.[4] Unlike many transition reports that just list priorities or propose policies, the Big Book was going to explain the steps to make change. It was going to focus on implementing policy, not just adopting it. One person involved in writing the Big Book said: "The idea was that we're not just saying what we want, we're actually going to walk through how you do it. So, every policy is going to have steps, and you're going to explain how to do it."[5]

A second factor that went into the writing of the Big Book was to make sure it reflected the moment in which it was written. One immigration group advocate said: "In terms of the arguments of 'defunding the police' and the militarization of [immigration] agencies, we adopted that framing."[6] That person continued: "Let's also think about this law enforcement that is oppressing immigrants, as well. We acknowledged the systematic racism in the immigration system. . . . We wanted to make sure that our recommendations were informed by the racial aspect and element of it, and then we tried to draw the connection between the surveillance and over-policing of Black communities and how that applies in the Brown space in terms of immigrants as well."[7] Similar to what we learned in the previous chapter, immigration advocates seemed to realize that their language and framing had to be responsive to the times.

The authors of the Big Book also had a third goal: to use the process of writing to mobilize activists, similar to what political scientist Hahrie Han (2014) described as the way certain organizations blend mobilizing and organizing. Explained one Big Book organizer, "The intent of this was to obviously get some policies in place, but also to use this to help people to know how to interact and also to engage with the administration. Like, 'How do you become an even better advocate?'"[8] This meant extensive training for organizations on the federal regulatory process and who to contact in the government with the authority to enact the recommendations.

As early as February 2020, before Joe Biden had even become the Democratic Party's candidate, the Immigration Hub held a workshop titled "The Big Book: Policy Priorities for the Next Administration" at a summit on immigration. There, representatives of Amnesty International USA, Service Employees International Union, and the National Immigration Project of the National Lawyers Guild spoke, encouraging activists in attendance to begin preparing early for the transition (Immigration Hub n.d.). Though many of those working on the Big Book had close ties to the Democratic Party, they didn't control the nominating process and had wide disagreement on who was the best Democratic candidate. One person said: "We had no idea who's going to be president, obviously, but we're planning for whoever the Democrat is."[9]

By the late spring, though, it was clear that Joe Biden was the candidate. One author of the Big Book said: "We were hoping to get it done for August. We knew it wasn't going to be public because Stephen Miller and his gang would immediately just take what's in there" and would begin to undermine the recommendations before they could even be considered.[10] "But we did want to have a public document for the convention because . . . we wanted the [immigration rights] movement to have like, 'Here's our baseline,'" the author explained.[11] So the editors of the Big Book had two sets of recommendations: the private and highly detailed Big Book, and a public and more general set of recommendations. This raises a subtle, and somewhat paradoxical, distinction on when groups choose to be public and when they choose to be private. While a novice might assume that if you are confident that you will get your way, you'd announce it to the world, the opposite was the case for immigration. One advocate explained: "Oftentimes those [transition] conversations are going to be more private and less public when we have an incoming friendly administration."[12] The advocate continued: "[That advice] may be more controversial. Maybe it involves regulation or detention or enforcement. Those are conversations that advocates don't necessarily want to be having in the public."[13] In those cases, "we are happy to have the vast majority of those conversations privately because we have a friendly administration, and these folks include many folks who were previously in the NGO space. Sometimes they include folks who helped write some of these recommendations."[14]

Indicative of this strategy, another advocate said: "For [the 2016] transition, we similarly developed a comprehensive memo of recommendations. Ultimately, after the 2016 election happened, we decided not to share those recommendations with the administration, because it would be a road map for them to be able to find where some of the weak points and vulnerabilities were and exploit them."[15] Instead, these groups wrote a much less detailed set of recommendations with a very different purpose: "when you have an unfriendly administration and you're trying to win the narrative, those [transition] recommendations may be geared toward the incoming administration, but they're not necessarily the audience. The audience is the media, the audience is the American public, the audience is the people that we want to rally in the public opinion, that we want to rally in order to support those recommendations."[16] Thus, rather than the private strategy used in 2020 to influence policy implementation, these groups had gone public in order to mobilize broad support and opposition to the incoming administration's plans four years earlier.

After the 2020 Democratic Convention, as pre-election transition planning ramped up, insiders had the access to make sure the transition team received a private copy of the Big Book with all its policy recommendations and advice for implementation. The timing was smart, but it also helped that many of those on the transition team and later the administration had worked on the Big Book. According to one organizer, "So many of the people that go in [to the transition and administration] are from the community. . . . A lot of them had worked on the Big Book, so it wasn't even new, but we had always intended for it to be a transition document . . . so [the transition team] had it by September or October before Election Day."[17]

That November, when the election was settled and transition planning accelerated, individual groups began to mention the Big Book in public. Hannah Matthews and Wendy Cervantes of the Center for Law and Social Policy (CLASP) publicly shared recommendations in November for the transition, noting that they supported "more comprehensive reforms to the country's immigration system as laid out in the 2021 Immigration Action Plan and Immigration Big Book" (Matthews 2020). Clara Long from Human Rights Watch wrote to the Department of Homeland Security transition team in January and referenced the Big Book "Border Response" chapter (Human Rights Watch 2021). The American Immigration Council and the American

Immigration Lawyers Association posted a policy brief to a website advising the incoming Biden administration to guarantee legal representation for those facing deportation. It referenced the Big Book chapter on the Department of Justice (American Immigration Council 2021). A group of organizations based in Mexico, including Asylum Access Mexico and Centro de Decheros Humanos Fray Matias de Cordova, offered recommendations to complement the Big Book chapter on "Humanitarian Protections" and cited statistics from the Big Book (Asylum Access 2020). The Big Book strategy, then, was private before the election but increasingly public once Biden won, implemented by a range of groups to make sure everyone on the transition team had a copy of the recommendations.

Not only did the team have it; they read it. One member of a transition team involved in immigration issues said: "The Big Book was used a lot."[18] Another said: "Given the extent of [Biden's] commitments during the campaign on immigration issues, the material in the Big Book was useful in executing on those commitments."[19] And a third said: "I never downloaded it because it was a *big* book . . . but really smart people put their perspectives into it . . . so I found it really helpful."[20]

The transition team also was listening to outsiders, calling immigrant rights leaders operating far from DC to set up meetings. One member of the transition team said, "What was useful was taking pieces of [the Big Book] . . . knowing who the authors were, being able to confer with them, and making that part of what we were recommending."[21] Illustrative of this, an advocate said, "I did not expect to have a voice at the table. . . . I did not identify as a policy person. . . . I didn't identify as a fancy DC person."[22] Nevertheless, shortly after Biden won, that person was on a Zoom call explaining what was happening at the border. And it wasn't just a single meeting. The meetings continued over the next two months, too many to count, and these regular check-ins led that person to be "extremely hopeful" about the signals coming from the transition team, especially the decisions on staffing key immigration policy jobs.[23] Another local immigration advocate concurred: "Advocates and attorneys realized the importance of these transition meetings and that we needed to make sure to get across certain very important talking points. . . . I do believe that the [transition team] was taking into account what we were saying, whether they wanted to act on it is a separate issue."[24]

Could it be that the Biden administration took all the advice and wanted to act? The Big Book had hundreds of recommendations from a vast array of organizations. Could all these groups, many outsiders, become insiders with the access and influence to win every battle?

The answers to these questions relate to a central theme of this book: the difference between access and influence as well as the limitations of the transition period. According to one immigration group advocate, outcomes from the transition ultimately relate to whether the issue is a priority, not for advocates, but for the new administration: "*Certain* issue areas and *certain* advocacy organizations that focus on *certain* topics are going to be a lot more successful."[25] Even an incoming administration that had prioritized immigration didn't necessarily mean it would agree with every proposed change in immigration policy. The leader continued: "[Groups] focusing on naturalization, on legal immigration, unemployment stuff . . . those things are easy to swallow for the administration."[26] Conversely, that person continued, "Organizations that focus on things like enforcement or border or immigration, those folks will not have as much success because even if you convince the immigration policy folks, you have the dynamic where the politicals are overruling the immigration folks."[27] Access is a necessary, but not sufficient, factor for influence, especially when policy and politics mix.

Additionally, the transition team's work was greatly constrained by Biden's priorities and his commitments during the campaign. Even those involved in policy on the transition agreed: the transition team didn't make policy, especially on areas where the candidate hadn't made a clear promise. One leader of the transition team explained: "The amount of work [the transition team] had on immigration was gargantuan because [Biden had] made huge commitments. But the Big Book was about everything that should ever happen, and our remit was smaller than that."[28] If there was an emergency issue that arose, the transition team had more leeway to act, but in 2020 this was primarily limited to COVID-specific issues.

This raises a central tension during the transition period between groups, which operate before, during, and after the transition period, and the transition team, which operates for just eleven weeks and then disbands. As we learned from the work of the HR 40 coalition earlier in the book, a typical group will have been advocating on a policy issue for years if not decades and has a time horizon that stretches far into the future. The transition team's work in 2020 was limited to seventy-eight days and focused on just the start of the administration; nothing beyond one hundred or two hundred days mattered much to it, according to several team members. One immigration advocate reflected this point based on a conversation with Ur Jaddou, the transition team's lead on the Department of Homeland Security: "Ur [Jaddou] said to me, 'You really need to get these [transition] things also to the people who will be in the administration, because we'll become pumpkins come January 21st.'"[29]

For other immigration advocates, this limited time period for the transition meant even their considerable access didn't lead to the influence for which they wished. And, when direct access to the transition team didn't work, some turned to more public and aggressive action. One advocate explained: "When the administration adopts our recommendations, we're happy to [lobby] internally, but if not, we need outside pressure to get them to move. . . . They have to feel pressure, whether that's getting the relevant committees to weigh in, investigatory bodies, or media exposés. You essentially gear into a campaign framework."[30]

As the Biden transition became the Biden administration, this was exactly what happened for immigration: "The [Biden] administration had a pretty big blow up on border-related stuff where a bunch of border advocates walked out of a meeting because the administration was just completely fucking up the border and still is. In those situations, you have to switch to a more external pressure campaign."[31]

Advocacy groups weren't alone in this frank assessment of how things were going on immigration policy for President Biden. Just three months into his administration, with trouble mounting, Biden changed course and chose Vice President Harris to be in charge of border issues (Shear, Kanno-Youngs, and Rogers 2021). Roberta Jacobson, a former ambassador to Mexico, soon stepped down from the role of "border czar." Then, in September, the special envoy to Haiti, Daniel Foote, resigned from his post, writing to Secretary of State Blinken: "I will not be associated with the United States' inhumane counterproductive decision to deport thousands of Haitian refugees and illegal immigrants to Haiti" (Jakes and Sullivan 2022). These staffing losses weren't just in the diplomatic corps; many of those who were integral to transition planning also left.

At the one-year mark, the *New Yorker* magazine featured the story of Andrea Flores, an immigration expert from the American Civil Liberties Union (ACLU), who had joined the Biden transition team and later the White House's National Security Council to direct border management (Blitzer 2022). Flores was one of the people who received a copy of the Big Book and understood the detailed immigration proposals. Yet, in frustration over Biden's failure to follow these recommendations to change Trump era policies, especially an unwillingness to phase out Title 42—the pandemic-era public health restriction on applications for asylum—Flores quit. And Flores wasn't alone. Tyler Moran, from the Immigration Hub, also left the White House, as did Esther Olavarria, another immigration policy expert.

Flores, Moran, and Olavarria all were insiders, and all three had access: first to the transition team and later to senior members of the White House. In the end, however, that access didn't lead to long-term influence. Though they were integral to the immediate actions of the White House following the inauguration, sustaining that influence to enact a broader immigration reform agenda that reflected many of the recommendations of the Big Book didn't happen. Factors outside of their control, such as the ongoing pandemic, an increase in migration across the Mexico border, and unfriendly rulings from the courts, not to mention a Republican Party eager to pounce, resulted in a political calculation by President Biden to go slow on immigration policy change. In the end, this proved too much for these immigration experts to accept and for immigration advocates to remain quiet on.

Looking Ahead

If, as the Heritage Foundation contended during the 1980 transition, "personnel is policy," then these departures were a huge loss to Biden's immigration plans. These were the staffers who understood the agenda of immigration activists and were ready to act. Once they were gone, many of those recommendations from the Big Book were gone, too.

Meanwhile, the Heritage Foundation, like many groups opposed to Biden's agenda, could see what this entailed for the future: another presidential transition could be just a couple of years away. This is why in April of 2022, it launched the "2025 Presidential Project" and hired a former chief of staff at the Office of Personnel Management (OPM), Paul Dans, to direct the project. Heritage could see the future but also knew the past. Dans was chosen for a reason: he knew people and he understood loyalty. In announcing the project, Heritage Foundation president Kevin Roberts wrote: "It is not enough to elect conservative leaders who articulate the right policies. We must ensure that the men and women surrounding these leaders also cherish American greatness" (Heritage Foundation 2022). Roberts explained that Heritage would "do everything we can to ensure the right people hold positions of influence in Washington—and are empowered to root out those who no longer serve the interests of the American people."

It was Dans, along with Trump's director of White House personnel, John McEntee, who pushed for many federal civil service jobs to be converted to political appointments that came out of Trump's so-called "Schedule F" executive order (E.O. #13957). In December 2020, in the middle of Trump's transition out of the White House, it was Dans who was elevated to chief of staff of OPM, the agency in charge of implementing Trump's executive order, described by political scientist Donald Moynihan (2022, 174) as "the most substantive change to the US civil service system since its creation in 1883."

Dans served at OPM along with acting director, Mike Rigas, who'd also spent time at the Heritage Foundation. Thus, in the waning days of the Trump administration, as the Biden transition team readied for Day 1, several of the most important figures in US personnel policies were working to institutionalize a core idea the Heritage Foundation offered to Ronald Reagan: personnel is policy. Dans and Rigas's previous work at Heritage, then, was not surprising, nor was Dans's central position in directing Heritage's transition planning for 2024–2025.

That Dans, McEntee, and Rigas largely failed to meet their aims during the fall of 2020 and Biden overturned Trump's executive order early in 2021 also was not surprising, as it demonstrated the paradox of the transition period: it is at once a period of enormous change as well as great stability. Hundreds of new officials are hired to loyally implement a new president's agenda, yet tens of thousands of civil servants remain, few with a stake in the campaign promises backed by a majority of the country. Groups like Heritage and the Immigration Hub, true party insiders, are given access during the transition to countless high-priority decisions that need to be made, but four years later, a new president with a new array of insiders can wipe those decisions out in less than a day. All the while, upstarts—those who energized the electorate in 2020 with new ideas and a vision for the country—are often left on the outside looking in, as frustrated as Jeannette Vizguerra was in Wilmington waiting to meet with Joe Biden.

The Biden-Harris transition wasn't the first time a social movement saw access fail to result in lasting influence. Urvashi Vaid witnessed the same thing in 1992–1993. Vaid was at the center of a movement for gay and lesbian rights, running an organization, the National Gay and Lesbian Task Force (NGLTF), and coordinating political strategies. As the AIDS crisis ravaged the country and Republicans committed to few planks of the movement's agenda, Vaid and other leaders backed Bill Clinton, helping raise millions of dollars for his campaign and mobilizing gay and lesbian voters for the election.

At the time, this seemed a logical decision. Though there were many more important issues to consider, including the need for a massive increase in federal funding to support the fight against AIDS, the military's ban on gay and lesbian service members emerged as one a new president would have the authority to quickly address. During the campaign, Clinton had promised several times to do just this: he would change military policy to allow all citizens to serve, regardless of sexual orientation.

Once Clinton won the election, the attention of the gay and lesbian movement shifted to the transition. For the first time, the movement seemed to have real access. Vaid (1995, 164) explained: "Overnight, gay donors to the Clinton campaign had received invitations to attend inaugural parties, to participate in the invitation-only economic summit held in Arkansas during the transition period, to join transition teams, to write position papers on gay rights issues . . . even to have dinner with Bill and Hillary." The movement launched a new headhunting organization, Coalition '93, to advocate for the appointment of gay and lesbian officials to the Clinton administration. The movement was on the verge of historic changes in Washington.

Upon reflection, certain people clearly had access, but, in practice, movement leaders remained on the outside. Vaid (1995, 163) concluded: "Although many gay individuals were involved in the campaign and eventually served on the transition team, leaders of the organized gay and lesbian movement did not enjoy direct access." This meant that those with the greatest expertise on the movement's policy agenda had to depend on information gleaned from "dinners with one another, from gossip on the phone with wealthy donors, or by reading the gay press reports" (Vaid 1995, 163).

This limited access also curtailed the movement's influence over administration policy, a problem when the transition team reevaluated Clinton's campaign promises. Vaid reported that Peter Feldman, who was leading the transition at the Department of Justice, asked a member of the transition team, Chai Feldblum, to evaluate the feasibility of a Clinton executive action on the military ban. Feldblum concluded that an executive order could be quickly overturned by Congress and an even more restrictive federal law enacted. Clinton's nominee to become secretary of defense, Les Aspin, seemed to agree with this assessment.

Soon after the inauguration, rather than immediately act to end the ban, Clinton gave the military six months to evaluate the policy. Even with the extra time, the military wouldn't budge, and by the end of 1993, Clinton had adopted the "don't ask, don't tell" policy, a compromise decision to maintain the military's status quo policy on who could talk openly about their sexuality and who could not. Vaid (1995, 149) later lamented: "We failed during the transition period of 1992–1993 to develop a coherent agenda with which to approach the new administration." The limited access during the transition, ultimately, cost the movement the influence needed to win this policy victory.

A lot changed between 1992 and 2020 for the groups and social movements that sought to influence the Clinton transition team, everyone from the NGLTF to the DLC. Rights were won and lost, organizations closed and opened, and agendas shifted and evolved. In between, there were two Republican transitions, as well, ushering in a different set of insiders with access and influence over the presidency and federal policymaking. Throughout, this book shows the limitations of the transition period as a source of change, especially for the vast array of groups representing people with diverse interests. Faith in the next transition to solve every problem is like Urvashi Vaid's assessment of the limitations of mainstreaming for the LGBTQ movement.

Vaid (1995, XVI) wrote: "The flaw in the strategy of mainstreaming is its confusion of access to power with power itself." This is in part because, Vaid (1995, XVI) argued, "The political access some have gained has translated poorly to genuine clout." In the end, Vaid (1995, XVI) developed the idea of "virtual equality": equality "based more on the appearance of acceptance by straight America than on genuine civic parity."

The 2020 transition team offered to many groups and movements this type of virtual equality: a "thank you" for submitting a letter of advice; an invitation to a meeting; sometimes even a seat at the table as a member of the transition team. In the end, the equality of the Biden transition was largely virtual, not just in the technological sense but also in the sense that Vaid intended it: an appearance rather than the genuine thing. Though the transition team was more diverse than any prior and the team infused a commitment to social equity and justice into its work, the institutionalized nature of the transition period and the many external and internal roadblocks faced in 2020 limited the influence of the very same groups that had championed these causes.

Much of this goes back to the power a party possesses—however diminished over time—to patrol the edges of its umbrella of intense policy demanders. Though this power may have waned during the nomination process, as a variety of factors have ushered outsider candidates like Bernie Sanders and Donald Trump into the spotlight, the transition period remains an effective buffer to change. Five decades of institutionalization of this process, including further modifications in the final days of 2022, has worked to stabilize the transfer of power, even during the most turbulent of times. With steadfast commitment to order and stability and ambivalence toward transparency, transitions—especially Democratic transitions—have evolved masterfully to accomplish the nearly impossible: preparing to lead the vast US government in just eleven weeks. In doing so with such institutionalized efficiency and precision, lasting change—that is, meaningful change aligned with the agenda of many groups—is virtually impossible.

Data Collection

Roadblocked is the result of a multi-method approach to data collection conducted from October 2020 to June 2023, including extensive qualitative information drawn from original interviews, secondary oral histories, and media interviews. All data collection and analysis related to original interviews conformed with human subject research standards established by the Institutional Review Board of the City University of New York (Project 2022–0098-JohnJay).

In total, I conducted 127 interviews with a variety of stakeholders in the 2020 transition, both members of the transition team and interest group, think tank, and civil society leaders. Those interviews were chosen using a non-random, snowball sampling approach based on an initial list of members of the agency review teams, then expanded based on recommendations and referrals by subjects. All interviews were conducted over the phone or Zoom, recorded, and then transcribed. Half of the subjects were white Americans (55%), one-quarter were Black Americans (24%), 14 percent were Asian American, and the remainder held other racial and ethnic identities. More than half (61%) were men, and less than half (39%) were women. All interview subjects verbally consented to participate in compliance with procedures established prior to the start of the project. Interviews lasted on average thirty minutes. I removed personal information from the transcribed interviews to protect the anonymity of all who participated. These interviews are used throughout the book, but most centrally in chapters 3, 4, 5, and the conclusion.

In addition, for the analysis in chapter 2, a team of graduate students and I collected the names and backgrounds of individuals on the Jimmy Carter, Bill Clinton, George W. Bush, Donald Trump, Barack Obama, and Joe Biden transition teams (complete lists for the Ronald Reagan and George H. W. Bush transition teams could not be located). This involved using publicly available sources, archived documents, and oral histories to search for biographical information on over two thousand individuals. I used the computer application gender.api (available at http://www.gender-api.com) to verify genders (using a female/male distinction only) and then conducted additional research to confirm the correct publicly identified gender when the program produced an accuracy score below 75 percent. In conducting this research, especially helpful were the Carter and Clinton presidential libraries as well as archival databases made available by the John Jay College of Criminal Justice.

Finally, for chapter 6, I searched and found archived letters and memorandums sent to the Obama, Trump, and Biden transition teams using a variety of methods. As indicated in the chapter, this method is far from ideal, but it did generate a sizable non-random sample of letters from each period. With these letters, I then developed a dictionary-based coding scheme with words, terms, and phrases associated with each variable. A small group of graduate students used the scheme to read and code each letter for key themes and concepts. For the sake of comparability, coders used the first two pages of each letter, since letter length varied (two pages was the average length of a letter). Once coders were trained on a sample of fifteen letters, updates were made to the scheme, and then the final coding of the full sample occurred. I then analyzed the coded letters using standard multivariate methods.

Notes

Introduction

1. Interview with subject 023 on June 15, 2022.

2. During the 2020 campaign, Biden told *Meet the Press* host Chuck Todd: "I would be 'most progressive' president in history." See https://www.nbcnews.com /meet-the-press/video/full-biden-i-would-be-most-progressive-president-in-his tory-78844485729?cid=sm_npd_nn_tw_mtp.

3. See https://www.sheriffs.org/about-nsa/faq.

4. Interview with subject 118 on May 26, 2023.

Chapter 1: A Model of Access and Influence during Presidential Transitions

1. Interview with subject 049 on November 24, 2022.

2. Figure based on data from: https://covid.cdc.gov/covid-data-tracker/#trends _dailydeaths_totalcasesper100k.

3. Interview with subject 021 on July 1, 2022.

4. Interview with subject 023 on June 15, 2022.

5. That change was included in the Intelligence Reform and Terrorism Prevention Act of 2004 and later amended by the Pre-Election Presidential Transition Act of 2010.

6. Edwin Meese, Reagan's chief of staff when he was California governor and later a professor of law at the University of San Diego, had attended a meeting organized by Heritage during the summer of 1980 and indicated that Reagan would be open to hearing from the new think tank (Edwards 1997).

7. In 2000 it was the AEI, not Heritage, that played the most prominent role in the Bush transition, due in part to the close relationship between Vice President–Elect Dick Cheney and the think tank.

8. In an oral history, Al From said: "Health care was a strange thing for us—not a strange thing. But it was the one item in all the Clinton agenda that we never really worked on here at the DLC with him. He had a separate person in the transition to work with the health care plan" (Riley 2007).

9. Interview with subject 029 on February 28, 2022.

10. Interview with subject 029 on February 28, 2022.

11. Interview with subject 029 on February 28, 2022.

Chapter 2: Securing a Seat at the Table

1. Data and original analysis drawn from https://www.bls.gov/cps/.

2. This figure is based on an estimate made by the author. The Biden-Harris transition team announced approximately eight hundred members of various transition and agency review teams in November 2020. Based on subsequent self-identification on social media, at least four hundred more individuals reported serving on a policy, appointments, or operation team, meaning the total number serving in 2020 could have as been as much as four times the Carter figure of approximately four hundred transition staff in 1976. The comparisons with past transitions are based on those publicly serving on agency review teams on each transition team.

3. Interview with subject 114 on May 12, 2023.

4. Other scholars have disputed some of Skocpol's conclusions that this era spelled the end of member-based groups (Walker, McCarthy, and Baumgartner 2011).

5. One high-ranking transition staffer interviewed reported that the total number involved in the transition "was in the thousands." Interview with subject 023 on June 15, 2022.

6. Data for the comparison of transition teams to appointments were generously provided by Kathryn Dunn Tenpas of the Brookings Institution. Complete data on Clinton appointments was not available.

7. Agency-specific data disaggregated by gender were only available for the Biden and Trump transitions.

8. With available data, it is impossible to compare other functions of the transition teams, such as appointments and staffing, since several transition teams only shared agency review team members publicly.

Chapter 3: Inside the Biden-Harris Transition

1. Interview with subject 018 on May 4, 2022.

2. Interview with subject 014 on April 27, 2022.

3. For these reasons, I used a snowball sampling approach to identify interviewees that started with individuals publicly identified on the agency review teams and those that self-identified on various social media platforms. The sample of interviewees grew based on recommendations and suggestions from those involved in various ways with the transition. Everyone who participated did so voluntarily and in confidence, so names and identifying details are not included throughout the chapter, except for those who were interviewed by journalists separate from this project for public news outlets. Additionally, a large portion of those who served on the Biden-Harris transition team later accepted positions in the administration. For these individuals, participating in a research project was a near impossibility. This means that I relied on interviews with members of the transition team, particularly the ARTs, most of whom did not go into government after the transition. The findings should be read with this in mind. It could be that the true insiders on the transition team were the ones chosen for positions in the Biden-Harris ad-

ministration, suggesting the possibility of a biased sample of interview respondents. Further, those who agreed to be interviewed may not have been fully candid about their experience, especially negative aspects, out of deference to the Biden-Harris administration. Even the promise of confidentiality may not have eliminated that concern outright. This chapter, then, reflects the experiences of what could be called the rank-and-file members of the transition team, those involved in the day-to-day planning efforts, not the large-scale work of those closest to the president-elect and vice president elect. Others will write that chapter of this time period.

4. Interview with subject 019 on April 27, 2022.

5. Interview with subject 025 on July 14, 2022.

6. Interview with subject 114 on May 16, 2023.

7. Interview with subject 022 on April 20, 2022.

8. Interview with subject 063 on December 7, 2022.

9. Interview with subject 054 on October 20, 2022.

10. Interview with subject 054 on October 20, 2022.

11. Interview with subject 060 on November 17, 2022.

12. Interview with subject 009 on June 7, 2022.

13. Interview with subject 022 on April 20, 2022.

14. Interview with subject 022 on April 20, 2022.

15. Interview with subject 019 on April 27, 2022.

16. Interview with subject 022 on April 20, 2022.

17. Interview with subject 029 on February 28, 2022.

18. Interview with subject 023 on June 15, 2022.

19. Interview with subject 023 on June 15, 2022.

20. Interview with subject 030 on March 18, 2022.

21. Interview with subject 025 on July 14, 2022.

22. Interview with subject 019 on April 27, 2022.

23. Interview with subject 023 on June 15, 2022.

24. Interview with subject 060 on November 17, 2022.

25. Interview with subject 023 on June 15, 2022.

26. Interview with subject 071 on January 18, 2023.

27. Interview with subject 026 on June 1, 2022.

28. Interview with subject 025 on July 14, 2022.

29. Interview with subject 030 on March 18, 2022.

30. Interview with subject 030 on March 18, 2022.

31. Interview with subject 082 on February 15, 2023.

32. A partial list of those serving on the Trump transition team can be found here: https://s3.documentcloud.org/documents/3217279/2016-11-10-Transition-Team-List.pdf.

33. Interview with subject 030 on March 18, 2022.

34. Interview with subject 096 on May 25, 2023.

35. Interview with subject 112 on May 10, 2023.

36. Interview with subject 096 on May 25, 2023.

37. Interview with subject 071 on January 18, 2023.

38. Abraham alternated between blue and gray suits and blue and white shirts, but the tie remained the same throughout. The briefings have been archived here: https://www.youtube.com/c/transition46/videos.

39. Interview with subject 022 on April 20, 2022.

40. Interview with subject 028 on February 25, 2022.

41. Interview with subject 017 on April 29, 2022.

42. Interview with subject 071 on January 18, 2023.

43. "Mini sprints" or "micro sprints" are a management strategy aimed to analyze what users identify as their problems and then work backwards from that information to design a business solution.

44. Interview with subject 023 on June 15, 2022.

45. Interview with subject 023 on June 15, 2022.

46. Interview with subject 071 on January 18, 2023.

47. Interview with subject 023 on June 15, 2022.

48. Interview with subject 014 on May 11, 2023.

49. Interview with subject 025 on July 14, 2022.

50. Interview with subject 105 on March 15, 2023.

51. Interview with subject 017 on April 29, 2022.

52. Interview with subject 017 on April 29, 2022.

53. Interview with subject 017 on April 29, 2022.

54. Interview with subject 028 on February 25, 2022.

55. Interview with subject 028 on February 25, 2022.

56. Interview with subject 017 on April 29, 2022.

57. Interview with subject 064 on December 12, 2022.

58. Interview with subject 114 on May 11, 2023.

59. Interview with subject 025 on July 14, 2022.

60. Interview with subject 016 on July 1, 2022.

61. Interview with subject 109 on April 19, 2023.

62. Interview with subject 014 on April 27, 2022.

63. Interview with subject 018 on May 4, 2022.

64. Interview with subject 018 on May 4, 2022.

65. Interview with subject 018 on May 4, 2022.

66. Interview with subject 018 on May 4, 2022.

67. Interview with subject 018 on May 4, 2022.

68. Interview with subject 020 on June 2, 2022.

69. Interview with subject 017 on April 29, 2022.

70. Interview with subject 017 on April 29, 2022.

71. Interview with subject 028 on February 25, 2022.

72. Interview with subject 028 on February 25, 2022.

73. Interview with subject 029 on February 28, 2022.

74. Interview with subject 014 on April 27, 2022.

75. Interview with subject 014 on April 27, 2022.

76. Interview with subject 026 on June 1, 2022.

77. Interview with subject 029 on February 28, 2022.

78. Interview with subject 048 on April 21, 2022.

79. Interview with subject 017 on April 29, 2022.

80. Interview with subject 003 on September 16, 2022.

81. Interview with subject 019 on April 27, 2022.

82. Interview with subject 022 on April 20, 2022.

83. Interview with subject 028 on February 25, 2022.

84. Interview with subject 023 on June 15, 2022.

85. Interview with subject 061 on November 22, 2022.

86. Interview with subject 061 on November 22, 2022.

87. Interview with subject 112 on May 10, 2023.

88. Interview with subject 053 on October 19, 2022.

89. Interview with subject 018 on May 4, 2022.

90. Interview with subject 018 on May 4, 2022.

91. Interview with subject 066 on December 15, 2022.

92. Interview with subject 014 on April 27, 2022.

93. Interview with subject 014 on April 27, 2022.

94. Interview with subject 017 on April 29, 2022.

95. Interview with subject 017 on April 29, 2022.

96. Interview with subject 025 on July 14, 2022.

97. Interview with subject 114 on May 16, 2023, confirmed by interview with subject 118 on May 26, 2023, as well as media reports from the time (Erickson et al. 2020; Frias 2020).

98. Interview with subject 025 on July 14, 2022.

99. Interview with subject 017 on April 29, 2022.

100. Interview with subject 017 on April 29, 2022.

101. Interview with subject 017 on April 29, 2022.

102. Interview with subject 019 on April 27, 2022.

103. Interview with subject 019 on April 27, 2022.

104. Interview with subject 014 on April 27, 2022.

105. Interview with subject 014 on April 27, 2022.

106. Interview with subject 014 on April 27, 2022.

107. Interview with subject 014 on April 27, 2022.

108. Interview with subject 009 on June 7, 2022.

109. Interview with subject 009 on June 7, 2022.

110. Interview with subject 009 on June 7, 2022.

111. Interview with subject 024 on May 25, 2022.

112. Interview with subject 049 on November 24, 2022.

113. Interview with subject 019 on April 27, 2022.

114. Interview with subject 024 on May 25, 2022.

115. Interview with subject 019 on April 27, 2022.

116. Interview with subject 023 on June 15, 2022.

117. Interview with subject 029 on February 28, 2022.

118. Interview with subject 030 on March 18, 2022.

119. Interview with subject 030 on March 18, 2022.

120. Interview with subject 017 on April 29, 2022.
121. Interview with subject 029 on February 28, 2022.
122. Interview with subject 082 on February 15, 2023.
123. Interview with subject 015 on April 29, 2022.
124. Interview with subject 064 on December 12, 2022.
125. Interview with subject 064 on December 12, 2022.
126. Interview with subject 064 on December 12, 2022.
127. Interview with subject 088 on May 1, 2023.
128. Interview with subject 116 on May 16, 2023.
129. Interview with subject 118 on May 26, 2023.
130. Interview with subject 060 on November 17, 2022.
131. Interview with subject 027 on January 26, 2022.
132. Interview with subject 027 on January 26, 2022.
133. Interview with subject 027 on January 26, 2022.
134. Interview with subject 060 on November 17, 2022.
135. Miguel Cardona was nominated as secretary of education on December 23, 2020.
136. Interview with subject 022 on April 20, 2022.
137. Interview with subject 022 on April 20, 2022.
138. Interview with subject 022 on April 20, 2022.
139. Interview with subject 028 on February 25, 2022.
140. Interview with subject 022 on April 20, 2022.

Chapter 4: The Biden-Harris Transition from the Outside

1. Interview with subject 099 on March 7, 2023.
2. Interview with subject 036 on March 16, 2022.
3. Interview with subject 031 on March 21, 2022.
4. Interview with subject 031 on March 21, 2022.
5. Interview with subject 044 on March 3, 2022.
6. Interview with subject 044 on March 3, 2022.
7. Interview with subject 044 on March 3, 2022.
8. Interview with subject 038 on March 10, 2022.
9. Interview with subject 038 on March 10, 2022.
10. Interview with subject 037 on March 16, 2022.
11. Interview with subject 037 on March 16, 2022.
12. Interview with subject 032 on April 1, 2022.
13. Interview with subject 032 on April 1, 2022.
14. Interview with subject 039 on March 10, 2022.
15. Interview with subject 032 on April 1, 2022.
16. Interview with subject 032 on April 1, 2022.
17. Interview with subject 032 on April 1, 2022.
18. Interview with subject 035 on March 18, 2022.
19. Interview with subject 039 on March 10, 2022.

20. Interview with subject 039 on March 10, 2022.

21. Interview with subject 101 on March 9, 2023.

22. Interview with subject 045 on February 22, 2022.

23. Interview with subject 045 on February 22, 2022.

24. Interview with subject 045 on February 22, 2022.

25. Interview with subject 039 on March 10, 2022.

26. Interview with subject 039 on March 10, 2022.

27. Interview with subject 039 on March 10, 2022.

28. Interview with subject 039 on March 10, 2022.

29. Interview with subject 045 on February 22, 2022.

30. Interview with subject 045 on February 22, 2022.

31. Interview with subject 040 on December 16, 2022.

32. Interview with subject 040 on December 16, 2022.

33. Interview with subject 043 on January 28, 2022.

34. Interview with subject 043 on January 28, 2022.

35. Interview with subject 032 on April 1, 2022.

36. Interview with subject 032 on April 1, 2022.

37. Interview with subject 039 on March 10, 2022.

38. Interview with subject 039 on March 10, 2022.

39. Interview with subject 050 February 11, 2022.

40. Interview with subject 041 on February 11, 2022.

41. Interview with subject 036 on March 16, 2022.

42. Interview with subject 036 on March 16, 2022.

43. Interview with subject 103 on March 7, 2023.

44. Interview with subject 039 on March 10, 2022.

45. Interview with subject 039 on March 10, 2022.

46. Interview with subject 039 on March 10, 2022.

47. Interview with subject 039 on March 10, 2022.

48. Interview with subject 040 on December 16, 2022.

49. Interview with subject 044 on March 3, 2022.

50. Interview with subject 035 on March 18, 2022.

51. Interview with subject 035 on March 18, 2022.

52. Interview with subject 032 on April 1, 2022.

53. Interview with subject 032 on April 1, 2022.

54. Interview with subject 032 on April 1, 2022.

55. Interview with subject 032 on April 1, 2022.

56. It was not until mid-January of 2021 that Movement for Black Lives organizers met with the Biden-Harris transition team (King 2021).

57. Interview with subject 032 on April 1, 2022.

58. Interview with subject 032 on April 1, 2022.

59. Interview with subject 032 on April 1, 2022.

60. Interview with subject 041 on February 11, 2022.

61. Interview with subject 041 on February 11, 2022.

62. Interview with subject 031 on March 21, 2022.

63. Interview with subject 031 on March 21, 2022.

64. Interview with subject 031 on March 21, 2022.

65. Interview with subject 036 on March 16, 2022.

66. Interview with subject 035 on March 18, 2022.

67. Interview with subject 035 on March 18, 2022.

68. Interview with subject 044 on March 3, 2022.

69. Interview with subject 035 on March 18, 2022.

70. Interview with subject 034 on March 22, 2022.

71. Interview with subject 037 on March 16, 2022.

72. Interview with subject 037 on March 16, 2022.

73. Interview with subject 037 on March 16, 2022.

Chapter 5: Healing the Nation in 2020

1. Interview with subject 007 on July 15, 2022.

2. A recording of the video call was published by *The Intercept*, available at https://theintercept.com/2020/12/10/biden-audio-meeting-civil-rights-leaders/.

3. Interview with subject 013 on July 25, 2022.

4. The full video is available at https://www.youtube.com/watch?v=uwkrCtxN1QE&t=134s.

5. Interviews with eight prominent activists in the TRHT coalition as well as archived documents serve as the basis for this analysis.

6. Interview with subject 004 on July 12, 2022.

7. Interview with subject 004 on July 12, 2022.

8. Interview with subject 008 on August 16, 2022. Interview with subject 005 on September 1, 2022. Interview with subject 005 on September 1, 2022.

9. Interviews with fourteen reparations activists and leaders in the HR 40 coalition as well as archived documents and newspaper articles serve as the basis of this analysis.

10. Interview with subject 010 on August 22, 2022.

11. Interview with subject 010 on August 22, 2022.

12. Interview with subject 008 on August 16, 2022.

13. Interview with subject 002 on September 21, 2022.

14. Interview with subject 002 on September 21, 2022. Interview with subject 001 on September 8, 2022.

15. Interview with subject 008 on August 16, 2022.

16. Interview with subject 008 on August 16, 2022.

17. Interview with subject 004 on July 12, 2022.

18. Interview with subject 004 on July 12, 2022.

19. Interview with subject 004 on July 12, 2022.

20. Interview with subject 004 on July 12, 2022.

21. Interview with subject 011 on August 16, 2022.

22. Interview with subject 012 on August 11, 2022.

23. Interview with subject 064 on December 12, 2022.

24. Interview with subject 011 on August 16, 2022.

25. Interview with subject 011 on August 16, 2022.

26. Interview with subject 006 on September 12, 2022.

27. Interview with subject 006 on September 12, 2022.

28. Interview with subject 007 on July 15, 2022.

29. Interview with subject 007 on July 15, 2022.

30. Interview with subject 007 on July 15, 2022.

31. Interview with subject 004 on July 12, 2022.

32. Interview with subject 007 on July 15, 2022.

33. Interview with subject 004 on July 12, 2022.

34. Interview with subject 011 on August 16, 2022.

35. Interview with subject 001 on September 8, 2022.

36. Interview with subject 064 on December 12, 2022.

37. Interview with subject 007 on July 15, 2022.

38. Interview with subject 007 on July 15, 2022.

39. Interview with subject 007 on July 15, 2022.

40. Interview with subject 006 on September 12, 2022.

41. Interview with subject 007 on July 15, 2022.

42. Interview with subject 004 on July 12, 2022.

43. Interview with subject 004 on July 12, 2022.

44. Interview with subject 004 on July 12, 2022.

45. Interview with subject 007 on July 15, 2022.

46. One activist explained, "One of the reasons why I think more energy ended up pointing to the legislative approach [was] because time after time [we] were thrown out of court on the litigation front." Interview with subject 010 on August 22, 2022.

47. Interview with subject 013 on July 25, 2022.

48. Interview with subject 068 on December 12, 2022.

49. Interview with subject 013 on July 25, 2022.

50. Interview with subject 013 on July 25, 2022.

51. Interview with subject 067 on December 16, 2022.

52. Interview with subject 062 on November 30, 2022.

53. Interview with subject 012 on August 11, 2022.

54. Interview with subject 002 on September 21, 2022.

55. Interview with subject 062 on November 30, 2022.

56. Interview with subject 013 on July 25, 2022.

57. Interview with subject 010 on August 22, 2022.

58. Interview with subject 010 on August 22, 2022.

59. Interview with subject 002 on September 21, 2022.

60. Interview with subject 012 on August 11, 2022.

61. Interview with subject 012 on August 11, 2022. Interview with subject 068 on December 12, 2022.

62. Interview with subject 047 August 9, 2022.

63. Interview with subject 012 on August 11, 2022.

64. Interview with subject 010 on August 22, 2022.

65. Interview with subject 013 on July 25, 2022.
66. Interview with subject 008 on August 16, 2022.
67. Interview with subject 013 on July 25, 2022.
68. Interview with subject 008 on August 16, 2022.
69. Interview with subject 012 on August 11, 2022.
70. Interview with subject 007 on July 15, 2022.
71. Interview with subject 004 on July 12, 2022.
72. Interview with subject 006 on September 12, 2022.
73. Interview with subject 004 on July 12, 2022.
74. Interview with subject 004 on July 12, 2022.
75. Interview with subject 004 on July 12, 2022.
76. Interview with subject 007 on July 15, 2022.
77. Interview with subject 004 on July 12, 2022.
78. Interview with subject 004 on July 12, 2022.
79. Interview with subject 001 on September 8, 2022.
80. Interview with subject 001 on September 8, 2022.
81. Interview with subject 011 on August 16, 2022.
82. Interview with subject 011 on August 16, 2022.
83. Interview with subject 047 August 9, 2022.
84. Interview with subject 012 on August 11, 2022.
85. Interview with subject 012 on August 11, 2022.
86. Interview with subject 047 August 9, 2022.
87. Interview with subject 047 August 9, 2022.
88. Interview with subject 047 on August 9, 2022.
89. Interview with subject 011 on August 16, 2022.
90. Interview with subject 011 on August 16, 2022.

Chapter 6: What to Advise the New President

1. Based on confidential email shared by subject 042.
2. Based on confidential email shared by subject 042.
3. Interview with subject 112 on May 10, 2023.
4. Interview with subject 043 on January 28, 2022.
5. Interview with subject 043 on January 28, 2022.
6. Interview with subject 039 on March 10, 2022.
7. Interview with subject 039 on March 10, 2022.
8. Interview with subject 032 on April 1, 2022.
9. Interview with subject 032 on April 1, 2022.
10. Interview with subject 032 on April 1, 2022.
11. Interview with subject 038 on March 10, 2022.
12. Interview with subject 038 on March 10, 2022.
13. Interview with subject 041 on February 11, 2022.
14. Interview with subject 031 on March 21, 2022.

15. Interview with subject 041 on February 11, 2022.

16. Interview with subject 039 on March 10, 2022.

Conclusion

1. A recording of the event and Vizguerra's speech can be viewed here: https://www.facebook.com/raicestexas/videos/474640057268802/.

2. Interview with subject 057 on November 2, 2022.

3. Interview with subject 031 on March 21, 2022.

4. Interview with subject 033 on April 1, 2022.

5. Interview with subject 033 on April 1, 2022.

6. Interview with subject 031 on March 21, 2022.

7. Interview with subject 031 on March 21, 2022.

8. Interview with subject 033 on April 1, 2022.

9. Interview with subject 033 on April 1, 2022.

10. Interview with subject 033 on April 1, 2022.

11. Interview with subject 033 on April 1, 2022.

12. Interview with subject 031 on March 21, 2022.

13. Interview with subject 031 on March 21, 2022.

14. Interview with subject 031 on March 21, 2022.

15. Interview with subject 031 on March 21, 2022.

16. Interview with subject 031 on March 21, 2022.

17. Interview with subject 033 on April 1, 2022.

18. Interview with subject 022 on April 20, 2022.

19. Interview with subject 023 on June 15, 2022.

20. Interview with subject 118 on May 26, 2023.

21. Interview with subject 078 on February 3, 2023.

22. Interview with subject 059 on November 16, 2022.

23. Interview with subject 059 on November 16, 2022.

24. Interview with subject 057 on November 2, 2022.

25. Interview with subject 031 on March 21, 2022.

26. Interview with subject 031 on March 21, 2022.

27. Interview with subject 031 on March 21, 2022.

28. Interview with subject 023 on June 15, 2022.

29. Interview with subject 113 on May 11, 2023.

30. Interview with subject 031 on March 21, 2022.

31. Interview with subject 031 on March 21, 2022.

Works Cited

Action Network. 2020. "URGENT: Tell Biden to Keep Cecilia Munoz Off His Transition Team and Administration." https://actionnetwork.org/petitions/tell-biden-to-keep-cecilia-munoz-off-his-transition-team-and-administration.

Adams, Biba. 2020. "Shaun King's Fundraising Called into Question Again in Expose Report." *The Grio* (blog), May 26. https://thegrio.com/2020/05/26/shaun-king-expose-report/.

Allen, Mike, and Jonathan Swan. 2022. "Scoop: Pentagon Halts Biden Transition Briefings." *Axios* (blog), December 18. https://www.axios.com/pentagon-biden-transition-briefings-123a9658-4af1-4632-a6e6-770117784d60.html.

American Immigration Council. 2017. "Summary of Executive Order 'Enhancing Safety in the Interior of the United States.'" American Immigration Council. https://www.americanimmigrationcouncil.org/immigration-interior-enforcement-executive-order.

———. 2021. "Policy Brief: The Biden Administration and Congress Must Guarantee Legal Representation for People Facing Removal."https://www.americanimmigrationcouncil.org/sites/default/files/research/the_biden_administration_and_congress_must_guarantee_legal_representation_for_people_facing_removal.pdf.

Associated Press. 2021. "White House Budget Chief Nominee Apologizes for Past Tweets." February 9. https://www.nbcnews.com/politics/white-house/white-house-budget-chief-nominee-apologizes-past-tweets-n1257158.

Asylum Access. 2020. "Recommendations from Mexican Civil Society Organizations to Biden-Harris Administration." December. https://asylumaccess.org/wp-content/uploads/2020/12/Recommendations-from-Mexican-CSOs-to-Biden-Harris-Administration.pdf.

Auletta, Ken. 1976. "The Waiting-for-Jimmy Blues." *New York*, July 12.

Azari, Julia R. 2014. *Delivering the People's Message: The Changing Politics of the Presidential Mandate*. Ithaca, NY: Cornell University Press.

Baker, Megan. 2021. InfluenceHER—Geovette Washington on Working with President Biden. https://www.facebook.com/watch/?v=535983040840079.

Banisky, Sandy. 1976. "Women's Caucus Works Up Ire at Carter's Club Selections." *The Sun*, December 22, 1976.

Baradaran, Mehrsa. 2020. "Closing the Racial Wealth Gap." *NYU Law Review* 95: 57–80.

Baumgartner, Frank, Jeffrey Berry, Marie Hojnacki, David Kimball, and Beth

Leech. 2009. *Lobbying and Policy Change: Who Wins, Who Loses, and Why*. Chicago: University of Chicago Press.

Baumgartner, Frank R., and Bryan D. Jones. 1993. *Agendas and Instability in American Politics*. Chicago: University of Chicago Press.

———. 2015. *The Politics of Information: Problem Definition and the Course of Public Policy in America*. Chicago: University of Chicago Press.

Bazan, Andrea, Monica Lozano, Ramon Murguia, Daniel Ortega, and Jose Villarreal. 2020. "Cecilia Munoz: A Wise Pick for Biden Transition Team." *UnidosUS* (blog), September 18. https://weareunidosus.medium.com/cecilia-mu%C3%B1oz-a-wise-pick-for-biden-transition-team-393de0e27d9a.

Bender, Bryan, and Theodoric Meyer. 2020. "The Secretive Consulting Firm That's Become Biden's Cabinet in Waiting." *Politico*, November 23. https://www.politico.com/news/2020/11/23/westexec-advisors-biden-cabinet-440072.

Biden, Joe. 2020. "Transcript of Gettysburg Speech." CNN. https://transcripts.cnn.com/show/cg/date/2020-10-06/segment/04.

———. 2021. *Proclamation on Termination of Emergency with Respect to the Southern Border of the United States and Redirection of Funds Diverted to Border Wall Construction*. https://www.whitehouse.gov/briefing-room/presidential-actions/2021/01/20/proclamation-termination-of-emergency-with-respect-to-southern-border-of-united-states-and-redirection-of-funds-diverted-to-border-wall-construction/.

Biden-Harris Transition Team. 2020a. "Biden-Harris Transition Team Ethics Plan." https://www.politico.com/f/?id=00000174-e388-dbd6-a9f4-e7ff81060000.

———. 2020b. "Biden-Harris Transition Team Announces Members of Agency Review Teams." American Presidency Project. https://www.presidency.ucsb.edu/documents/press-release-biden-harris-transition-team-announces-members-agency-review-teams.

———. 2020c. "Biden-Harris Presidential Transition Briefing." November 13. https://youtu.be/aZLaTTbYJaI.

———. 2020d. "Ascertainment Briefing." November 20. https://www.youtube.com/watch?v=rFoaLLxN31U.

———. 2020e. "Press Briefing with Members of the Biden-Harris Transition." December 18. https://www.youtube.com/watch?v=IzmPcXdYDX4.

Biden-Sanders Unity Task Force. 2020. "Combatting the Climate Crisis and Pursuing Environmental Justice." https://joebiden.com/wp-content/uploads/2020/08/UNITY-TASK-FORCE-RECOMMENDATIONS.pdf.

Birkland, Thomas A. 1997. *After Disaster: Agenda Setting, Public Policy, and Focusing Events*. Washington, DC: Georgetown University Press.

Bjerre-Poulsen, Niels. 1991. "The Heritage Foundation: A Second-Generation Think Tank." *Journal of Policy History* 3 (2): 152–172.

Black Lives Matter. 2020. "BLM Letter to Biden-Harris." https://blacklivesmatter.com/wp-content/uploads/2020/11/blm-letter-to-biden-harris-110720.pdf.

Blitzer, Jonathan. 2022. "The Disillusionment of a Young Biden Official." *New*

Yorker, January 28. https://www.newyorker.com/news/the-political-scene/the
-disillusionment-of-a-young-biden-official.

Bohn, Michael K. 2003. *Nerve Center: Inside the White House Situation Room*, 1st
ed. Washington, DC: Brassey's.

Box-Steffensmeier, Janet M., Dino P. Christenson, and Matthew P. Hitt. 2013.
"Quality over Quantity: Amici Influence and Judicial Decision Making." *American Political Science Review* 107 (3): 446–460.

Bravender, Robin. 2021. "Inside the 7-Minute Workout the Biden Transition Team
Used to Stay Connected." *Business Insider*, February 4. https://www.businessin
sider.com/biden-white-house-transition-team-administration-remotely-work
outs-2021-2.

The Brian Lehrer Show, dir. 2021. "Taking Up the Mantle of Dr. King's Leadership." WNYC. https://www.wnyc.org/story/taking-mantle-dr-kings-leader
ship/.

Brookings Institution. 1960. "Brookings Institution Studies: Transition [Book Project and Advisory Committee]." https://www.jfklibrary.org/asset-viewer/archives
/CCPP/MF03/CCPP-MF03-019.

———. 2008. "Johnson to Nixon: Brookings and the 1968–69 Presidential Transition." https://www.brookings.edu/articles/johnson-to-nixon-brookings-and
-the-1968-69-presidential-transition/.

Brooks, David. 2019. "The Case for Reparations." *New York Times*, March 7.
https://www.nytimes.com/2019/03/07/opinion/case-for-reparations.html.

Brown, Heath A. 2012. *Lobbying the New President: Interests in Transition*. New
York: Routledge.

Brown, Seyom. 2015. *Faces of Power: Constancy and Change in United States Foreign
Policy from Truman to Obama*, 3rd ed. New York: Columbia University Press.

Buble, Courtney. 2020. "Trump Signs Bill to Strengthen Presidential Transition
Ethics Requirements." *Government Executive* (blog), March 4. https://www
.govexec.com/management/2020/03/trump-signs-bill-strengthen-presidential
-transition-ethics-requirements/163506/.

Buchanan, Larry, Quoctrung Bui, and Jugal Patel. 2020. "Black Lives Matter May
Be the Largest Movement in US History." *New York Times*, July 3. https://www
.nytimes.com/interactive/2020/07/03/us/george-floyd-protests-crowd-size
.html.

Burke, John P. 2000. *Presidential Transitions: From Politics to Practice*. Boulder:
Lynne Rienner Publishers.

———. 2017. *"The Contemporary Presidency* : The Trump Transition, Early Presidency, and National Security Organization: National Security in Trump's Transition and Early Presidency." *Presidential Studies Quarterly* 47 (3): 574–596.
https://doi.org/10.1111/psq.12402.

Burstein, Paul. 2006. "Why Estimates of the Impact of Public Opinion on Public
Policy Are Too High: Empirical and Theoretical Implications." *Social Forces* 84
(4): 2273–2289.

Caldwell, Leigh Ann. 2016. "Trump Transition Team Filled with Hardline Anti-

Immigration Advocates." NBC News, November 11. https://www.nbcnews
.com/politics/2016-election/trump-transition-team-filled-hardline-anti-immi
gration-advocates-n682651.

Canelo, Kayla S. 2022. "The Supreme Court, Ideology, and the Decision to Cite or
Borrow from Amicus Curiae Briefs." *American Politics Research* 50 (2): 255–264.

CAPE. 1976. "Outlook." Council for American Private Education. https://web.ar
chive.org/web/20101120175613/http://www.capenet.org/pdf/Outlook026.pdf.

Carnes, Nicholas. 2013. *White-Collar Government: The Hidden Role of Class in Economic Policy Making.* Chicago: University of Chicago Press.

Carroll, Susan J. 1986. "Women Appointed to the Carter Administration: More or
Less Qualified?" *Polity* 18 (4): 696–706.

Carter Library. 1976. "Political Problems—Political File, 8/76–1/77." Jimmy Carter
Library. https://www.jimmycarterlibrary.gov/digital_library/sso/148838/2/SSO
_148838_002_17.pdf.

"Carter Transition." 1976. https://americanarchive.org/catalog/cpb-aacip_507-pk06
w9752q.

Center for Presidential Transitions. 2022a. "The 2020–21 Presidential Transition:
Lessons Learned and Recommendations." https://presidentialtransition.org
/publications/2020-21-lessons-learned/.

———. 2022b. "Joe Biden's First Year in Office: Nominations and Confirmations."
https://presidentialtransition.org/publications/joe-bidens-first-year-in-office/.

———. n.d. *Exploring Job Opportunities.* Accessed September 26, 2022. https://
presidentialtransition.org/readytoserve/exploring-job-opportunities/.

Chalfant, Morgan. 2020. "Biden: 'More People May Die' If Trump Refused to
Coordinate on Vaccine Plans." *The Hill*, November 16. https://thehill.com
/homenews/administration/526197-biden-more-people-may-die-if-trump
-refuses-to-coordinate-on-vaccine?utm_source=&utm_medium=email&utm
_campaign=34897.

Chisthti, Muzaffar, Sarah Pierce, and Jessica Bolter. 2017. "The Obama Record on
Deportations: Deporter in Chief or Not?" Migration Policy Institute. https://
www.migrationpolicy.org/article/obama-record-deportations-deporter-chief
-or-not.

Christenson, Dino P., and Douglas L. Kriner. 2020. *The Myth of the Imperial Presidency How Public Opinion Checks the Unilateral Executive.* Chicago: University
of Chicago Press.

Christopher, Gail C. 2021. "Truth, Racial Healing, and Transformation: Creating
Public Sentiment." *Health Equity* 5 (1): 668–674.

Clinton Presidential Records. 1993. "Health Care Task Force." Clinton Presidential
Library. https://clinton.presidentiallibraries.us/files/original/883fbe57c1b3d9f
d7fe62d92efcba0b6.pdf.

Cobb, Roger W., and Charles D. Elder. 1983. *Participation in American Politics: The
Dynamics of Agenda-Building,* 2nd ed. Baltimore: Johns Hopkins University Press.

Cohen, Marty, David Karol, Hans Noel, and John Zaller. 2008. *The Party Decides:
Presidential Nominations before and after Reform.* Chicago: University of Chicago
Press.

Cohen, Michael. 2020. *Disloyal: The True Story of the Former Personal Attorney to President Donald J. Trump.* New York: Simon & Schuster.

Consortium for Citizens with Disabilities. 2020. "Email to Biden-Harris Transition Team." https://www.c-c-d.org/fichiers/CCD-Letter-to-COVID19-taskforce -final-11-20-20.pdf.

Conway, Madeline. 2016. "Trump and Romney's 10 Harshest Insults." *Politico,* November 25. https://www.politico.com/story/2016/11/trump-romney-insults -231839.

Costa, Mia, Bruce A. Desmarais, and John A. Hird. 2019. "Public Comments' Influence on Science Use in U.S. Rulemaking: The Case of EPA's National Emission Standards." *The American Review of Public Administration* 49 (1): 36–50.

Cowan, Edward. 1974. "50% Cut Proposed in Energy Growth." *New York Times,* October 18. https://www.nytimes.com/1974/10/18/archives/50-cut-proposed -in-energy-growth-a-ford-foundation-report-sees-no.html.

Dark, Taylor E. 2018. "Partisan Polarization and Political Access: Labor Unions and the Presidency." *Interest Groups & Advocacy* 7 (2): 126–49. https://doi .org/10.1057/s41309-018-0035-3.

Derysh, Igor. 2020. "Progressives Praise Early Biden Picks, But Worry His Team Is Staked with 'Corporatists.'" *Salon* (blog). November 24, 2020. https://www .salon.com/2020/11/24/progressives-praise-early-biden-picks-but-worry-his -team-is-stacked-with-corporatists/.

DNC. 2020. "2020 Democratic Party Platform." https://democrats.org/wp-con tent/uploads/2020/08/2020-Democratic-Party-Platform.pdf.

Downs, Anthony. 1972. "Up and Down with Ecology: The Issue Attention Cycle." *Public Interest* 28: 38–50.

Drutman, Lee. 2015. *The Business of American Is Lobbying: How Corporations Became Politicized and Politics Became More Corporate.* New York: Oxford University Press.

Dwidar, Maraam A. 2022. "Diverse Lobbying Coalitions and Influence in Notice and Comment Rulemaking." *Policy Studies Journal* 50 (1): 199–240.

The Economist/YouGov Poll. 2020. "Econ Tab Report." https://docs.cdn.yougov .com/vgqowgynze/econTabReport.pdf#page=194.

Edwards, George C. 2016. *Predicting the Presidency: The Potential of Persuasive Leadership.* Princeton, NJ: Princeton University Press.

Edwards, Lee. 1997. *The Power of Ideas: The Heritage Foundation at 25 Years.* Ottawa, Ill: Jameson Books.

"Eleven Weeks between Presidents." 1960. *Kiplinger's Personal Finance.*

Erickson, Bo, Paula Reid, Grace Segers, and Fin Gomez. 2020. "Trump Administration and Biden Transition Team Have 'Marginal' Backchannel Communications." CBS News, November 19. https://www.cbsnews.com/news/biden-tran sition-trump-administration-communication/.

Eshbaugh Soha, Matthew, and Kenlea Barnes. 2021. "The Immigration Rhetoric of Donald Trump." *Presidential Studies Quarterly* 51 (4): 781–801.

FACT Coalition. 2016. "2016 Transition Memo." https://thefactcoalition.org/wp -content/uploads/2016/11/FACT-2016-Transition-Memo-FINAL.pdf.

———. 2020. "Transition Memo to President-Elect Biden." https://thefactcoali
tion.org/wp-content/uploads/2020/11/FACT-Transition-Memo-to-President
-Elect-Biden-11.9.2020.pdf.

Fagan, E. J. 2020. "What the 2020 Democratic Party Platform Tells Us about Joe
Biden's Issue Priorities." *Medium* (blog), August 17. https://medium.com
/3streams/what-the-2020-democratic-party-platform-tells-us-about-joe
-bidens-issue-priorities-fa8f15dd8f24.

Fagan, E. J., and Zachary A. McGee. 2022. "Problem Solving and the Demand for
Expert Information in Congress." *Legislative Studies Quarterly* 47 (1): 53–77.

Faulders, Katherine, Anne Flaherty, and Benjamin Siegel. 2020. "GSA Official
Blocking Biden's Transition Appears to Privatively Plan Post-Trump Career."
ABC News, November 16. https://abcnews.go.com/amp/Politics/gsa-official
-blocking-bidens-transition-privately-plans-post/story?id=74234794.

Fenton, Jeron, and LaFleur Stephens-Dougan. 2022. "Are Black State Legislators
More Responsive to Emails Associated with the NAACP versus BLM? A Field
Experiment on Black Intragroup Politics." *Journal of Race, Ethnicity, and Politics*
7 (2): 203–218.

Flemming-Hunter, Sheila. 2016. "Conversations about Reparations for Blacks in
America." *Phylon (1960-)* 53 (2): 100–125.

Ford Library Museum. 1968. "Nixon, Richard—Transition Expenditures: GAO Accounting Office Audit (2)." https://www.fordlibrarymuseum.gov/library/docu
ment/0067/7773945.pdf.

Frey, William F. 2020. "The Nation Is Diversifying Even Faster than Predicted, According to New Census Data." *Brookings Institution* (blog), July 1. https://www
.brookings.edu/research/new-census-data-shows-the-nation-is-diversifying
-even-faster-than-predicted/.

Frias, Lauren. 2020. "Current and Former Officials Quietly Reaching out to
Biden Transition Team." *Business Insider*, November 19. https://www.busines
sinsider.com/trump-officials-quietly-reaching-out-to-biden-transition-team
-cnn-2020-11.

Friedman, Rebecca. 2011. "Crisis Management at the Dead Center: The 1960–1961
Presidential Transition and the Bay of Pigs Fiasco." *Presidential Studies Quarterly* 41 (2): 307–333.

Furnas, Alexander C., Timothy M LaPira, Alexander Hertel-Fernandez, Lee Drutman, and Kevin Kosar. 2022. "More than Mere Access: An Experiment on Mon-
eyed Interests, Information Provision, and Legislative Action in Congress." *Political Research Quarterly*, May, 10659129221019887.

Galston, William. 2004. "William Galston Oral History." Miller Center. https://
millercenter.org/the-presidency/presidential-oral-histories/william-gals
ton-oral-history.

Galston, William, and Elaine Kamarck. 1989. "The Politics of Evasion: Democrats
and the Presidency." Progressive Policy Institute. https://www.progressivepo
licy.org/wp-content/uploads/2010/01/Politics_of_Evasion.pdf.

Goldmacher, Shane. 2020. "A Small Staff of Advisers and Other Trusted Figures
Will Start Planning What a Biden Administration Will Look Like If He Wins in

November." *New York Times*, June 30. https://www.nytimes.com/2020/06/30/us/politics/biden-transition-team.html?referringSource=articleShare.

Grossmann, Matt, and Casey B. K. Dominguez. 2009. "Party Coalitions and Interest Group Networks." *American Politics Research* 37 (5): 767–800.

Grossmann, Matthew. 2012. *The Not-so-Special Interests: Interest Groups, Public Representation, and American Governance*. Stanford, CA: Stanford University Press.

Grossmann, Matthew, and David A. Hopkins. 2016. *Asymmetric Politics: Ideological Republicans and Group Interest Democrats*. New York: Oxford University Press.

Grove, Rashad. 2022. "Activist Shaun King Accused of Scamming Customers in Regards to His 'Real One' Clothing Line." *Ebony*, May 16. https://www.ebony.com/shaun-king-accused-of-scamming-customers-in-regards-to-his-real-one-clothing-line.

Gunderson, Anna. 2021. "Ideology, Disadvantage, and Federal District Court Inmate Civil Rights Filings: The Troubling Effects of Pro Se Status." *Journal of Empirical Legal Studies* 18 (3): 603–628.

Gutierrez, Jose Angel. 1996a. Oral History Interview with Alicia Chacon. https://library.uta.edu/tejanovoices/xml/CMAS_002.xml.

———. 1996b. Oral History Interview with Marc Campos. https://library.uta.edu/tejanovoices/xml/CMAS_140.xml.

———. 1997. Oral History Interview with Linda Yanez. https://library.uta.edu/tejanovoices/xml/CMAS_105.xml.

Hall, Richard, and Alan Deardorff. 2006. "Lobbying as Legislative Subsidy." *American Political Science Review* 100 (1): 69–84.

Halpin, Darren R., Bert Fraussen, and Anthony J. Nownes. 2018. "The Balancing Act of Establishing a Policy Agenda: Conceptualizing and Measuring Drivers of Issue Prioritization within Interest Groups." *Governance* 31 (2): 215–237.

Han, Hahrie. 2014. *How Organizations Develop Activists: Civic Associations and Leadership in the 21st Century*. Oxford : Oxford University Press.

Han, Hahrie, Elizabeth McKenna, and Michelle Oyakawa. 2021. *Prisms of the People: Power and Organizing in Twenty-First-Century America*. Chicago : University of Chicago Press.

Hansford, Thomas G. 2004. "Information Provision, Organizational Constraints, and the Decision to Submit an Amicus Curiae Brief in a U.S. Supreme Court Case." *Political Research Quarterly* 57 (2): 219–230.

Hardy-Fanta, Carol, Pei-te Lien, Dianne M. Pinderhughes, and Christine Marie Sierra. 2006. "Gender, Race, and Descriptive Representation in the United States: Findings from the Gender and Multicultural Leadership Project." *Journal of Women, Politics & Policy* 28 (3-4): 7–41.

Harvard Institute of Politics, dir. 2020. *Youth Vote Discussion at Harvard Institute of Politics*. https://www.c-span.org/video/?507005-1/youth-vote-discussion-harvard-institute-politics.

Heatherly, Charles L., ed. 1981. *Mandate for Leadership: Policy Management in a Conservative Administration*. Washington, DC: Heritage Foundation.

Heclo, Hugh. 1977. *A Government of Strangers: Executive Politics in Washington*. Washington, DC: Brookings Institution.

Heritage Foundation. 2022. "Heritage Announces 2025 Presidential Transition Project, Hiring of Paul Dans." April 14, 2022. https://www.heritage.org/press /heritage-announces-2025-presidential-transition-project-hiring-paul-dans -direct-new.

Herz, Michael, and Katherine A. Shaw. 2021. "Transition Administration." *Minnesota Law Review* 106: 607–688.

Hill, Gladwin. 1976. "Carter Advisor on Resources Quits, Citing Friction." *New York Times*, November 20. https://www.nytimes.com/1976/11/20/archives/car ter-adviser-on-resources-quits-citing-friction.html.

Hojnacki, Marie, and David Kimball. 1998. "Organized Interests and the Decision of Whom to Lobby in Congress." *American Political Science Review* 92 (4): 775–790.

Holyoke, Thomas. 2004. "By Invitation Only: Controlling Interest Group Access to the Oval Office." *American Review of Politics* 25 (November): 221–240.

Horowitz, Juliana Menasce. 2021. "Support for Black Lives Matter Declined after George Floyd Protests, but Has Remained Unchanged Since." *Pew Research Center* (blog), September 27. https://www.pewresearch.org/fact-tank/2021/09/27 /support-for-black-lives-matter-declined-after-george-floyd-protests-but-has -remained-unchanged-since/.

Howell, William. 2003. *Power without Persuasion: The Politics of Direct Presidential Action*. Princeton, NJ: Princeton University Press.

Hufbauer, Gary Clyde, ed. 2007. *Economic Sanctions Reconsidered*, 3rd ed. Washington, DC: Peterson Institute for International Economics.

Hula, Kevin W. 1999. *Lobbying Together: Interest Group Coalitions in Legislative Politics*. Washington, DC: Georgetown University Press.

Hult, Karen. 2022. "Trump's Management of the Executive Branch." In Steven E. Schier and Todd E. Eberly, eds., *The Trump Effect: Disruption and Its Consequences in US Politics and Government*. Lanham, MD: Rowman & Littlefield.

Human Rights Watch. 2021. "HRW Letter to the Biden Transition Team." January 14, 2021.

———. 2022. "'Why We Can't Wait' Coalition Statement on US Failure to Establish HR 40 Commission." *Human Rights Watch* (blog), August 23. https://www .hrw.org/news/2022/08/23/why-we-cant-wait-coalition-statement-us-failure -establish-hr-40/s-40-commission.

Hundt, Reed. 2019. *A Crisis Wasted: Barack Obama's Defining Decisions*. New York: RosettaBooks.

Hunnicutt, Trevor. 2020. "Biden Weighs Naming Cabinet Officials before Election, including Republicans." *Reuters* , April 29. https://www.reuters.com/article /us-usa-election-biden/biden-weighs-naming-cabinet-officials-before-election -including-republicans-idUSKBN22B384.

Immigration Hub. n.d. "Ignite Agenda." Accessed September 18, 2022. https:// theimmigrationhub.org/ignite-agenda.

Infectious Disease Society of America. 2016. "Letter to Trump Transition Team." https://www.idsociety.org/globalassets/hivma/policy-and-advocacy/idsa-let ter-to-vice-president-elect-mike-pence.pdf.

Ioffe, Julia. 2016. "The Believer: How Stephen Miller Went from Obscure Capitol Hill Staffer to Donald Trump's Warm-Up Act and Resident Ideologue." *Politico Magazine*, June. https://www.politico.com/magazine/story/2016/06/ste phen-miller-donald-trump-2016-policy-adviser-jeff-sessions-213992/.

Itkonen, Tiina. 2009. "Stories of Hope and Decline: Interest Group Effectiveness in National Special Education Policy." *Educational Policy* 23 (1): 43–65.

Jackson-Lee, Sheila. 2019. "H.R. 40—Commission to Study and Develop Reparations Proposals for African-Americans Act." US Congress. https://www.congress.gov/bill/116th-congress/house-bill/40.

Jakes, Lara, and Eileen Sullivan. 2022. "A Senior US Diplomat to Haiti Resigns, Citing the Biden Administration's 'Inhumane Deportation Policy.'" *New York Times*, September 23. https://www.nytimes.com/2021/09/23/us/politics/haiti-diplomat-resign-biden.html.

Jamieson, Dave. 2021. "Union Allies Call on Joe Biden to Fire Trump's Labor Board Attorney Immediately." *Huffington Post* (blog), January 14. https://www.huff post.com/entry/joe-biden-peter-robb-nlrb-unions_n_6000a47cc5b62c0057b b6301?ypf.

Jenkins, Chris L., and Hamil R. Harris. 2002. "Slavery's Children Seek Reparations." *Washington Post*, August 18. https://www.washingtonpost.com/archive /local/2002/08/18/slaverys-children-seek-reparations/26948fd5-b0fa-471f -b12d-b68ee5e78720/.

Jenkins, Jack. 2020. "Biden Talks Faith and Poverty at Poor Peoples Campaign Event." *Religion News*, September 15. https://religionnews.com/2020/09/15 /biden-talks-faith-and-poverty-at-poor-peoples-campaign-event/.

Jimmy Carter Library. 1976. "Transition Budget, 11/76." https://www.jimmycarter library.gov/digital_library/sso/148838/2/SSO_148838_002_23.pdf.

———. 1977. "Office of Staff Secretary; Presidential Files; Folder: 1/25/77." https://www.jimmycarterlibrary.gov/digital_library/sso/148878/4/SSO_148878 _004_05.pdf.

Johnson, Katanga. 2020. "US Public More Award of Racial Inequality but Still Rejects Reparations." *Reuters*, June 25. https://www.reuters.com/article/us-usa -economy-reparations-poll/u-s-public-more-aware-of-racial-inequality-but -still-rejects-reparations-reuters-ipsos-polling-idUSKBN23W1NG.

Jones, Charles. 1998. *Passages to the Presidency: From Campaigning to Governing*. Washington, DC: Brookings Institution.

Kalla, Joshua L., and David E. Broockman. 2016. "Campaign Contributions Facilitate Access to Congressional Officials: A Randomized Field Experiment." *American Journal of Political Science* 60 (3): 545–558.

Kaufman, Ted. 2021. "I Led the Biden Presidential Transition. Its Leadership Lessons Can Apply to Any Organization." *Fortune*, May 4. https://fortune .com/2021/05/04/joe-biden-campaign-transition-administration/.

Kernell, Samuel. 2007. *Going Public: New Strategies for Presidential Leadership*, 4th ed. Washington, DC: CQ Press.

Kessler, Glenn, Salvador Rizzo, and Meg Kelly. 2021. "Trump's False or Misleading

Claims Total 30,573 over 4 Years." *Washington Post*, January 24. https://www.washingtonpost.com/politics/2021/01/24/trumps-false-or-misleading-claims-total-30573-over-four-years/.

King, James D., and James W. Riddlesperger. 2018. "The Trump Transition: Beginning a Distinctive Presidency: The Trump Transition." *Social Science Quarterly* 99 (5): 1821–1836.

King, Maya. 2021. "Biden Racial Equity Executive Orders 462917." *Politico*, January 26. https://www.politico.com/news/2021/01/26/biden-racial-equity-executive-orders-462917.

King, Shaun. 2020. *About Our Meeting with the Biden-Harris Transition Team*. Podcast. https://podcasts.apple.com/us/podcast/ep-366-about-our-meeting-with-the-biden-harris/id1457725100?i=1000500832292.

Kingdon, John. 1995. *Agendas, Alternatives, and Public Policies*. New York: Harper Collins.

Kollman, Ken. 1998. *Outside Lobbying: Public Opinion and Interest Group Strategies*. Princeton, NJ: Princeton University Press.

Kopan, Tal. 2021. "One Year in Biden Has Been Slow to Unwind Trump." *San Fransisco Chronicle*, December 27. https://www.sfchronicle.com/politics/article/One-year-in-Biden-has-been-slow-to-unwind-Trump-16725642.php.

Kumar, Martha Joynt. 2017. *Before the Oath: How George W. Bush and Barack Obama Managed a Transfer of Power*. Baltimore: Johns Hopkins University Press.

———. 2021. "Joseph Biden's Effective Presidential Transition: 'Started Early, Went Big.'" *Presidential Studies Quarterly* 51 (3): 582–608.

Lamb, Brian. 2005. Q&A with Paul Weyrich. https://www.c-span.org/video/transcript/?id=7958.

LaPira, Timothy M., and Herschel F. Thomas. 2017. *Revolving Door Lobbying: Public Service, Private Influence, and the Unequal Representation of Interests*. Lawrence: University Press of Kansas.

LaPira, Timothy M., Herschel F. Thomas, and Frank R. Baumgartner. 2014. "The Two Worlds of Lobbying: Washington Lobbyists in the Core and on the Periphery." *Interest Groups & Advocacy* 3 (3): 219–245.

Lee, Barbara. 2020. "H. Con. Res 100—Urging the Establishment of a United States Commission on Truth, Racial Healing, and Transformation." US Congress. https://www.congress.gov/bill/116th-congress/house-concurrent-resolution/100/text?q=%7B%22search%22%3A%5B%22billOriginalCosponsor%3AA000371%22%2C%22billOriginalCosponsor%3AA000371%22%5D%7D&r=99&s=1.

Lee, Kyuwon, and Hye Young You. 2023. "Bureaucratic Revolving Doors and Interest Group Participation in Policymaking." *Journal of Politics* 85 (2): 701–717.

Leher, Lisa. 2008. "Economic Team Users 'Data-Driven Approach.'" *Politico*, November 25. https://www.politico.com/story/2008/11/economic-team-uses-data-driven-approach-015958.

Lesniewski, Niels. 2020. "Budget Process, COVID Spending Being Undermined by OMB, Biden Transition Says." *Roll Call* (blog), December 30. https://rollcall

.com/2020/12/30/budget-process-covid-spending-being-undermined-by-omb
-biden-transition-says/.

Levinthal, Dave, and Robin Bravender. 2021. "New 1,021-Page Document Shows
How Mary Trump, Leonardo DiCaprio, and Jennifer Aniston Helped Fund
Biden's Transition Effort as Trump Dragged His Heels." *Business Insider*, February 22. https://www.businessinsider.com/joe-biden-presidential-transition
-funding-democrats-megadonors-donald-trump-2021-2.

Lewis, David E., and Mark D. Richardson. 2021. "The Very Best People: President
Trump and the Management of Executive Personnel." *Presidential Studies Quarterly* 51 (1): 51–70.

Lewis, David E., Patrick Bernhard, and Emily You. 2018. "President Trump as
Manager: Reflections on the First Year: Trump's First Year." *Presidential Studies
Quarterly* 48 (3): 480–501.

Lewis, Michael. 2018. *The Fifth Risk*. New York: W. W. Norton.

Locin, Mitchell. 1992. "Clinton Finishes Cabinet of Diversity." *Chicago Tribune*, December 25. https://www.chicagotribune.com/news/ct-xpm-1992-12-25-920427
0273-story.html.

Lowande, Kenneth, Melinda Ritchie, and Erinn Lauterbach. 2019. "Descriptive and
Substantive Representation in Congress: Evidence from 80,000 Congressional
Inquiries." *American Journal of Political Science* 63 (3): 644–659.

Mahler, Jonathan. 2018. "How One Conservative Think Tank Is Stocking Trump's
Government." *New York Times Magazine*, June 20. https://www.nytimes
.com/2018/06/20/magazine/trump-government-heritage-foundation-think
-tank.html.

Mahler, Jonathan, and Steve Eder. 2016. "'No Vacancies' for Blacks: How Donald
Trump Got His Start, and Was First Accused of Bias." *New York Times* , August
27. https://www.nytimes.com/2016/08/28/us/politics/donald-trump-housing
-race.html.

Manigault, Omarosa. 2019. *Unhinged: An Insider's Account of the Trump White
House*. New York: Gallery Books.

Marchick, David. 2021. *Yohannes Abraham on Leading the Biden Transition*. Podcast.
https://podcasts.apple.com/us/podcast/yohannes-abraham-on-leading-the
-biden-transition/id1495404153?i=1000504940482.

Marcus, Ruth. 1992. "Clinton Berates Critics in Women's Groups." *Washington Post*,
December 22. https://www.washingtonpost.com/archive/politics/1992/12/22/clin
ton-berates-critics-in-womens-groups/f035a4fc-8203-42c9-8f52-bb418301fcc7/.

Martin, Paul. 2006. Alphonso Michael Espy Oral History. https://millercenter.org
/the-presidency/presidential-oral-histories/alphonso-michael-espy-oral-history.

Matthews, Hannah. 2020. "Transition Briefing and Recommendations: Stop the
Harm and Start Healing for Children in Immigrant Families." *CLASP* (blog),
November . https://www.clasp.org/wp-content/uploads/2022/04/CLASP_im
migration20recommendations_Jan2021.pdf.

McKay, Amy. 2022. *Stealth Lobbying: Interest Group Influence and Health Care Reform*. New York: Cambridge University Press.

Meyer, Theodoric, and Alex Thompson. 2020. "Goldman Sachs Vets Quietly Added to Biden Transition." *Politico*, December 14. https://www.politico.com/newslet ters/transition-playbook/2020/12/14/goldman-sachs-vets-quietly-added-to -biden-transition-491143.

Michelson, Melissa R. 2002. "The Black Reparations Movement: Public Opinion and Congressional Policy Making." *Journal of Black Studies* 32 (5): 574–587.

Milbank, Dana. 2000. "White House Hopes Gas Up a Think Tank." *Washington Post*, December 8. https://www.washingtonpost.com/archive/politics/2000/12 /08/white-house-hopes-gas-up-a-think-tank/77661a31–89bd-4322-b6c2 –0873a2c287df/.

Milkis, Sidney M., and Daniel J. Tichenor. 2019. *Rivalry and Reform: Presidents, Social Movements, and the Transformation of American Politics*. Chicago : University of Chicago Press.

Miller, David Ryan. 2022. "The President Will See Whom Now? Presidential Engagement with Organized Interests." *American Political Science Review* 117 (3): 1019–1035.

Minta, Michael D. 2021. *No Longer Outsiders: Black and Latino Interest Group Advocacy on Capitol Hill*. Chicago: University of Chicago Press.

Miroff, Bruce. 1981. "Presidential Leverage over Social Movements: The Johnson White House and Civil Rights." *Journal of Politics* 43 (1): 2–23.

Monmouth University Polling Institute. 2020. "Protestors' Anger Justified Even If Actions May Not Be." *Monmouth University* (blog), June 2. https://www.mon mouth.edu/polling-institute/reports/monmouthpoll_us_060220/.

Moynihan, Donald P. 2022. "Public Management for Populists: Trump's Schedule F Executive Order and the Future of the Civil Service." *Public Administration Review* 82 (1): 174–178.

Murphy, Emily. 2020. "GSA Letter." GAO. https://www.gsa.gov/cdnstatic/2020-11 -23_Hon_Murphy_to_Hon_Biden_0.pdf.

Neustadt, Richard. 1960. *Presidential Power: The Politics of Leadership*. New York: Wiley.

New York Times. 1976. "Louise Dunlap, Joseph Browder Wed in Virginia." *New York Times*, January 4. https://www.nytimes.com/1976/01/04/archives/louise -dunlap-joseph-browder-wed-in-virginia.html.

———. 1992. "The 1992 Campaign; Excerpt from Clinton's Speech on His Economic Proposals." June 23. https://www.nytimes.com/1992/06/23/us/the-1992 -campaign-excerpts-from-clinton-s-speech-on-his-economic-proposals.html.

New York Times Editorial Board. 1993. "The Lesson of Zoe Baird." *New York Times*, January 23. https://www.nytimes.com/1993/01/23/opinion/the-lesson -of-zoe-baird.html.

NLIHC. 2008. "Obama-Biden Transition Letter." National Low Income Housing Coalition. https://web.archive.org/web/20081126202258/http://www.nlihc.org /doc/Obama-Biden-Transition-letter.pdf.

———. 2016. "Opportunities to End Homelessness and Housing Poverty in a Trump Administration." https://nlihc.org/sites/default/files/NLIHC_Transi tion-Memo_1216.pdf.

————. 2020. "NLIHC Memo to Biden Transition Team." National Low Income Housing Coalition. https://nlihc.org/sites/default/files/NLIHC_Biden-Transition-Memo.pdf.

Noble, Barbara Presley. 1992. "World Markets: The Britain-First Cure Is Working." *New York Times* , December 13. https://www.nytimes.com/1992/12/13/business/world-markets-the-britain-first-cure-is-working.html.

North, Douglass C. 2009. *Institutions, Institutional Change, and Economic Performance*. Cambridge: Cambridge University Press.

Obama White House Archive. n.d. "Vice President Joe Biden." Accessed October 28, 2022. https://obamawhitehouse.archives.gov/vp.

Orsmeth, Matthew. 2020. "S. David Freeman, Public Power Chief and Energy Advisor, Dies at 94." *Los Angeles Times*, May 13. https://www.latimes.com/california/story/2020-05-13/s-david-freeman-public-power-chief-and-energy-adviser-dies-at-94.

Peterson, Mark A. 1992. "The Presidency and Organized Interests: White House Patterns of Interest Group Liaison." *American Political Science Review* 86 (3): 612–625.

Pettypiece, Shannon, and Geoff Bennett. 2020. "Legacy Civil Rights Groups Feel Left Out of Biden Transition." NBC News, December 1. https://www.nbcnews.com/politics/white-house/legacy-civil-rights-groups-feel-left-out-biden-transition-n1249495.

Pew Research Center. 2020. "Important Issues in the 2020 Election." August 13. https://www.pewresearch.org/politics/2020/08/13/important-issues-in-the-2020-election/.

Politico Staff. 2016. "Trump Adds Vice Chairs to Transition Team, including Several Women." *Politico*, November 29. https://www.politico.com/blogs/donald-trump-administration/2016/11/trump-adds-vice-chairs-to-transition-team-including-several-women-231975.

POLITIFACT. n.d. "Obameter." Accessed September 26, 2022. https://www.politifact.com/truth-o-meter/promises/obameter/.

Poor People's Campaign, dir. 2020. *Our First Meeting with the Biden-Harris Transition Team Is Today*. https://www.facebook.com/watch/?v=410748083495033.

————. 2021. "14 Policy Priorities to Heal the Nation." https://www.poorpeoplescampaign.org/wp-content/uploads/2021/03/Final_14-Points_State-Demand-Delivery.pdf.

Porier, Shar. 2021. "Q&A with Sheriff Mark Danells on the Border." *Herald/Review*, March 21. https://www.myheraldreview.com/news/cochise_county/q-a-with-sheriff-mark-dannels-on-the-border/article_d8c3a486-8903-11eb-b8c6-9f6f5561615d.html.

Posthumus, Daniel, and Kelebogile Zvobgo. 2022. "Democratizing Truth: An Analysis of Truth Commissions in the United States." *International Journal of Transitional Justice* 15 (3): 510–532.

Potter, Rachel Augustine. 2019. *Bending the Rules: Procedural Politicking in the Bureaucracy*. Chicago: University of Chicago Press.

Potter, Rachel Augustine, Andrew Rudalevige, Sharece Thrower, and Adam L.

Warber. 2019. "Continuity Trumps Change: The First Year of Trump's Administrative Presidency." *PS: Political Science & Politics* 52 (4): 613–619.

Prakash, Varshini. 2020. "I'm Joining the Sanders-Biden Taskforce on Climate. Here's Why." *Medium* (blog), March 13. https://medium.com/sunrisemvmt/im-joining-the-sanders-biden-taskforce-on-climate-here-s-why-90a3ddoff546.

Ramos, Jorge. 2020. *Joe Biden: The Interview.* https://www.facebook.com/RealAmericaWithJorgeRamos/videos/joe-biden-the-interview/696144000990829/.

Reagan, Ronald. 1981. "Inaugural Address." Reagan Foundation. https://www.reaganfoundation.org/media/128614/inaguration.pdf.

Reichelmann, Ashley V., and Matthew O. Hunt. 2022. "White Americans' Attitudes toward Reparations for Slavery: Definitions and Determinants." *Race and Social Problems* 14 (3): 269–281.

Rein, Lisa, Jonathan O'Connell, and Josh Dawsey. 2020. "A Little-Known Trump Appointee Is in Charge of Handing Transition Resources to Biden—and She Isn't Budging." *Washington Post*, November 8. https://www.washingtonpost.com/politics/trump-gsa-letter-biden-transition/2020/11/08/07093acc-21e9-11eb-8672-c281c7a2c96e_story.html.

Reingold, Beth, Kerry Lee Haynie, and Kirsten Widner. 2021. *Race, Gender, and Political Representation: Toward a More Intersectional Approach.* New York: Oxford University Press.

Reny, Tyler T., and Benjamin J. Newman. 2021. "The Opinion-Mobilizing Effect of Social Protest against Police Violence: Evidence from the 2020 George Floyd Protests." *American Political Science Review* 115 (4): 1499–1507.

Resh, William G. 2014. "Appointee-Careerist Relations in the Presidential Transition of 2008–2009: Appointee-Careerist." *Presidential Studies Quarterly* 44 (4): 697–723.

———. 2015. *Rethinking the Administrative Presidency: Trust, Intellectual Capital and Appointee-Careerist Relations in the George W. Bush Administration.* Baltimore: Johns Hopkins University Press.

Riley, Russell. 2007. Al From Oral History. https://millercenter.org/the-presidency/presidential-oral-histories/al-oral-history-2007.

———. 2008. Elaina Kamarck Oral History. https://millercenter.org/the-presidency/presidential-oral-histories/elaine-kamarck-oral-history.

Roberts, Russ. n.d. "Lisa Cook on Racism, Patents, and Black Entrepreneurship." https://www.econtalk.org/lisa-cook-on-racism-patents-and-black-entrepreneurship/#audio-highlights.

Roosevelt Institution. 2021. *What Makes for a Strong Presidential Transition.* https://rooseveltinstitute.org/event/what-makes-for-a-strong-presidential-transition/.

Rudalevige, Andrew. 2005. *The New Imperial Presidency: Renewing Presidential Power after Watergate.* Ann Arbor: University of Michigan Press.

———. 2012. "'A Majority Is the Best Repartee': Barack Obama and Congress, 2009–2012" *Social Science Quarterly* 93 (5): 1272–1294.

Saad, Lydia. 2022. "Concern about Race Relations Persists after Floyd's Death." *Gallup* (blog), May 19. https://news.gallup.com/poll/392705/concern-race-relations-persists-floyd-death.aspx.

Schickler, Eric. 2013. "New Deal Liberalism and Racial Liberalism in the Mass Public, 1937–1968." *Perspectives on Politics* 11 (1): 75–98.

Schlesinger, Arthur M. 2004. *The Imperial Presidency.* Boston: Houghton Mifflin.

Schlozman, Daniel. 2015. *When Movements Anchor Parties: Electoral Alignments in American History.* Princeton, NJ: Princeton University Press.

Schlozman, Daniel, and Sam Rosenfeld. 2019. "The Hollow Parties." In Frances E. Lee and Nolan McCarty, eds., *Can America Govern Itself?*, 120–152. Cambridge: Cambridge University Press.

Schlozman, Kay Lehman, and John Tierney. 1986. *Organized Interests and American Democracy.* New York: Harper & Row.

Schram, Sanford F. 2022. "The Biden Racial Justice Policy Agenda: Combating Systemic Racism with Targeting within Universalism." *International Review of Public Policy* 4 (1).

Scott, Eugene. 2019a. "Democratic Candidates Are Backing Reparations for African Americans. That Could Be Politically Risky." *Washington Post* , February 26. https://www.washingtonpost.com/politics/2019/02/26/democratic-candidates -are-backing-reparations-african-americans-that-could-be-politically-risky/.

———. 2019b. "What Obama Actually Said about His Rejection of Reparations." *Washington Post* (blog), July 9. https://www.washingtonpost.com/poli tics/2019/07/09/what-obama-actually-said-his-rejection-of-reparations/.

Sharpe, Jared. 2021. "UMass Amherst/WCVB Poll." *UMass* (blog), April 29. https:// www.umass.edu/news/article/umass-amherstwcvb-poll-finds-nearly-half.

Shear, Michael, Zolan Kanno-Youngs, and Katie Rogers. 2021. "White House Border Coordinator to Step Down." *New York Times*, April 9. https://www.nytimes .com/2021/04/09/us/politics/biden-border-czar.html.

Shogan, Colleen. 2004. "Presidential Campaigns and the Congressional Agenda: Reagan, Clinton, and Beyond." Washington, DC: Wilson Center. https://www .wilsoncenter.org/sites/default/files/media/documents/event/shogan.pdf.

Sides, John, Chris Tausanovitch, and Lynn Vavreck. 2022. *The Bitter End: The 2020 Presidential Campaign and the Challenge to American Democracy.* Princeton, NJ: Princeton University Press.

Sifry, Micah. 2017. "Obama's Lost Army." *New Republic*, February 9. https://newre public.com/article/140245/obamas-lost-army-inside-fall-grassroots-machine.

Skocpol, Theda. 2001. "Associations without Members." *American Prospect* (blog), December 19. https://prospect.org/power/associations-without-members/.

Skocpol, Theda, and Lawrence Jacobs. 2012. "Accomplished and Embattled: Understanding Obama's Presidency." *Political Science Quarterly* 127 (1): 1–24.

Skowronek, Stephen. 1997. *The Politics Presidents Make: Leadership from John Adams to Bill Clinton.* Cambridge, MA: Belknap Press of Harvard University Press.

Skowronek, Stephen, John A. Dearborn, and Desmond S. King. 2022. *Phantoms of a Beleaguered Republic: The Deep State and the Unitary Executive*, rev. ed. New York: Oxford University Press.

Smith, Hedrick. 1976. "Strains in Carter Transition." *New York Times*, December 10. https://www.nytimes.com/1976/12/10/archives/strains-in-carter-transition -aides-discovering-that-power-brings.html.

Smith, James Allen. 1993. *Strategic Calling: The Center for Strategic and International Studies, 1962–1992.* Washington, DC: Center for Strategic and International Studies.

Smith, Robert C. 2022. "Presidential Responsiveness to Black Interests from Grant to Biden: The Power of the Vote, the Power of Protest." *Presidential Studies Quarterly* 52 (3): 648–670.

Sprunt, Barbara. 2020. "Biden Says Trump's Refusal to Concede Won't Impede Transition." NPR , November 10. https://www.npr.org/sections/biden-transition-updates/2020/11/10/933533575/biden-says-trumps-refusal-to-concede-wont-impede-transition.

Sullivan, Jake. 2016. "Jake Sullivan Statement on Breaking News that Confirms Russia Is Behind the Hack of John Podesta's Emails." *American Presidency Project* (blog), October 20. https://www.presidency.ucsb.edu/documents/jake-sullivan-statement-breaking-news-that-confirms-russia-behind-the-hack-john-podestas.

Supovitz, Jonathan, and Patrick McGuinn. 2019. "Interest Group Activity in the Context of Common Core Implementation." *Educational Policy* 33 (3): 453–485.

Tarrow, Sidney. 2022. *Power in Movement: Social Movements and Contentious Politics,* 4th ed. Cambridge: Cambridge University Press.

Tenpas, Kathryn Dunn. 2018. "White House Staff Turnover in Year One of the Trump Administration: Context, Consequences, and Implications for Governing White House Staff Turnover." *Presidential Studies Quarterly* 48 (3): 502–516.

———. 2022. "Waiting for Advice and Consent: Record Level Diversity amidst an Exceedingly Slow Confirmation Pace during the First 300 Days of the Biden Administration." *Presidential Studies Quarterly* 52 (3): 709–717.

Think Tank Watch. 2022. "Ranking of Think Tanks." University of Pennsylvania. https://repository.upenn.edu/cgi/viewcontent.cgi?article=1019&context=think_tanks http://www.thinktankwatch.com/2020/11/dozens-of-think-tankers-helping-with.html.

Thomas, Jacqueline Rabe, and Adria Watson. 2021. "Miguel Cardona's Ideas about Education Were Forged in Meriden, CT. Now He Will Bring Them to Washington, DC." *The CT Mirror* (blog), January 19. https://ctmirror.org/2021/01/19/miguel-cardonas-ideas-about-education-were-forged-in-meriden-ct-now-he-will-bring-them-to-washington-d-c/.

Toosi, Nahal, Daniel Lippman, and Dan Diamond. 2020. "Before Trump's Inauguration, a Warning: 'The Worst Influenza Pandemic since 1918.'" *Politico,* March 16. https://www.politico.com/news/2020/03/16/trump-inauguration-warning-scenario-pandemic-132797.

Transition Lab. 2020. *The Biden Transition to Power.* https://presidentialtransition.org/blog/the-biden-transition-to-power/.

Troy, Tevi. 2017. "The Dilemma of the D.C. Think Tank." *The Atlantic,* December. https://www.theatlantic.com/politics/archive/2017/12/presidents-and-think-tanks/548765/.

Truman, David. 1951. *The Governmental Process. Political Interests and Public Opinion.* New York: Knopf. https://onlinelibrary.wiley.com/doi/10.1002/ncr.4110400915.

Trump, Donald. 2016. "Transcript of Donald Trump's Immigration Speech." *New York Times,* September 2. https://www.nytimes.com/2016/09/02/us/politics/transcript-trump-immigration-speech.html.

———. 2017. "Executive Order 13768." White House. https://www.govinfo.gov/content/pkg/FR-2017-01-30/pdf/2017-02102.pdf.

US Congress. 1992. "Implementation of the Intermodal Surface Transportation Efficiency Act of 1991." Washington, DC. https://www.google.com/books/edition/Implementation_of_the_Intermodal_Surface/6of_beTbGMoC?hl=en&gbpv=1&bsq=transition.

Vaid, Urvashi. 1995. *Virtual Equality: The Mainstreaming of Gay and Lesbian Liberation.* New York: Anchor Books.

Viser, Matt. 2020. "Biden's Vision Comes and It's Much More Liberal than It Was." *Washington Post,* July 12. https://www.washingtonpost.com/politics/bidens-vision-comes-into-view-and-its-much-more-liberal-than-it-was/2020/07/11/f260830a-c2f2-11ea-b178-bb7b05b94af1_story.html.

Vitali, Ali. 2020. "Biden Transition Boast Majority-Female Staff, 40 Percent People of Color." NBC News, November 15. https://www.nbcnews.com/politics/meet-the-press/blog/meet-press-blog-latest-news-analysis-data-driving-political-discussion-n988541/ncrd1247875#blogHeader.

Vought, Russell. 2020. "Letter to Ted Kaufman." Executive Office of the President. https://trumpwhitehouse.archives.gov/wp-content/uploads/2020/12/Kaufman.pdf.

Walker, Edward T., John D. McCarthy, and Frank Baumgartner. 2011. "Replacing Members with Managers? Mutualism among Membership and Nonmembership Advocacy Organizations in the United States." *American Journal of Sociology* 116 (4): 1284–1337.

Walker, Jack. 1991. *Mobilizing Interest Groups in America: Patrons, Professions, and Social Movements.* Ann Arbor: University of Michigan Press.

Warshaw, Shirley Anne. 2009. *The Co-Presidency of Bush and Cheney.* Palo Alto, CA: Stanford University Press.

Wayne, Stephen. 2021. "The Politics of the Biden Transition." *Routledge* (blog), January 20. https://www.routledge.com/blog/article/the-politics-of-the-biden-transition.

———. 2023. *The Biden Presidency: Politics, Policy, and Polarization.* New York: Routledge.

Weiss, Janet A. 1989. "The Powers of Problem Definition: The Case of Government Paperwork." *Policy Sciences* 22 (2): 97–121.

Weko, Thomas. 1995. *The Politicizing Presidency: The White House Personnel Office, 1948–1994.* Lawrence: University Press of Kansas.

Whipple, Christopher. 2022. "Inside the Shtshow that Was the Trump-Biden Transition." *Vanity Fair,* October. https://www.vanityfair.com/news/2022/10/exclusive-inside-the-shtshow-that-was-the-trump-biden-transition.

————. 2023. *The Fight of His Life: Inside Joe Biden's White House.* New York: Scribner.

Wide Eye. n.d. "The Biden-Harris White House." Accessed September 27, 2022. https://wideeye.co/case-study/the-white-house-biden-harris-transition/.

Wolbrecht, Christina, and Michael T. Hartney. 2014. "'Ideas about Interests': Explaining the Changing Partisan Politics of Education." *Perspectives on Politics* 12 (3): 603–630.

Workman, Samuel. 2015. *The Dynamics of Bureaucracy in the United States Government: How Congress and Federal Agencies Process Information and Solve Problems.* New York: Cambridge University Press.

Wright, Lauren A. 2016. *On Behalf of the President: Presidential Spouses and White House Communications Strategy Today.* Santa Barbara, CA: Praeger.

Yukich, Grace. 2013. "Constructing the Model Immigrant: Movement Strategy and Immigrant Deservingness in the New Sanctuary Movement." *Social Problems* 60 (3): 302–320.

Index

Page references in *italics* indicate an illustration; page references in **bold** indicate a table.

Printed in the USA
CPSIA information can be obtained
at www.ICGtesting.com
CBHW032154150624
10154CB00004B/320